YOUNG MR SMITH IN UPPER CANADA

MARY LARRATT SMITH

Young Mr Smith in Upper Canada

University of Toronto Press
Toronto Buffalo London

© University of Toronto Press 1980
Reprinted in 2018
Toronto Buffalo London
Printed in Canada

ISBN 0-8020-2376-2
ISBN 978-1-4875-7169-6 (paper)

Canadian Cataloguing in Publication Data

Smith, Larratt William Violett, 1820–1905.
    Young Mr. Smith in Upper Canada

ISBN 0-8020-2376-2

1. Smith, Larratt William Violett, 1820–1905.
2. Toronto, Ont. – Social life and customs – 19th century. I. Smith, Mary Larratt. II. Title.
FC3097.41.S64A3   971.3'02'0924   C80-094413-5
F1059.5.T6853S64

This book has been published with the assistance of the Canada Council and the Ontario Arts Council under their block grant programs.

'... My epitaph is in my diary ...'

Excerpt from the codicil to the will of
Larratt William Violett Smith, September 1905

Contents

Preface ix

Introduction xi

1 'We have sprung from Thomas Smythe' 3

2 'Rough quarters in Orillia' 7

3 'Another kingly spirit fled' 11

4 'The infernal housekeeping business' 14

5 The Happy Go Lucky Club 29

6 Parties, politics, pretty girls 51

7 'Myself the most lively' 74

8 'All my spare time ... writing Briefs' 85

9 'Great fun with Miss Thom' 92

10 'Our long cold winter journey' 95

11 'At Home' on Front Street 99

12 'Not such a wilderness as some imagine' 106

Contents / viii

13 No lack of parties – or of travel 118

14 'Sowed my early peas ... made my Will' 129

15 'Here, there, and everywhere' 136

16 'Sixth Anniversary of our Wedding Day' 143

17 'Now green in youth, now withering ...' 155

18 'Leave everything to circumstance & opportunity' 161

19 'She certainly strikes my fancy' 163

20 Always carefully chaperoned 165

21 'Behaving as strangely as usual' 168

22 One passage to Southampton 172

23 Meanwhile Mrs Thom is packing 176

The Accession of Queen Victoria, by Larratt Smith 179

Notes 185

Bibliography 197

Index 199

Picture credits 216

Preface

Young Mr Smith in Upper Canada is taken from some of the diaries and letters of my paternal grandfather, Larratt William Violett Smith, who was born in Plymouth, England, in 1820, brought to Canada by sailing ship when he was twelve, and died at Toronto in 1905 in his eighty-fifth year.

He bequeathed his diaries to my father, his fifth son, Goldwin Larratt Smith. After his death my grandfather's diaries and letterbook, and several miscellaneous letters, came into my possession. Faded ink in the diaries, tattered pages in the letterbook, grandfather's handwriting – always difficult, sometimes illegible – made the deciphering and the transcribing a terrific task which occupied much of ten years. The diaries, a few of them bound in leather, most of them oilcloth notebooks, are now safely deposited in the Canadian History Department of the Metropolitan Toronto Library.

My grandfather kept a journal from the year 1839 until just before his death in 1905. Since I was fascinated by the exuberance of his youthful days, between the ages of eighteen and thirty-eight, I have used only the sections from autumn 1839 until August 1858, and letters written during that time. There are also two letters from his father, Captain Smith, one written in Canada, one in England; one letter from his brother George, also from England; and two from a friend. The originals of all these letters are in my possession.

The information about the Smith ancestry, both English and French, is taken from twentieth-century letters written by my father's first cousin Bernard Smith, in England, to my aunt Violett Georgina Larratt Smith, in Toronto.

Although I have occasionally changed Larratt Smith's syntax and often the punctuation to make his meaning clear, I have left his spelling unchanged. For example, he wrote the past tense of the verb 'eat' as 'eat,' instead of 'ate' as we spell it today; he used the past tense of 'lie' to denote the present: 'The snow did not "lay."' He spelt 'pony,' 'poney,' 'beef,' 'beaf,' and 'plums,' 'plumbs,' and often capitalized certain nouns. Also, since French was Larratt Smith's second language, there are French words and phrases (and some Latin and Greek ones) in his writing, a few of which he has translated in parentheses.

ACKNOWLEDGEMENTS

Young Mr Smith in Upper Canada took a very long time to transcribe and a long time to edit and put together; indeed, had it not been for the enthusiastic encouragement of certain of my relatives and friends, the book might never have come into being.

I am indebted to my friend Marion Gilroy, librarian, associate professor emerita, University of British Columbia, who upon first sight of the diaries and letters in the 1960s urged me to transcribe them.

After I had copied out a great many journals and most of Larratt Smith's correspondence from his difficult handwriting and was faced with the task of editing them, I was fortunate in being able to turn to the poet Marya Fiamengo for criticism and advice. Her interest in the diarist and the social history of his time, not to mention her sensitivity and literary taste, inspired me to finish the manuscript.

I am most grateful to Sally Creighton, whose knowledge of Canadian history and whose professional help with the format of the manuscript were of inestimable assistance.

I would also like to thank my friend Edith Firth, head of the Canadian History Department, Metropolitan Toronto Library, who has followed the fortunes of *Young Mr Smith* for about ten years.

I owe debts of gratitude to my cousins, George Cassels-Smith of Baltimore, Maryland, Hamilton Larratt Smith of Peterborough, Ontario, and Hugh Larratt Henderson of Victoria, British Columbia, for their cooperation in contributing family information.

Finally, my special thanks are due to Dorothy Miller who typed and retyped the manuscript with unfailing cheerfulness and whose experienced eye caught the errors that I had missed.

M.L.S.

Introduction

'... And who are you?' asked the lady in the fashionable flowered hat, looking over my head and not pausing for a reply. This question was put to me at a Toronto reception a long time ago. I was young and shy, and beyond some half-remembered family anecdotes, had not the faintest idea who I was, so I said, 'My name is Smith.' She turned her head for a moment, then looked away.

Standing shyly in the midst of a garrulous crowd of society people in twentieth-century Toronto, I was aware that her question really meant, did my family have money or prestige? Although I vaguely knew we had ancestors lurking in the backwoods of Canadian history, I was pretty sure they were neither wealthy nor very important, so I simply answered 'Smith,' which is a perfectly good name and my own.

Some time after this episode I was approached at a cricket match by yet another lady. This one was English and enquired what part of England did I come from. 'I am not English,' I replied, but could think of nothing more to add. Eventually I did become curious, and slowly and haphazardly began to take an interest in finding out about my family and other people who lived in Canada long ago.

I did not have to search very far, as almost at my hand were some diaries and a letterbook written by my grandfather Larratt Smith more than a hundred years before, which had lain unnoticed by his family ever since.

My grandfather Smith and I must have encountered each other soon after my entry into the world. My birth was carefully noted in his diary as were the births of his other grandchildren, and no doubt I was presented for his inspection from time to time.

I have one quite clear memory of him when I was taken to see him sometime in the summer of 1905. My grandfather was eighty-five years old; I was not quite three. He was sitting outside on the verandah in an armchair, a rug over his knees, and a glass of something they called 'whisky' at his side. I am not sure whether any words passed between us, although I remember a gentle admonition from someone holding my hand to be very quiet, a warning I somehow understood. I knew he did not really care whether I was there or not: his face was turned away, and he seemed to be looking out over the garden at something far away.

He died a few weeks later on 18 September 1905. According to the funeral notice in the Toronto *Globe*, 'the casket was covered with maple leaves, evergreens and flowers gathered from the grounds of "Summerhill."' His grave is in St James' Cemetery in Toronto where he lies buried, like the patriarch he was, with his two wives and ten of his fourteen children.

My grandfather's full name was Larratt William Violett Smith. He lived in a large, early Victorian house that sat on the high land above the Rosedale ravine in what is now midtown Toronto. Behind the house were the stables, a cow barn, and a hen house. A long, gravelled driveway, winding around tennis and croquet lawns, connected the house and stables with the front gate on what was to become Summerhill Avenue. At the back of the property were two orchards; beyond them, the woods ran down to the spring-fed creek in the ravine below. The place was called Summer Hill.

The old house was pulled down in 1909 to make a subdivision, Summer Hill Gardens. The street, Summerhill Avenue (once a part of the property), is still there, but the city reservoir in the park where my father and my uncles used to race beetles and wash their dogs when no one was looking has been pushed underground and covered with cement.

There is a subway station in Toronto called Summerhill. When the trains come to a clattering stop and the passengers get on and off, there is nothing but the name of the station to remind them of the original Summer Hill, first owned by a man called Charles Thompson, and no one now alive can tell of seeing Mr Thompson driving his stage-coach on Yonge Street.

Charles Thompson's main business was the stage-coach line he bought in 1840. His coaches, in which he carried passengers as well as providing a postal service, were drawn by four and sometimes six horses; they rolled and lurched up and down the rough track known as Yonge Street, which linked Toronto with the upper lakes. In his youth Larratt Smith often rode in a Thompson stage-coach when his own father, Captain Smith, lived at Twickenham Farm, Richmond Hill.

Introduction / xiii

In addition to the stage-coach business, Mr Thompson had a sideline, an amusement park he had set up on a pretty piece of land he owned in what was then the country. There he had built an inn with a tavern. It was said that William Lyon Mackenzie got a horse from Thompson's stables when he was hard pressed in the Rebellion of 1837, but this I doubt since the house and stables were not built before the 1840s. After the inn and the tavern were completed, the park was made accessible to Toronto by a horse-car that ran on wooden rails. This pleasure ground became very popular with the townspeople for picnics and outings; it was called Thompson's Park, and sometimes (perhaps because the inn itself sat on top of the escarpment) Summer Hill.

Larratt Smith bought Summer Hill sometime in 1866 or 1867 when, according to Dr Scadding's *Toronto of Old*, 'The new owner developed it into a handsome property ...'[1] Smith was by then a prosperous, middle-aged barrister whose second wife Minnie, daughter of James F. Smith, a wealthy Montreal merchant, had brought him a dowry. But I am ahead of my story; let us go back to the beginnings of this family called Smith.

On that summer day of our last meeting, I was too young to realize I was in the presence of a man who had been born in Plymouth in the reign of King George IV. What could a child less than three years old know of England, or of her own country, Canada, for that matter. I was very young, my grandfather was very old; more than eighty years stretched between us. Somewhere in old Summer Hill House lay the history of those years: in his journals, letters, and in the Smith family Bible, where births, marriages, and deaths were all carefully recorded in Larratt Smith's own hand.

The list of names in the Bible begins with his own: 'Larratt William Violett Smith, son of Captain Larratt Hillary Smith and Mary Violett, born 29th November, 1820 (Wednesday 9 p.m.). Christened at Stonehouse Chapel (Devonshire, England) on the 31st of December 1820.'

ILLUSTRATIONS

Toronto harbour in 1835

King Street East, Toronto, 1835; the jail, the courthouse, and St James' Church are on the left

Captain Larratt Hillary Smith, 1782–1860, young Mr Smith's father, detail from a portrait painted by George Theodore Berthon about 1840

Mary Violett Smith, 1796–1886, young Mr Smith's mother, also painted by Berthon

The Parliament Buildings, with the military guardhouse and storehouse at the right; young Smith boarded at the Greenland Fishery tavern, on the left, in 1839

Larratt William Violett Smith as a young man

Upper Canada College, King Street West, as it looked in Larratt Smith's time

The prayer hall of Upper Canada College, on the occasion of the laying of the cornerstone of King's College, 23 April 1842. Watercolour by John George Howard

Robert Baldwin, 1804–58, who brought 'responsible government' to the Canadas

William Henry Draper, 1801–77, attorney-general of Upper Canada, under whom Larratt Smith articled as a law student

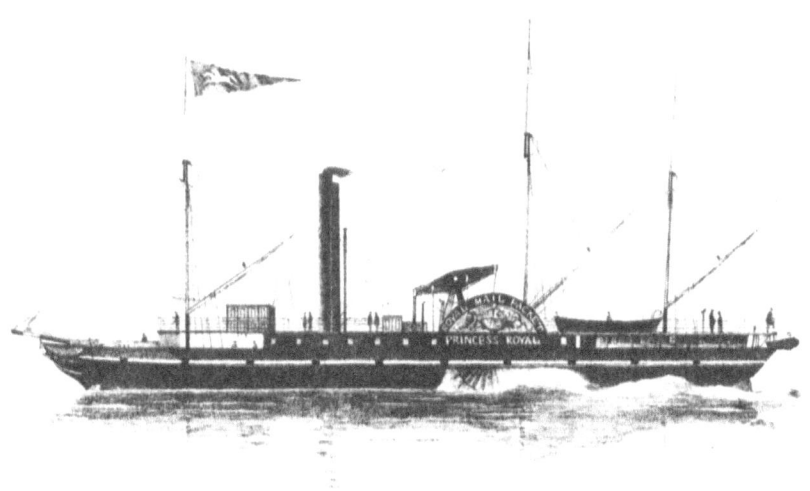

The Royal Mail steam packet *Princess Royal*, Lake Ontario, on which young Smith sailed to get his bride in 1845

Charles Dickens visited Toronto in May 1842

Jenny Lind, another prominent visitor in October 1851

Toronto harbour in 1849, Helliwell's wharf and rear of city hall

Ontario House, corner of Church and Market (Wellington) streets, 1840s

Yonge Street south of King in the 1840s, showing F.C. Capreol's Commercial Sales Rooms

The Bank of British North America, Yonge Street at Wellington

Eliza Smith's monument in St James' Cemetery

John Street, looking north from Queen Street West, 1851; the funeral of Larratt Smith's first wife Eliza was held in St George's Church (centre) in December 1851

Mary Elizabeth (Minnie) Smith, 1838–1922, second wife of Larratt William Smith

King's College, Queen's Park

Deering's Theatre at Front and Scott streets, 1840s

Toronto Bay in 1852, showing the steamer *Chief Justice Robinson* landing passengers on the ice

Toronto in 1854 from the top of the jail

The Provincial Exhibition on University Avenue, September 1852

Government House, Simcoe Street at King, celebrating the Queen's birthday on 24 May 1854. Lithograph by Lucius O'Brien

Williams Omnibus in front of the Red Lion Hotel, Yonge Street north of Bloor, 1850s

The tollgate on Dundas Street West, between Sheridan and Brock avenues, 1850s

St Patrick's Market on Queen Street, 1850, with St George-the-Martyr Anglican Church on John Street

The Queen's Own Rifles on the Normal School grounds; presentation of the silver mace by Mrs Draper, 25 May 1863

Summer Hill House, purchased by Larratt Smith about 1867

Larratt Smith, about 1894

The patriarch: Larratt Smith, his wife Minnie, and their ten children, about 1887

YOUNG MR SMITH IN UPPER CANADA

1: 'We have sprung from Thomas Smythe'

Apart from the information given in my grandfather's journals and letters, all I know about my Smith forbears was gleaned from a short family tree and from some letters to my father's sister, my Aunt Violett Smith, from her English cousin Bernard Smith. Aunt Violett, who was of a religious disposition, had refused marriage and spent her life keeping track of the family and making sure that her nephews and nieces were safely in the fold of the Anglican Church. In keeping the living Smiths together, Aunt Violett incidentally became interested in their ancestors.

Violett's cousin Bernard, who was also of course my father's first cousin, was a London architect, and in his spare time an amateur genealogist. In one of his letters to my aunt, he told of their grandfather's endeavour to trace the Smith lineage: 'Our grandfather, Captain Larratt Hillary Smith, went to the College of Heralds with such data as his father had given him, and he came away convinced that we have sprung from Thomas Smythe medical attendant and boon companion of James IV of Scotland who in 1477 conferred certain lands and hereditaments on his friend together with allusive arms, viz:- Azure; a flaming cup between two Chess-Rooks gold; and the motto "mediis tranquillus in undis," meaning "calm amidst the waves." The crest you probably know as it was on a ring of your father's ...'[1]

The Smith crest is a dolphin, shaped like an S, with a comb of ragged scales running down its back to an acanthus-shaped tail; this creature sits on what appears to be a striped sugar stick, its dolphin lips curled in either a simper or a sneer. Below the stick is a scroll bearing the caption mentioned in Bernard's letter; as a Smith kinsman once remarked, a more unsuitable motto could not have been devised, for no family could have been less calm amidst the waves than the passionate, hot-tempered Smiths, as he remembered them.

4 / Young Mr Smith in Upper Canada

Cousin Bernard says nothing more about King James's convivial medical friend, but he does give the names of some of his posterity: 'In a dwelling known as the Mill of Ogle lived a certain George Smith and his wife (who was born Isobel Wilson). They christened their son George, (I call him George II) in the Parish of Tannandice. This is in the Glen of Ogle in the County of Forfar, Scotland'. Although Bernard gives no dates for George Smith I or for his wife, they were the great-grandparents of the Devonshire-born Larratt William Violett Smith who emigrated to Canada

George Smith II was born in 1746, and when old enough to go to work he obtained a character reference from the minister of the Parish of Tannandice, witnessed by the sessions' clerk. With this testimonial in his pocket, young George left the Mill of Ogle in the Highlands of Scotland to seek his fortune in England. He evidently had expertise in farming and land management for he entered the service of Lord Aberdeen, and subsequently that of the Earl of Dartmouth. He eventually became one of the sheriffs of London. This George Smith appears to have made a rather interesting marriage: 'While acting as Lord Dartmouth's agent, George Smith came to know Miss Mary Larratt, who was gentlewoman to Lady Dartmouth, and sometime in the late 1770's he married Miss Larratt ... Mary Larratt was Irish-born. I have not as yet come across any of her family history, I think she transmitted her high spirits and gaiety to her sons and grandsons ...'

George Smith and Mary Larratt had three sons: the first was George, who became a wine merchant and had an unhappy end. The second was William, a soldier, who was said to have red hair. A portrait of a young, red-headed, British army officer wearing a red uniform with gold epaulettes hung in my father's dining room in Toronto for years without anyone knowing who he was. The unknown soldier turned out to be great-grand-uncle William Smith, who was killed in the Napoleonic Wars.

George and Mary's third son, Larratt Hillary Smith, also went into the army. It was this British army officer who became the father of Larratt William Violett Smith, the diarist and my grandfather. His grandson Bernard described his career:

Larratt Hillary Smith entered the Royal Artillery as a Cornet. He later transferred to the Paymaster branch as an Ordinance Officer, known then as His Majesty's Field Train. Smith made the campaign into North Germany & got as far as Bremen, where a French army marching from Belgium threatened to cut off our army from its base on the sea. It retreated and was re-embarked, after which Smith served in Scotland until 1805, when he embarked at Deal for Quebec where he was in charge of the Field Trains as Chief Commissary and Paymaster. Whilst in Quebec Garrison he was noted as a great amateur actor, a good raconteur and conversationalist. He hated the taste of spirits so much so that he jumped out of the window on one occasion when they locked the doors of the Mess Room until a case of wine was finished ... the escapade earned him the nickname of the 'Flying Commissary.'

He served in Canada all through the War of 1812, and was present at the battle of Queenston Heights – the report of this battle was reprinted and sold on the streets of Toronto whilst I was at Summer Hill [about 1899]. It is signed Larratt Smith. Smith then returned to England where he commanded his branch of the service at Woolwich, and when peace was made, left the service and went on a Grand Tour of the continent. He did not get further than Bordeaux where, at the house of Robert Violett (who had been a long time in the British Navy), he fell in love with Violett's younger sister, Mary ...

Who were these Violetts? What possible connection could Robert Violett, a Frenchman living in Bordeaux, have with the British navy? Bernard Smith supplied the answers:

The Violett family who were originally French, were Huguenots. In 1699 to escape persecution (after the Revocation of the Edict of Nantes) they fled from La Rochelle, France and settled in Seaton, Devonshire, England, where they occupied the Manor House. One of their descendants, our great-grandfather, Robert Violett married an English girl, Amy Benson, and went to live in the largest of a row of houses known as Violett Row ... Robert and Amy had several children, among them; Robert, William and Mary. It was Mary Violett who married Captain Larratt Hillary Smith and became the mother of Larratt William Violett Smith of Toronto.

Robert Violett Senior, the father of Mary Violett was (privately) a smuggler of French brandy and lace (but mostly brandy). He had a wharf by the catwater in Plymouth whence his luggers sailed to and from the Channel Islands, where they shipped the 'stuff' or exchanged it at sea with French correspondents ...

After his death, the wharf came into the possession of his daughter, Mary Violett Smith. But she was in Canada at this time and there was no one in Plymouth to look after her interests, so the buildings were swept away to make a better view of the Mayflower landing stage ...

Judging by what little I know of my great-grandmother's disposition, I don't think she would have wanted the wharf or approved of her father's smuggling activities. She was probably very young when she left England to live with her brother in France.

Robert Violett, who was named after his smuggler-father, became a French citizen through a series of extraordinary circumstances, as related by Bernard Smith:

6 / Young Mr Smith in Upper Canada

Our great-uncle, Robert, entered the Royal Navy as a midshipman and during the Napoleonic Wars, rose to the command of a dispatch brig. He was carrying dispatches when he became engaged with a French ship which lured him inshore under the guns of a masked battery so as to sink him. He had no choice but to surrender. After quickly sinking his dispatches, he and his crew came ashore ...

Now Robert Violett and his father had enemies at the British Admiralty who made his case look as black as possible. His French ancestry was brought up against him, and he was court martialed in absentia for surrendering his ship and his dispatches to the enemy. The French were informed by cartel that there was no officer named Violett on the British Navy list. In consequence he was herded in with non-commissioned men and deck ratings ... and was a prisoner for many years. During that time, he and all the other prisoners were marched about France from one prison to another. Wherever they were, the local drummers came out and drummed the column triumphantly through the place. This was done to put the local inhabitants in good spirits about the war.

It happened that on one of these marches near Bordeaux, Robert Violett noticed the profusion of plum trees along the roads, much of the fruit fallen and rotting on the ground. This struck him as a waste of good fruit. The memory remained until he was able to turn it to his profit. After the war he brought proof from French sources that he had not deserted to the enemy or given up his dispatches. The verdict was reversed and he was offered reinstatement or a sum of money in compensation.

He took the money and used it in fitting out a ship to trade between England and France. Back he went to Bordeaux and became a brandy shipper. He then bought plums, bottled them for export to England and did very well indeed. The capsule on the plum bottles sold today still bear his trade mark – a sprig of violets.

When this same Robert Violett, the merchant captain, settled in France after the Napoleonic Wars, he took his sister Mary to live with him. Sometime in the year 1819, while on his Grand Tour, Larratt Hillary Smith came to Bordeaux, met Mary Violett, fell in love with her, and married her.

... There was some opposition at first, but they were married and came to England to live at 4 Emma Place, at Stonehouse, adjoining the seaport of Plymouth, in Devonshire, England. There their children were born. The eldest of these children was born 29 November, 1820, and baptised Larratt William Violett Smith.

Then in 1833, Chartist Riots, general unrest, and some persuasion by Sir John Colborne,[2] made Captain Smith decide to return to Canada, where he had been popular and very happy.

2: 'Rough quarters in Orillia' 1833-6

Canada offered land: either the uncleared, unbroken land granted to war veterans by the British government or the farms that had already been cleared, which semi-retired army officers could buy reasonably and finance with their half pay. In 1833 Captain Larratt Hillary Smith, acting on the advice of the lieutenant-governor of Upper Canada, Sir John Colborne, took up a large tract of land at Oro in Simcoe County. It was not a good choice.

There are no scraps of letters or even a fragment of a diary left to tell of the Smiths' voyage to Canada in 1833. With them were their four children, ranging in age from Larratt who was twelve to Adelaide aged three. Whether they came by way of New York or Quebec is not known. They may have followed the example of some of their friends and taken passage in one of the fast sailing packets that, in good weather, left Liverpool for New York once a week. The crossing took about thirty-eight days, which at that time was considered fast, and the cabin fare included wines and liquors. Some of these ships even carried a cow to provide milk for the children.

It was cheaper to take a packet to Quebec, but the voyage took much longer. People said that the journey from Quebec to the Town of York[1] was a nightmare, whereas the trip from New York to Oswego on the New York State side of Lake Ontario was comparatively easy. Oswego travellers could then board a comfortable lake vessel for the crossing to Canada.

Whichever route Captain Smith and his family took, they eventually reached York. There they stopped long enough to enrol Larratt and his ten-year-old brother George as boarders at Upper Canada College. This boys' school had been founded by Sir John Colborne in January 1829, four years before the Smiths arrived in Canada. Leaving their sons behind and keeping the little girls, Mary and Adelaide, with them, Captain Smith and his wife Mary Violett left for their new property at Oro.

The journey (either by stage-coach or wagon) took them northward through the woods over the muddy, rutted track known as Yonge Street to Holland Landing in the marshy country of the Holland River. There they went on board a wooden boat, a bateau, which, propelled by oars and sail, carried them up the Holland River to Lake Simcoe and north across the water to Lake Couchiching in the Township of Oro.

This village and township, named after the Spanish word for gold, had been opened up in 1820 with the vague idea of making it a settlement for freed slaves from the Spanish African colonies. Despite its name, Captain Smith found his Oro land to be stony and unproductive. Why Sir John Colborne talked him into buying it remains a mystery.

The Smiths were not the first immigrants to buy land they had never seen, or to find themselves doing rough, unfamiliar work. I vividly recall a family housekeeper, Sarah Standish, whose ancestors had escaped to Canada during the French Revolution, telling me that her great-grandmother had never so much as done her own hair in France; moreover, these immigrants had even brought their tutor with them. On their arrival in Upper Canada, the entire family, including the tutor, had sat about on packing cases looking hopelessly at the forest which had to be cleared before they could begin to farm. No one seeing Sarah milking cows, churning butter, feeding chickens and turkeys, or expertly baking soda biscuits in the wood stove, would have believed for a moment that she was the descendant of helpless French nobility.

Here is a glimpse of Mary Violett Smith, my ancestor from France, who, although not of aristocratic stock and likely able to do her own hair, had probably never lifted a finger to much else. Her grandson, Bernard Smith, wrote: '... They went at first to Oro & settled in rough quarters in Orillia – whilst there, Grandmother did hard work cooking and washing, and on Sundays she started teaching the children of other settlers to read and write and read the Bible to them. Many of these children spoke Gaelic and my father gave me an imitation of their songs ...'[2] Mary Violett Smith's granddaughter, my Aunt Violett, told me that the 'rough quarters in Orillia' were a one-storey log house; Mary Violett, she said, cooked the meals for her family over an open hearth, rinsed the clothes in the lake, and did indeed keep a school in the log cabin.

The Smiths struggled to farm their land at Oro for nearly four years. It was quite long enough for Mary Violett to become disenchanted with life in the clearings of the bush. I think she hated Oro from the moment she set foot in the place.

Sometime in 1836 Captain Smith bought Twickenham Farm on the west side of Yonge Street just north of Richmond Hill, and moved the family there, leaving the Oro property behind unsold. Soon after the move, he was appointed a member of the Grand Jury for the Home District.[3]

In the meantime, the Smith sons, Larratt and George, continued to attend Upper Canada College in Toronto. The fees were two pounds a quarter with an additional five shillings for quill pens, ink, candles, and firewood. The pupils began Latin in the first form and by the time they reached the sixth form they could construe Horace, Cicero, and Virgil, and were proficient in Greek as well. The principal of Upper Canada College was the Reverend Joseph Harris, an eminent English scholar, a Fellow of Clare Hall, Cambridge, and brother-in-law of Sir John Colborne.

Dr Harris seems to have made little or no impression on Larratt Smith. There was, however, a teacher at the school who not only befriended the homesick boys but became a lifelong friend of the entire Smith family. He was a young Englishman called John Kent, who became headmaster of Upper Canada preparatory school about the time the young Smiths were enrolled. Through his interest in the boys, Kent soon came to know their parents, and often spent the holidays with them at Oro, and later at Twickenham Farm. In 1897, when they were both old men, John Kent, then living in Funchal, Madeira, wrote to Larratt Smith: '... I sometimes meet Violetts, your kin I assume, but I do not send their names to George for I believe he is not genealogically minded as he made no response to some I sent him. To me "Time consecrates, and what is hoary with age becomes religion." And the humblest forefather is as much cherished by me as if he had been a Duke ... I hope that some one of your children will take down from your lips recollections of Oro & Richmond Hill, ere they fade & are lost ... of while at Oro our little dilemma, when on Lake Simcoe we nearly drifted oarless – almost ...'[4]

In the same year that Captain Smith and Mary Violett moved to Twickenham Farm, a relative of theirs named Francis Boyd bought a farm on Yonge Street adjoining the Smith property. These farms, each containing two hundred acres, were described by Dr Henry Scadding in his book, *Toronto of Old*: 'We recall two instances of property with the appreciation of the elegant and comfortable, a little way beyond Richmond Hill on the left ... the cosy English looking residences not far apart, of an improved style with a cluster of appurtenances round each ... lawns, sheltering plantations, winding drives, well constructed entrance gates ... of Mr. Larratt Smith and Mr. Francis Boyd. Mr. Boyd who emigrated hither from the County of Kent was one of the first to import from England improved breeds of cattle. In his house was to be seen a collection of really fine paintings, amongst them a Holbein ...'[5]

Although Mr Francis Boyd had a Holbein, neither he nor the Smiths (or anyone else) had running water in their houses. They did, however, have wells. They also had servants, country girls and boys who carried water, chopped firewood, cleaned the lamps, and helped with the cooking and the washing. A two-storied house with these amenities, and cultured, amiable neighbours, was a far cry from the lonely log cabin in Oro, but Mary Violett never got over her nostalgia for the old country. Eventually, after eight years at Twickenham Farm, Captain Smith, his wife, and their two young daughters, preceded by their son George, returned to England, leaving only their eldest son, Larratt, in Canada.

Just before their departure the Smiths had their portraits painted by Theodore Berthon, who was said to be very good at capturing a likeness. Captain Smith, in his portrait, looks to be a very handsome man, with olive skin, black hair, and a cheerful expression. His wife, Mary Violett, who must have been pretty in a pale sort of way, looks out at the world as though it had displeased and disappointed her, as perhaps it had.

3: 'Another kingly spirit fled' 1837-8

In the year 1837, while Larratt and his brother were still boarding at Upper Canada College and his sisters were comfortably ensconced with their parents at Twickenham Farm, two historic events occurred. The first of these was Queen Victoria's accession to the throne in England; the second was a rebellion in the Canadas.

Sometime in July 1837 news of the death of King William IV and of the accession to the throne of Princess Victoria, the King's niece, reached the colony. When the royal proclamation was announced, it was still term time at Upper Canada College. To celebrate the occasion, since summer vacation did not begin until 19 August, the school held a competition for the best poem on the accession of the young Queen. Larratt Smith won the prize. His poem, published in the Montreal *Gazette* on 10 February 1838, bravely begins:

> And has another kingly spirit fled
> To swell the mansions of the silent dead?

and goes on to say:

> But as we wistful gaze, admiring yet
> The mellow glories of the sun that's set,
> Hail to the rising star that cheers the scene,
> Shedding around new light and joy – Our Queen;
> Our virgin Queen; the herald loud proclaims ...
> Thus while thy presence gilds this earthly scene,
> Each Briton loud will shout, GOD SAVE THE QUEEN.

There are five stanzas altogether, and for the curious the entire poem is reprinted at the end of this book (pages 179-84).

The Queen's poem was barely finished when its author was called to arms to defend her against the rebellious William Lyon Mackenzie and his followers.

In those uncertain times in Upper Canada, even young boys bore arms: by the time he had reached his fifteenth year young Larratt Smith had been gazetted as an ensign (the lowest rank of officer) in the Oro Militia. After the Smith family moved to Richmond Hill, Larratt was promoted to a lieutenancy in the 4th North York Militia.

Mackenzie was no stranger to Larratt Smith. Some forty years later Smith recalled a scene from his boyhood when, shortly before the revolt in 1837, the erratic Sir Francis Bond Head, then lieutenant-governor of Upper Canada, had evacuated the entire Toronto garrison to Montreal, leaving the city and the surrounding countryside unprotected: 'I saw the 24th Regiment, the last to leave, defile up King Street and down Simcoe Street, as they marched to the boat, and when William Lyon Mackenzie, who sat in his buggy at the corner of King and Simcoe Streets saw the last of them pass, he remarked in a loud tone of voice, "I'll make it hot for you before you return." I, with the other Upper Canada College boys who were looking on, threw stones at him.'[1] The stones, which were probably only pebbles, missed their mark.

When rebellion broke out in 1837 Larratt Smith left Upper Canada College to serve as a lieutenant in the Home District Militia. His father, as a half pay officer attached to the 4th North York Regiment, was also called to full military duty. Captain Smith was then a man of nearly fifty-six, his son had just turned seventeen.

There are no records of their military service, but after the rebellion was over young Larratt Smith went to England at the invitation of his uncle George, the wine merchant. Uncle George, with no sons of his own, proposed to adopt his nephew, train him in the wine business, and eventually make him his heir. Larratt reluctantly went, tried the business, didn't like it, and came back to Canada. There was a flaming family row: Smith tempers on both sides of the Atlantic flared, to be cooled only when Larratt's brother George, then seventeen, gave up a prospective career as a farmer and went to England in his stead. Years later Bernard Smith wrote: 'My father gave me a few letters ... at a time when he was burning a lot of old letters that he would not let me read – I believe that there was some heart burning when my father was adopted by his uncle, George Smith, & that rather unpleasant letters were written on the subject ...'[2]

There is a hint of this in a letter from Larratt to his maternal uncle, William Violett, in England, written 1 May 1847: '... How much I should like to see you again, for you of all my relatives were kind and considerate when all condemned me and I have never forgotten it, I can assure you ...'

At all events young George left Canada for England in the autumn of 1839, never to return.

The homesick George wrote regularly to his family in Canada. None of his letters survive, save one written from his uncle's counting house in Greenwich on 18 July 1841, carried by a fast clipper ship to Halifax and received by his father at Richmond Hill, Upper Canada, on 11 August 1841: '... Your letter as usual was so short that it but excited my longing for more of it ... I should be delighted to hear from you oftener and more at length ... The wine business of late has been very flat ... I by chance heard Uncle Geo tell Aunt (not in my presence) "that there was not one quarter of the business doing now that he did a few years ago. That I must consequently bestir myself and seek new customers as many of his old ones were defunct, and others had diminished their consumption." No very dazzling prospect this ...'

George's money worries ended on 7 May 1843 when his uncle, the unhappy merchant, hanged himself (no one knows why). Young George inherited the wine business, which prospered under his hand; he eventually became a wealthy man, acquired a yacht, the *Danitza* (steam and sail), and a wife, Mary Charlotte Pingo Bucknell, whose family owned all the cork in Portugal and a line of ships that ran to South Africa. George Smith and Mary Bucknell had many children, including of course Bernard, the genealogist and letter writer.

4: 'The infernal housekeeping business' 1839

SEPTEMBER 1839

Larratt Smith, not quite nineteen, decided to go into law. Since there was no law school in Toronto in 1839, after passing an examination he was admitted as a student by the benchers of the Law Society of Upper Canada[1] and articled to William Henry Draper, the solicitor-general of Upper Canada, one of the most eminent jurists and politicians of his time. When Smith became his student, Draper was already known in parliamentary circles for his pleasant and persuasive powers as a speaker, and had been nicknamed 'Sweet William.'

When his diaries begin in September 1839, young Mr Smith is apprenticing in the Draper law office and living in a well-known Toronto tavern, the Greenland Fishery, which he is about to leave in order to move into a rented cottage he will share with two brothers, Thomas and Edward Hind. I don't know how long Smith boarded at the Greenland Fishery, with its unusual signboard showing a landscape of Greenland on one side and a whaling scene on the other; he began his journal the day he moved out.

Thursday 12th September 1839. Threatening to rain. Today is the 2nd day of the Olympic Games. Left Mrs. Wright's Greenland Fishery this morning for a cottage belonging to Thomas Kinnear on Garrison Common. Having moved all my things in, I went shopping with Tom Hind & dined with him at Mrs. Leckie's boarding house, also took evening tea there. Tom & I slept at the cottage. Ned Hind at Mrs. Leckie's.

The entries in Smith's journals, which are short, reveal him to be preoccupied with the weather, though he also frequently mentions sporting items. '... Climbing greased pole & chasing pig,' he later cheerfully recorded of the 'Olympic Games' celebrated in Toronto on 29 June 1843; perhaps Smith himself was a participant and valiantly tried to shinny up the greasy pole for the amusement of the Toronto beau-monde who arrived in their carriages to watch.

On 12 September 1839, however, Smith did not attend the games for he was too busy moving into the cottage on Garrison Common. The common, a large piece of waste land lying west of the old fort and the Queen's Wharf, bordered Lake Ontario. People frequently grazed their cows on these acres: Smith's journal for the summer of 1849, written when he was living on Front Street, relates how he lost a cow in the bush on Garrison Common for more than a week. The cottage Smith rented in 1839 was somewhere on the east side of the common near the lake.

The owner of the cottage, Thomas Kinnear, was a gentleman farmer who lived some eighteen miles north of Toronto, on the east side of Yonge Street near the farm belonging to Smith's parents at Richmond Hill. A journalist of the time wrote that Mr Kinnear was possessed of considerable means and that he lived a life of careless ease and self-indulgence with his housekeeper, Nancy Montgomery, a very attractive woman. Aside from this association there was little to distinguish Thomas Kinnear from anyone else in the surrounding countryside until 18 July 1843 when he and his housekeeper were killed by an Irish manservant.[2] Then, as a victim in the most notorious murder case in Upper Canada, Kinnear became famous. Larratt Smith and the Hind brothers had severed their business connection with him three years before. In 1839 Kinnear was still living his easeful life at his farm near Richmond Hill, although he does not appear to have been a member of the Vaughan Township social circle, possibly on account of his relationship with Miss Montgomery. The whole district no doubt knew he owned a ramshackle cottage on Garrison Common and that young Larratt Smith and Major Hind's sons had rented the place and were busily fixing it up.

Smith's account book shows the payment of five shillings to have the cottage cleaned. On the shopping expedition the day of the move he and Tom Hind spent nearly three pounds on furnishings; among other things, they bought a little Dutch stove to heat the parlour. and, since cooking stoves were rare and costly, they purchased a gridiron with which to cook meat over the kitchen hearth. They also bought two chairs, a sofa, a candlestick, several yards of print for curtains, some carpeting with fringe, an earthenware crock, a saw, a hammer, a toasting fork, and a pair of dog irons for the fireplace. Tom Hind kept the accounts, carefully dividing the costs three ways.

These were only a few of their expenses. Smith's own ledger makes no mention of the cost of food and drink, but it does show the rent charged by Thomas Kinnear, which was thirty pounds a year, payable quarterly. The tenants were also liable for property tax and repairs to the building. Smith's income at this time was eight pounds a month, allowed him by his father, since he was not paid for his work in Mr Draper's office. The Hind brothers, who had government jobs, were not much better off, as Smith explained in a letter written to a friend, Tom Keefer, in January 1840: 'Tom Hind & Ned & I are keeping Bachelors' Hall together here – the former is in the Executive Council office – the latter is a kind of confidential Secretary at Government House where he writes dispatches from Sir George Arthur's dictation – a good berth but damned bad pay ...'[3]

Neither Smith nor his friends suspected that a year and a half later he would record in his journal: 'Paid Tom Hind 11 shillings & 3 pence to pay Execution for Taxes, putting in window glass in cottage & some other little expenses, this being the last amount I owe him on account of the infernal housekeeping business.'

In September 1839, however, everything appeared to be going well.

Saturday 14th. I stayed in the house all day today making carpet & putting the parlor to rights. Got into the cottage in toto to tea in the evening. 3 Fitzgibbons looked in & spent the evening with us.

Monday 16th. A fine day. Sam Jarvis came to the office again from Manitoulin Island after 8 weeks absence. I did some shopping & when I came home found the Fitzgibbons here leaping about the house. Walked with them to the 9 o'clock drums, stole a cat on my way home.

Smith's friends, the Fitzgibbons, were the sons of Colonel James Fitzgibbon, a British veteran of the Napoleonic Wars, who distinguished himself in the War of 1812 by receiving the surrender of the American forces at Beaver Dam in 1813.[4] In 1822 James Fitzgibbon was assistant adjutant-general of Upper Canada. In 1837 he commanded the troops that dispersed the rebels at Montgomery's Tavern, and was unjustly dismissed the next day by Sir Francis Bond Head, the lieutenant-governor, who falsely accused him of disobeying orders. Colonel Fitzgibbon eventually returned to England where he was appointed a military knight of Windsor.

1839 / 17

Larratt Smith had been at Upper Canada College with the young Fitzgibbons. When he moved into the cottage on Garrison Common, the Fitzgibbon family was living in a large two-storied roughcast house on Colonel Fitzgibbon's land grant at the corner of Brock Street (now Spadina Avenue) and Lot Street (now Queen). The Fitzgibbons' well-kept garden contained fruit trees and flower beds; the lawn was screened from the road by four immense weeping willows. Situated as it was, the Fitzgibbon house was within easy walking distance of Garrison Common: 'Tom Hind & I spent a most pleasant evening at the Fitzgibbons, drinking tea & talking. I had a polemical discussion with Miss Fitzgibbon & was invited to eat Michaelmas goose with them but declined.'

The Fitzgibbons were often at Smith's easy-going establishment. 'Fitzgibbon, Loring & Alex McDonell spent a long evening here with me playing whist & vingt un.' After a few gatherings such as this it was not long before the cottage on the common came to be known as the Happy Go Lucky Club.

The Jarvis who had appeared at the Draper office on 16 September was young Samuel Jarvis, an articled student to Christopher Hagerman, solicitor-general of Upper Canada. Sam Jarvis's relative and namesake, Samuel Peters Jarvis, had shot his best friend, John Ridout, in a duel in Elmsley's field near Grosvenor Street in 1817. Jarvis was tried and acquitted of manslaughter, but it took some time for the Jarvis family to live down the disgrace.

More duels were fought in Canada than people cared to admit. Our own great-grandfather, Captain Larratt Hillary Smith, owned a pair of duelling pistols; I was told that he fought a duel in a clearing in the woods near his farm at Richmond Hill. And I'm sorry to say his hot-headed son Larratt came very close to fighting the last duel in Toronto when *he* challenged *his* best friend, Aemilius Irving, in the summer of 1841.

Years later the very same duelling pistols reposed in a glass case in the drawing room of Larratt Smith's house, Summer Hill. His sons, my father and my uncles, sometimes purloined them to go rabbit shooting. But that was more than fifty years after their father began to study law in William Henry Draper's office in 1839.

Young Larratt Smith's duties as a first-year articled student in the Draper firm consisted of making up accounts, copying letters and documents with a quill pen, running errands, and serving subpoenas, six days a week. He was allowed his first time off in late September 1839, and travelled the sixteen miles to his parents' farm in Richmond Hill.

Saturday 21st. Intended to have gone home today but Stanley the tailor did not send my clothes, so I took a nice cup of chocolate & went to bed. Bitten by a bed bug in the night – got up at ½ past 2 A.M. & killed him. In the morning nothing came from the tailor so I finally started at 11 A.M. & walked out to Finch's Tavern[5] where I met Captain Stuart & his men coming from a shooting match so I rode in their vehicle to the Cricket Ground & played there from 2 to 5. Left there on foot without waiting for Capt. Stuart's vehicle. Arrived home by 6 o'clock & found Mamma very ill – supposed liver complaint. Aunt Mary Boyd & Mary called over to see her & Frank Boyd brought medicine.[6]

Sunday 22nd. A rainy Sunday morning. I went to church at Thorn Hill on horseback & John Boyd also went on horseback, but none of the families went from Richmond Hill. Sat with John in Boyd's pew as ours was being limed. Later in the afternoon I picked blackberries with my little sister, Adelaide, till pitch dark. George thought us lost & blowed the farm horn for us. All home safe at last. The wind very high indeed to-night. We spent the evening talking over about George going to England to live with Uncle George. Papa decided to write to Uncle George in England.

Tuesday 24th. Waited all yesterday morning for Papa to write his letter to England, but as the letter was not finished I walked over to Mr. Boyd's field & picked blackberries. Mamma still very ill, Mr. Kent & Mr. & Mrs. Barwick called to enquire. Papa's letter not finished till ½ past 10 last night. I started for Toronto per stage this morning, got in early & after dinner put Papa's letter in the post for England, by *British Queen* & paid 2 shillings, tenpence halfpenny postage. I then played whist & went to bed, (found my dear little pussy cat Tommy missing).

Thursday 26th. Kent called at the office to ask me down to Westmacott's last evening. I went down there at 8 o'clock & found Barber & a good many others at Westmacott's but no wine or anything else – very shabby of Westmacott. Barber walked home with me & we eat bread & butter & drank milk & water (most horrible) till 12 o'clock. Found Mr. Fitzgibbon & Mr. E. Hind at home, they had just come in from Major Hind's farm & told us there was snow in the country.

Friday 27th. I made a Record in the Crown Office first thing this morning & sent it off by the steamboat *Gore*[7] at 2 o'clock. Invited to Sheriff Jarvis's this evening. Went first to Benjamin's where I bought a pair of garters (5 shillings). Spent a delightful evening at the Jarvis's & came home at ½ past 4 in the morning, hanging onto the Jarvis carriage – ladies in it. Upper

Canada College opened today, I went down there & fetched up an axe, a cake, & a tablecloth which Walter Boyd had brought from home.

Monday 30th. Fine but desperately cold, ice for the first time this season. We asked Alex McDonell to come & see us on Saturday night. He came with Loring, bringing us a melon & some plumbs. We spent a long pleasant evening with 2 Fitzgibbons, cards, etc. Fitzgibbons brought us plenty of apples. By Sunday the cottage was so dreadfully cold (no firewood) that Fitzgibbon asked me to dine with them, the Hinds being in the country. They came back today & Ned Hind drew his money from Government House & bought 1 cord of wood.

OCTOBER 1839

Friday 4th October. Cleaned my gun last night & bought percussion caps & powder & went shooting this morning. Saw large quantities of plover on the island, but shot only 1 snipe. After 3 o'clock, or rather after dinner, went again & shot 2 plover, then fired my ramrod out of my gun & lost it in the dark. Went to the theatre & saw Miss Davenport perform in the *Merchant of Venice* and in *Old & Young.* Very much pleased indeed with her performance.

Travelling theatrical companies were again visiting Toronto despite a spot of trouble some twelve years earlier when a troupe of American players, stranded by a snowstorm in the early winter of 1827, had given an impromptu performance of Shakespeare's *Richard III* for the British officers at the garrison. The trouble had occurred during the curtain calls when a certain Captain Matthews was alleged to have derided *Rule Britannia* and called for *Yankee Doodle.* Hats were knocked off, there was a scuffle, and, later, an investigation into Captain Matthews' conduct. He was exonerated mainly because he and the rest of the audience had been very drunk that evening, it being New Year's Eve. Canadian tempers still ran high in Captain Matthews' day, for there were people living in York who had been through the War of 1812 and could never forget the American invasions of the town in 1813.

By Larratt Smith's time war was almost forgotten and American circuses and theatrical companies came regularly to Toronto. Miss Davenport was no doubt a member of one of them.

Young Smith was said to have been a born actor, only dissuaded from going on the stage by his father, who had had the same inclination himself before he became a soldier. Both father and son were devoted to the theatre and never missed a performance if they could help it. When Larratt joined a theatrical group, the Toronto Amateurs, he not only produced and directed but played every role offered him. He sometimes put on one-man shows at home: 'Dressed myself in Tom's aide-camp's coat – cocked hat – knee breeches & silk stockings – played Poor Richard (alias played the fool).'

Soon after Larratt Smith began to study law with William Henry Draper, his mentor's wife discovered that the new student was very musical and could play the violin; when she heard his fine singing voice, she invited him to join her choir.

Augusta Draper had been a Miss White, a daughter of Captain George White of the Royal Navy. In her younger days she had been a member of Lord Byron's literary circle and a close friend of John Trelawny. After she married Draper and came to live in Toronto, she gathered about her other people with literary and musical interests. According to Smith's journals there was singing nearly every night of the week at Mrs Draper's house. In the autumn of 1839 her little choir not only practised anthems and hymns but also sang the entire Psalter.

St James' Church (later St James' Cathedral), a wooden building, was still in the process of construction after the original church had been destroyed by fire. It was close to completion by late October 1839 and reopened on 22 December of that year: '... saw them get up last timber for steeple & touched the top of it ...' wrote Larratt Smith.

Sunday for Smith, and for most Church of England people in the colony, was a gloomy Upper Canada Protestant day: dancing, playing or singing secular music, reading novels, were all forbidden, and no one ever dared to play cards. Everybody who was anybody, and Church of England to boot, went to church twice a Sunday. Since there were no free seats, the well-to-do rented their own pews; the nobodies – servants, children, law students – squeezed in wherever they were allowed. William Henry Draper, as solicitor-general, had his own family pew in St James' Church, in which Larratt Smith was allowed to sit.

Smith, however, soon became a member of St James' choir, led by Mrs Draper. As the church at this time lacked an organ, the choir sang the hymns and canticles accompanied by one of the regimental bands. Smith sang counter-tenor and later became the soloist. On the subject of music he was a perfectionist: 'The singing today was abominable. Fitzgibbon trying to play the flute, failed. I was therefore obliged to lead the treble without it ... Cozens & Hepburn managed to sing the afternoon Psalm very badly by themselves.'

On the second Sunday in October 1839 Larratt Smith was absent from the choir. Mr Draper had given him a week's leave to go home to Richmond Hill where an important meeting was to take place, a meeting called by the farmers and settlers of the townships of Vaughan and Markham to discuss Lord Durham's report on 'responsible government.'[8]

Friday 18th October. When I arrived home last Friday I found Papa & Mr. Boyd deep in discussion about the intended Meeting. A very rainy weekend, but the weather cleared on Monday. Mr. Carthew came down from Newmarket & slept at our house. The Durham Meeting took place on Tuesday with about 1000 people present. Mr. Boyd was Chairman & Papa moved the Resolution. Later, a fight broke out in which the Orangemen thrashed the rebels so badly that one man was killed almost on the spot. I came home a little after dinner & at nightfall loaded all our guns & pistols & went round the house before I went to bed.

I spent most of yesterday spreading out onions, picking up potatoes & putting the cellar in order to receive the turnips. In the evening, read a law book by Sir James Stephens on Pleading. To-day opened with a violent thunderstorm. I got up at 6 o'clock to see it, then started for Toronto with Mr. Boyd in his private waggon. As we drove down Yonge Street, noticed sky very curious in appearance.

Tuesday 22nd October. Yesterday morning as I was arranging papers in the office, my brother, George suddenly appeared. He had come in from Richmond Hill with Papa and was about to leave for England in the morning. I left the office at once and went about town making calls with George. Bought some biscuits for Papa, and after dinner took them down to Ontario House where I spent the evening with Papa & George.

Ontario House, later called the Wellington Hotel and since demolished, was built in 1832 on the corner of Church and Wellington streets. The hotel, with three tiers of balconies held up by columns of peeled pine logs, looked out over Toronto Bay; it was advertised as keeping a good table and its beds were warranted to be free of insects of any kind. The Smiths often stayed there, as did many of their friends from the country settlements. This was to be the last time young George Smith stayed at Ontario House; his brother Larratt wrote: 'Got up very early & went down to breakfast with Papa and George, then to the wharf where I wished George farewell on board the lake vessel *St. George.*[9] Mamma sent me in a quilt, another blanket & a knife tray.'

Wednesday 23rd October. I left the office at 12 today & went to Brigade. Very splendid troops fired. The Artillery, Cavalry, & 93rd & 32nd Regiments were reviewed by Colonel Foster & Colonel Bankhead of the United States Army. In the evening I went to the singing at Mrs. Draper's. Found Mrs. Maynard, Miss Mary Jane Hagerman, & Mrs. Cozens all there warbling. I came home pretty early, took a glass of grog, played cards & went to bed. Sir George Arthur went below to Montreal to see Sir John Colborne off & meet Poulett Thomson,[10] the new Governor-General.

Thursday 24th. A very fine day. Tom took the day off & went shooting. I went down to the Court, then called at the Club to see Hickory Irving. He was not there. Saw him later at the lich gate of Upper Canada College. In the evening we went to Shaw's to tea. Spent a pleasant evening playing cards with the Shaws & brought home a cat about 3 years old.

Hickory Irving, whose real name was Aemilius, was the son of Captain Jacob Aemilius Irving, a veteran of the Napoleonic Wars. When Captain Irving brought his wife and children to Canada in 1834 and settled at Niagara, young Aemilius was sent to board at Upper Canada College where he met Larratt Smith. A few years later, Captain Irving was appointed First Warden for the District of Simcoe and moved his family to a farm called Bonshaw in the North Yonge Street, Newmarket, area, some fourteen miles from Twickenham Farm.

Aemilius Irving and Larratt Smith – despite some stormy interludes, and despite Smith's hopeless passion for Irving's sister – became lifelong friends. The club where they met on that October day in 1839 was a makeshift affair in rented quarters which later became the Toronto Club. In one of his later journals Smith observed: 'Great meeting at the Club House about its affairs. Papa, Mr. Francis Boyd, Captain Irving etc. making plans to form new Club at Ontario House.'

The Shaws with whom Smith and Irving were playing cards must have been relatives of Major-General Aeneas Shaw, a Loyalist who had lived in the first house built in York in 1793. The young Shaws were frequent visitors at the Happy Go Lucky Club. Later in the month Smith wrote: 'William Shaw & his brother George here to tea this evening, they brought us some apples & a Cock & 6 hens.' And still later, when all Toronto was celebrating Queen Victoria's marriage: 'The Shaws came down here this evening & let off squibs & rockets in honour of the Queen.'

This event, however, did not take place until the spring of 1840. In 1839 Smith had barely begun to study law.

Wednesday 30th October. Raining all day today. Went to Court rather punctual & staid there all day. Judge Jonas Jones called on father & son for assisting soldiers to desert. Attorney-General Hagerman made a good speech for the Crown. I did not get home till 7 o'clock nor did I go to Mrs. Draper's. No one with us tonight. I spent the evening reading Brougham's Defence of Queen Caroline.

Henry Peter Brougham, the distinguished British statesman and jurist, was counsel for Caroline of Brunswick, wife of King George IV of England, when she was accused of adultery and tried before the House of Lords in 1820. Long after Larratt Smith's time I heard a counting-out rhyme at a children's party in Toronto. It went:

> Queen Queen Caroline
> Washed her face in turpentine
> Turpentine made it shine
> Queen Queen Caroline.

As a child my knowledge of English history was scanty: I thought this an odd little verse, whereas my grandfather, who had had history dinned into him from the time he could read, must have known about the lampooning of Queen Caroline long before that autumn night in Toronto when he sat reading Brougham's defence of her by candlelight.

Next day young Smith went to a different kind of trial: '*Thursday 31st October*. I was in Court all day & heard Flood tried for conspiracy. The case was not finished when I left at ½ past 5. Came home only to find that a dog had carried off my dinner. All Hallow Eve.'

NOVEMBER 1839

Why a hungry dog was allowed to roam about the cottage at dinner-time is not explained! Smith's journals are vague about the haphazard house-keeping arrangements at the Happy Go Lucky Club. 'Very late cooking a leg of mutton for dinner, kept it on the spit till 7 o'clock – not done after all ... horrible beafsteak today ...'

After some weeks of struggling with the cooking, all of which was done over the open kitchen hearth, the club members, despite being strapped for money, acquired some domestic help: 'Boy came, cleaned out my bedroom today & gave us a very good dinner of nice pork & tongue & pumpkin pie Tom brought in from the country.' This, however, did not last: 'Boy never came to give us any dinner & when we found he had been stealing in our absence, we sent for his mother to talk to her about him. Dismissed him after paying his month's wages. We have now engaged a housekeeper, Mrs. Davis. Our new cook very handy, on the day she arrived, gave us a capital dinner with plum pudding.'

Mrs Davis had barely settled in when her employers discovered the cottage on Garrison Common was not in a state of good repair.

Tuesday 5th November. It began to rain about midday, as I was going about Town to get an Affidavit sworn for Major Colclough. I came home only to discover that the rain had found its way in, all over the house, under & through the window frames & had leaked in dreadfully through the ceiling of the front parlor. Tom & Ned's bedroom so wet we all brought our beds into the back parlor & slept there. Mrs. Davis got so desperately frightened in the night sleeping before the kitchen fire, to find the water surrounding her, that she brought her things up to my bedroom & slept there.

Wednesday 6th. Found nearly 1 foot of water in the cellar this morning & took up the carpet in the front parlor as it was wet through. Late to the office & went about town again with Major Colclough. When I came home Mrs. Davis had the house very tidy indeed. Snowing all day & too wet for Mrs. Draper's singing. No one with us in the evening, so we played cards.

Saturday 9th. Very cold, ground frozen. Left the office at ½ past 2 & went out to Thornhill in Thorne's waggon, walked to Parsons[11] who lent me his horse. Terrible roads. I got home by 7, up to the neck in mud. Found all well at home & a letter lying on the ground covered with snow, from George in England.

Monday 11th. No church yesterday, roads too bad. Service at home. In the afternoon I exercised Mr. Parsons' horse in the fields, cleaned the stirrups, bridle, etc. In the evening Papa gave me a 5£ check and a striped neck handkerchief. Very hard frost this morning. I got up a little before 7 & started for Toronto on Mr. Parsons' horse. Breakfasted & left the horse at Mr. Parsons' & started to walk to Toronto when I was picked up by Crookshank's team. But it broke down & I was obliged to walk in after all. Got to the office before 1 & went to work till 4, then left for home & went to bed early.

Thursday 21st. Very fine but most horribly cold. All the ponds will bear, but the wind too high all night for the Bay to freeze. Poulett Thomson & staff arrived in the steamboat *Traveller*. I ran down to see him land. Sir George Arthur went down to meet him, very few people present. Most bitter cold.

Saturday 23rd. Poulett Thomson was sworn in yesterday. Went down to see him but did not go in. Much milder day. Poulett Thomson went to Niagara at 6 A.M.!!! I went to the market in the morning & ordered 6 lbs of Beaf steaks & they sent a leg of mutton! Busy all morning writing Bill in Chancery, Billings helped me. I stole Jarvis's stick, he gave chase & I flung it away after being chased from the office to Dr. McCaul's[12] house. Billings came home with me, we took some luncheon & went skating till dinner time on the Garrison Common pond opposite our house.

Tuesday 26th. Blowing a gale from the North West yesterday. The *Gore* nearly capsized in putting back to Toronto Bay, but despite the wind, the *Transit* went to Niagara carrying Brown of the 93rd Regiment with dispatches for the Queen, he is to sail from New York on 1st December. Today is the coldest day yet & most bitter cold all night in spite of all the clothing I could heap on. Went down to Harrington about a stove, but he wanted my note which I would not give. I therefore went to Ridout's[13] who let me have what I wanted. Wrote to Papa for money.

Thursday 28th. Stayed from the office yesterday, mended my bed & put in pane of glass in the parlor window & papered my own bedroom window to keep out the cold. Musson's men put up the stoves in the hall & parlor. A very lovely mild day. Skated early & had beaf steak for breakfast. The Major, Miss Hind, & servant came in so I was obliged to take it in my bedroom, then scampered off to the Crown office. A letter came from Papa saying he could not send in my goose etc. 3 Fitzgibbons & Wright here in the evening.

Friday 29th November. Entered my 19th year today. Went to the office pretty early & read Sir Francis Bond Head's *British Policy* (copy sent out by himself) to Joseph in the office. Jarvis & Billings made an appointment to meet here at our house to make further arrangements for shooting (damned impertinent of them). William Powell came so I was obliged to borrow things for tea, in the end we had a supper of sausages, cold tongue & beer & sang songs till 12 o'clock.

Saturday, St. Andrew's Day. Major Hind brought in $\frac{1}{2}$ of a pig, also a kitchen table & a bunk bed with straw for same. Governor-General Poulett Thomson reviewed the Artillery, the Lancers & 32nd & 93rd Regiments, great firing. The 93rd walked in the St. Andrew's procession. I drank tea with Fitzgibbons, Hepburn & wife there, kept it up till past 1 on Sunday morning.

DECEMBER 1839

Monday 2nd December. The Governor-General was at church yesterday morning, the singing pretty middling. After dinner I walked as far as the Yorkville toll-gate with Tom & Ned on their way home, returned & went to bed soon after tea. Awakened by dog barking very violently, got up & loaded Tom's gun with snipe shot & went out but could see nothing. Got up early today & took breakfast before Tom & Ned got in, their waggon broke down with Major Hind, Miss H, Tom & Ned, about 5 miles from town, which they walked. I left the office early & met Ed Davis after cutting him once, he was dressed so ruffian-like. Irving drank tea & spent the evening here.

With some encouragement from Mrs Draper, Larratt Smith was beginning to find his way into Toronto society.

Friday 6th December. A fortnight ago, Mrs. Draper, after choir practise talked a good deal about calls, she wished me to call at Government House. I therefore called there, put my name down & left my card & just a week later got invitation to Govt. House Ball for 3rd December. Went down to Murchison's after dinner that same day & was measured for a pair of best black trowsers £2.10, & a satin waistcoat at £1.12.6. Bought a pair of carpet slippers at Dodsworth's and wrote to Papa about his evening cloak.

Met Papa yesterday morning coming from the stables at Ontario House, introduced Tom Hind to him. Papa gave me £2 & I went shopping with him after taking lunch. After dinner I went down to Ontario House & sat till past 8 with Mamma and her friends, Mrs. Gapper & Mrs. Paget. When I left, I took with me a cake, a loaf of bread, 2 pair of flannel waistcoats, & Papa's cloak to wear at the Ball.

Went to Govt. House & found upwards of 600 people present – a regular crush with the 32nd Regiment Band playing overtures, & the 93rd Regiment Band playing Quadrilles etc. Had a capital supper & danced with the Misses White, Fitzgibbon, & Hind. Walked home at ½ past 3 with Miss Hind, then turned in very tired. Up late. Did not go to the office today. Took back cloak & bought biscuits for Papa. Went shopping all the morning with Papa & Mamma, then brought them to see this house & called at Mrs. Fitzgibbon's. Papa & I left our names at the Governor-General's & at Government House. Mamma called at Mrs. Blake's about putting Mary to school there. Papa & Mamma went out at 4 o'clock p.m. to sleep at Finch's Inn on their way home. Ned Hind broke a pane of glass in the cottage playing singlestick.[14]

Thursday 12th. It snowed nearly all day yesterday but did not lay very deep. Up very early & took a walk to Garrison Wharf & back before breakfast. Went to the office but shut up the office & went, all of us, to Parliament House to hear the Debating on the Union of Upper and Lower Canada. Draper made a good speech – many ladies present. When the meeting adjourned I left & went home. 3 Fitzgibbons & Sam Jarvis here in the evening making Latire,[15] did not succeed. Ned & I quarreled about cards, I called him a cheat. Went to bed directly after tea with a headache.

Sunday 15th. Very fine & cold. Short of wood, borrowed some of Lyons. Tom & Ned went home on foot. I went to church with James Fitzgibbon. The Gov.-General came in late. Singing very good indeed. No flute, the ladies sung loud for the first time. After church Billings came in his cutter & drove me on Dundas Street & about town.

Wednesday 18th. Threatening to snow, but too cold. Resolution regarding the Union of Upper & Lower Canada passed on Monday by a majority of 7. Before going to the office today I bespoke a pair of red stockings at Dodsworth's, 4 shillings. Wrote to Papa about going home for Christmas. Fitzgibbons came in to tea this evening, a great disturbance & a row as usual between Jim Fitzgibbon & Ned Hind, upsetting everything. Ned victorious. After they went off, Ned & I walked before going to bed. Washed my feet.

Thursday 19th. Fine & very cold, the Bay frozen over to bear. I went to the office & asked leave of Mr. Draper to go home, granted of course. After dinner Tom & I went to Dodsworth's shoemaker, Smith's grocers, Dixon's Post Office & the Boarding House, met Shaw in town & Tom treated us. In the evening in the middle of tea Papa unexpectedly came in & spent the evening with us all. I walked home to the Club with him at $\frac{1}{2}$ past 11, came back & packed up my things.

Friday 20th. Went down first thing in the morning to meet Papa at the Club House, then went about town with him. Bought a cutter[16] at Stranges & left our own to be sold. Looked in at the office, then called on Mrs. Blake & made arrangements for Mary to go to her school. I came home, lunched & went with Papa to the distribution of prizes at Upper Canada College. We went out of town rather late. Very fine and thawing in the sun, no sleighing until we came to Mrs. Heath's[17] place, Deer Park, where we found plenty of snow & were able to spin along in the new cutter. Found all well at home.

Tuesday 31st. A very cold week with drifting snow. Just before Christmas one of our servant boys ran away, when the second boy ran away too, I became busy about the house and cellar, keeping the fires on, plastering to keep the frost out and stowing away carrots etc. Went to church in the big sleigh on Xmas Day – Sacrament. Although it snowed terribly on Saturday, I took my sisters, Mary & Adelaide to Mrs. Parsons, then came home, dressed & drove a fresh horse down to the Parsons' delightful evening party. This morning, Papa drove me in the cutter to Thornhill, where I met J. Parsons who drove me to Toronto. Went to town & bought gloves & at ½ past 10 went to Mrs. Draper's party, a very pleasant one indeed. Came back to the cottage at 3 A.M., then left at noon for Richmond Hill in John Parsons' sleigh.

5: The Happy Go Lucky Club 1840

JANUARY 1840

Monday 6th January. Am now back in Toronto after spending New Year's at Twickenham Farm. Whilst there I helped with the pig killing and made myself useful in other ways. It was too desperately cold to make any calls on New Year's Day, but the following evening being milder, we drove in the cutter to a most delightful party at Mr. Thorne's farm. Papa, Mamma, Mary & I, came into town in the big sleigh this morning. Mary to go to school at Mrs. Blake's. Brought in Potatoes, carrots, parsnips, & turkey for the Happy Go Lucky Club.

Friday 10th. Fine & mild. Mr. Draper sent me off again on Wednesday to King Township about the Sandwich Lands.[1] I rode home to our farm with Lawrence Sothers & arrived at 4 o'clock. Mrs. Gapper's party in the evening, a very delightful one & much the pleasantest as yet. Started from home about 10 yesterday morning & rode into King, reached Snook's farm at 2 o'clock, had some dinner & slept there last night right in the same bed with him. Killed a mad ox at Snook's.

Saturday 11th. Left Snook's yesterday about ½ past 9 & rode to Watson's where I was very favourably received then rode into Tecumseth to see Marken – not at home. In the afternoon I rode over to see the Sandwich Lands – snowing hard – slept at Watson's. Still mild this morning & a heavy fall of snow, it became dreadfully cold about midday. I started for home & got into Yonge Street at Crosford's, dined & stopped 2 hours at McLeod's tavern – got home by 4 o'clock in the afternoon. Drove Papa's cutter to Richmond Hill for papers etc.

Monday 13th. Up very early in the morning at 5 & left home at 7 with John our handyman & 3 pigs. After remaining in the market till 2 o'clock, I sold 2 pigs for 4$ & ¼ and 4$ & 3 York shillings² likely to be cheated out of 4 York shillings, made the fellow pay. Wrote to Papa by John – went to bed very early indeed.

Wednesday 15th. To office early yesterday – then left at 1 for the Cottage to dress etc. Got into chance sleigh & arrived at Thornhill a little after 4 & drank tea at Parsons preparatory to going to Barwick's party. Only Harriet, John & Mrs. Parsons went. Papa there & no one else from home. Mrs. Draper, Miss White & Miss Cox & numbers of people from Toronto – 93rd Band there. Delightful party – I danced all evening – came away at 3 o'clock in Bill Jarvis's Cutter & arrived in town at 6 A.M. Went to bed at 7 & to the office at ½ past 11.

Thursday 16th. Fine & very cold – to office early making up Agency papers to put away. Papa called & we went to the Cottage at ½ past 1 where we took some lunch, fed the horse & went down to Smith's grocers, took some things in there & at Scott's grocers & went home with Papa. Stopped & dined at Finch's, got home very late – Papa's ear frozen.

Friday 17th. Papa's birthday. Very fine & still very cold. I went into the woods to cut branches to decorate supper room at Twickenham Farm but only succeeded in embellishing part – Aunt Mary Boyd & John came over in the morning to see how we were getting on. I borrowed Neil's fiddlestick after sending a note down to Thornhill by teamster in the afternoon as Harris the builder would not lend me his fiddlestick. Papa's birthday party in the evening. Ned Hind & Bill Jarvis came up in a hired double sleigh. They slept together in the spare room. I slept upstairs. Tom Hind too unwell with rheumatism to come out. Rather a pleasant party of Richmond Hill & Thornhill families. Parsons, Barwicks, the 2 Miss Lees, Mr. Thorne, and the Boyds down to Mary, omitting little Frank. The Gappers & Mrs. & Miss Sharpe also came. I played the fiddle to quadrilles & country dances till the party broke up at 2 o'clock in the morning. Walked home with Elizabeth Boyd & the Boyds. Much milder this evening.

Saturday 18th. Jarvis & Hind staid to breakfast & dinner. In the morning we all drove to Bond Lake. After dinner, we loaded the hired sleigh with potatoes, onions & peas & drove to Toronto in a blinding snowstorm in 3 hours, horses very tired. Found Tom Hind much better. Brought cakes in for him & my sister Mary.

On the evening of 20 January 1840 Smith took some paper and quills to his sister Mary at Mrs Blake's school, and on his return to the cottage on Garrison Common took his own quill in hand and answered a letter from his friend, Tom Keefer, in Thorold, Upper Canada.

Thomas Coltrin Keefer, who was of Loyalist descent, was born in Thorold and went to school with Smith at Upper Canada College. After he left school Keefer went to the United States where he worked for a time on the construction of the Erie Canal. He had just returned to Canada and was planning an army career when Smith wrote this letter. Fortunately for Canada, Keefer did not join the army as Smith's letter suggests: instead he helped to build the Welland Canal, then went on to plan waterworks, railways, and the navigation routes of the lower St Lawrence River. He eventually became one of the most distinguished Canadian engineers of his time.[3] When this letter was written, Keefer was eighteen years of age, Smith had just turned nineteen.

Monday 20th January 1840

Dear Tom:

... I received your amusing epistle a few days ago but I had not time to reply till to day – So you have left the land of Egypt and are safely deposited in the land of your fathers ... I think that you could not do better than play the soldier particularly so if the Incorporated Battalions are to be placed on a permanent footing as Fencible Regts & which there is every reason to believe will be the case & some of the Regts of the Line withdrawn; then we should see Tommy Laddy gazetted in the Army List – With all due deference to your opinion (as Matthews[4] used to say) about our happenings at Upper Canada College. I should be sorry to return to it again, for as you remarked I never saw such a stunted set – the biggest lout in the College being Charley Kingsmill – Jade has been seen once only in town since he left the College – wearing a *complete* suit of worn out fustians, his boots outside his breeches as usual – & his beak etc. more holy than righteous.

My brother George went to England in November last, not to return again – and I think it more than likely that all the family will be on their way before very long leaving myself their only son out here.

William Jarvis is my Junior in this office – Sam Jarvis is in Hagerman's – the two McDonells in Henry Sherwood's, Master Calico I have not seen since I left in August 1838 – I shall be very glad to see you should you pay your intended visit to Toronto– I saw Hale in the summer at Hamilton whilst there on business for a couple of days – He is no small potatoes among the gals there I am told – I hope he may be equally successful at Fort Erie ... It is currently reported that Draper is Atty General vice Hagerman resigned – & Baldwin Solicitor General, vice, Draper promoted – but I have not heard it confirmed – Hagerman has been offered a seat on the Bench but has not as yet made up his mind to accept it – What is your opinion about the Union? James Fitzgibbon has been appointed without purchase to the 24th Regt & will join in May next – '*What a long tail our cat has got!*' We have magnificent sleighing here the snow being better than 2 feet in depth – The officers here at the Toronto garrison are keeping the town all alive – Their tandem Club makes a great show – I am quite tired of parties I have been to so many lately, up in the country as well as in town.

Sister Sal [likely Mary] has got over the teeth ache and is anxious to know how the gals are down your parts – Poor Joe Harris instead of getting his expected fortune of £1500 per annum has not succeeded to a farthing and is devilish glad to accept a living in England, so somebody has told me – Irving has returned from England and is living near Newmarket about 26 miles from town, where his father has purchased a farm. Little Sarah Henderson is quite a belle at Davidtown and Newmarket & I think you would have a fight & hard work to win her over from the Philly – she is so deeply in love ...

John Powell has been re-elected Mayor of Toronto for the third year in succession. The Clergy Reserve Question[5] is settled, $\frac{1}{4}$ for the Church of England, $\frac{1}{4}$ for Scotland, & the other $\frac{1}{2}$ for all other denominations. So much for legislation!

I must now wind up this tedious epistle and wishing you the compliments of the season

Believe me,
Yours very sincerely
Larratt W. Smith.

P.S. They are holding Hunters' Lodges in Markham & Vaughan etc. – north of Toronto.

The 'Hunters' Lodges' Smith so casually mentions were groups dedicated to freeing Canada from British domination. They were originally formed to assist William Lyon Mackenzie and Joseph Papineau and their followers in the Rebellion of 1837. In Lower Canada they were known as 'Les Frères Chasseurs,' in Upper Canada as the 'Patriot Hunters' Lodges.' In 1840 they were still holding secret meetings with codes and signals supposedly known only to their members. Their program was one of intrigue and sabotage. In April 1840 the Hunters were suspected of blowing up the monument to General Brock at Queenston Heights. The explosion was a great shock to everyone in the colony, including Smith, who had no idea when he heard of the Hunters' winter meetings that they were scheming another gunpowder plot.

Politics aside, young Smith had a problem of his own – money. From the time they had moved into Kinnear's cottage on Garrison Common, Smith and the Hind brothers were short of money. By the end of January 1840 their financial situation had become so acute they turned to a friend of Smith's called Gifford for help. Gifford worked in the government office, and through his connections there found them temporary jobs: '*Tuesday 28th January* ... Tom & Ned writing extra work till 4 in the morning ... Tom staid at home in the evening on Thursday while Ned & I went to Govt Office copying & comparing from near 7 in the evening to 2 in the morning.' According to his accounts, Smith wrote twenty hours extra work for the government and made himself a total of three pounds, two shillings, and sixpence. His entry also shows the receipt of two pounds from his father. 'Went with Tom to Smith's & ordered about $4 worth of groceries – played cards, drank grog, and rode about town in Shaw's sleigh with Hinds – singing & making a great row.'

FEBRUARY 1840

About this time the housekeeper who had promised so well, Mrs Davis, disappointed them: 'While Ned & I were at the Government office doing extra work, Mrs. D sat up in the parlor & amused herself drinking ...'

Monday 3rd February. Obliged to cater for ourselves on Saturday, Mrs. Davis still very drunk did not get up till past 12. House in a beastly mess with 3 weeks washing lying about. In the afternoon she went to the post office – as she said – came home dreadfully drunk & worse than ever. Tom, Ned & I lifted her into bed & covered her up. Tom gave her a dreadful scolding & she was very furious on being told she was drunk. She later confessed & promised to give it up ...

Wednesday – Mrs. D nearly recovered but drank some more from the bottle she brought in on Monday ... I was gabbing with her all evening, then after she got into bed, took her bottle away.'

A few weeks later, while Smith was at Twickenham Farm, Mrs Davis left the house on an errand and never came back.
 February brought colder weather and snow to Toronto and influenza to some of the inhabitants.

Monday 3rd. I spent a restless night and felt ill in the morning. Took Seidlitz Powder & Tom very kindly got me some medicine from Dr.

Wilkinson at the Hospital. Could not go to the office or to Hepburn's in the evening altho invited to a musical soirée. A very cold night. Slept by the stove in the parlor.

Wednesday 5th fine & mild – first breakup of winter & commencement of thaws. I felt very much better & went to the office then took a sleigh ride with J. Billings about town, upset into the snow in the hollow behind Government House – felt very much worse towards evening. Irving came up here & brought me some tamarinds & hickory ramrod. Played the fiddle, took 2 pills & went to bed.

Saturday 8th. Felt very weak yesterday – did not go to the office. Took 2 pills & went to bed. Lovely this morning & quite a thaw. Tom Hind & I borrowed Jarvis's cutter & left Toronto at 2 P.M. for home. Yonge street flowing with water, the thaw so rapid the snow fast disappearing. Met Papa at Finch's a little before 3, took lunch & drove home reaching there 20 minutes before Papa.

Monday 10th – went to church yesterday in double sleigh, I drove. Sleighing almost gone. Mr. Fay read prayers – Mortimer preached. After we arrived home I left Papa & Tom drinking port and went over to see the Boyds. It began to rain hard & continued so till near morning when it began to snow fast & drift from the North West. Tom Hind & I left home this morning at 25 minutes to 11. We had some little trouble with Tom's horse on Thorn Hill. Stopped 25 minutes at Finches & arrived in Toronto at precisely 1. The town running with water – our house flooded with about 3 feet of water. Saw Poulett Thomson go down to dissolve the House.

Wednesday 12th – very hard frost. Went to the office very early & saw Mr Draper who told me of his appointment to Attorney-General & of my being his clerk. I went at once to Hocken's where I ordered a pair of long boots for myself to wear in Court on Thursday. Skated till 8 P.M. this evening. Afterwards played the fiddle then read & went to bed. Queen Victoria married.

Friday 14th. Went shopping yesterday with Tom & bought some things for the house. 93rd Regiment marched through town. Billings treated me & Tom. Walter Boyd came to me for ½ a dollar for a pair of velvet gloves belonging to another Upper Canada College boy which Walter had lost. Very mild today & raining tremendously, thus I got very wet coming from

1840 / 35

the office. We went to Jarvis's in the evening to tea where we spent a delightful evening getting pretty well corned, waltzing, galloping,[6] just acting. Danced Sir Roger de Coverly[7] for 1½ hours. Quite the pleasantest evening I have spent this winter. Came away near 2 in Jarvis's sleigh with Fitzgibbons, Miss Steer etc.

On Saturday, 15 February, the official government newspaper, the *Upper Canada Gazette*, published the appointments of William Henry Draper to attorney-general, Robert Baldwin to solicitor-general, and Christopher Alexander Hagerman to judge of the Court of the Queen's Bench. 'Saw Hagerman take his seat on the Bench,' wrote Smith.

Sunday 16th – Cold & snowing. In the morning I went to St. James' Cathedral Church & sang in the choir. Bishop Strachan preached, a stranger read the prayers & a collection was taken up for the family of William Butcher, the man who fell off the steeple and was killed last October. Poulett Thomson at church.

Monday 17th. A lovely day – Poulett Thomson took his departure for Montreal at 6 A.M. in a Russian Droshky built especially for him. He took with him Baring, as aide de-camp. I was up earlier than usual & exceedingly busy all day – moved Attorney-General's desks into our office but had not time to see my sister Mary. William Jarvis came to the cottage in the evening & we had red herrings & tamarinds for tea. After tea Bill & I walked with Jim Fitzgibbon who was going to fetch his little sister from Mrs. Draper's juvenile party. I shot a mad dog at the Draper house. Wrote a few lines of poetry on office business before I went to bed.

Friday 21st. Raining almost all day yesterday. Went to the office till ½ past 1 – came home & rode out on Tom's poney to Mr. Boyd's party at Richmond Hill. Rain in the evening prevented many from coming, but the Duries, the Gappers, the Barwicks, John Parsons, Mrs. & Miss Cameron all came. I spent a very pleasant evening, came home & went to bed at 4 A.M. Left home at 10 A.M. this morning, beautiful day & freezing hard, arrived in Toronto by 12 o'clock, cleaned Tom's poney & went to the office.

APRIL 1840

When he recorded Queen Victoria's marriage to Prince Albert of Saxe-Coburg-Gotha on 12 February 1840, Smith did not say how long the news took to come from London to Toronto. He did, however, describe the festivities in the city some six weeks later.

Thursday 2nd April – weather very fine indeed. Great ball at Government House last night in honour of the Queen's marriage. General Holiday today by Proclamation. An ox was roasted whole and people sat down to dinner in the market place with the 32nd & 93rd Regiment bands playing all the time. In the evening there was a general illumination. Mary and I walked about the town until 11 o'clock.

Friday 10th April. Very fine. Came home very early from the office yesterday as Mr. Draper was at Council. In the evening I went to the Theatre to see Monsieur Schioghoff juggle, found plenty of ladies there. Sat in the pit, very cold there. We were to have gone to Shaw's or Fitzgibbon's this evening but it rained & Ned Hind & I had bad colds so we took pills & went to bed.

Sunday 12th. Raining very hard, did not go to church. Tom Hind came in with their waggon for us. About 12 o'clock when the weather got a little finer we went out to Major Hind's farm, Tom Hind & Jim Fitzgibbon on horseback, I driving Captain Fitzgibbon & Ned Hind in the waggon. This was the first time I saw their farm & met Mrs. Hind. We spent a very pleasant day there. I came in to Toronto on Tom's poney about 9 P.M. He & Captain Fitz walking.

Saturday 18th. We gave a dinner party last Wednesday at the Happy Go Lucky Club for Jim Fitzgibbon who is leaving Toronto to join his regiment, the 84th. All the Fitzgibbon brothers came, also Sam & Bill Jarvis, & Christopher Robinson who arrived after dinner. Gave them a very good dinner, with wines, & later, coffee. Left town next day with Papa, Mamma & Mary, in our waggon. Roads dreadfully bad. Showery all day on Good Friday making the roads too bad to go to church. Still raining today so I planted trees all day. Brock's Monument at Queenston Heights blown up at 4 A.M. this morning.

As every Canadian schoolchild learns, Brock's monument was erected in the year 1824 in memory of General Sir Isaac Brock who had been killed in battle against the Americans at Queenston Heights on 13 October 1812. His body and the body of his aide-de-camp, Attorney-General John Macdonell who fell with him, were buried at the foot of the memorial

1840 / 37

column. The blowing-up was done in the darkness of the very early hours of 18 April 1840 by a mysterious insurgent group. Were the conspirators members of the 'Hunters' Lodges'? Larratt Smith says nothing. Of course he did not learn of the destruction of the monument on the day he recorded the event in his diary; he may not have known until he arrived back in Toronto late in Easter week. Captain Larratt Hillary Smith, Larratt's father, with sixteen miles of miry Yonge Street his only link with Toronto, would not have received the news until much later. Having commanded the field trains in the War of 1812, Captain Smith may have known Brock personally; he had been at the battle of Queenston Heights and had published an account of the engagement. He may even have seen General Brock fall. One can only guess his emotions when he heard of the wanton vandalism of this gallant soldier's tomb.

MAY–JUNE 1840

On 28 May 1840 Captain Smith and his son went over to Queenston on the steamboat *Transit* to have a look at the damage. Official plans were made for a mass excursion to arouse public interest and raise money to rebuild Brock's monument. This excursion took place on Thursday, 30 July 1840. Larratt, by this time, had been promoted to a lieutenancy in the 4th North York Militia.

My sword & cap & uniform came by stage from home on Tuesday. Got up very early before 4 o'clock yesterday morning & walked down to the wharf to see the vanguard of the party to Brock's Monument off by the *Transit*. Today was very beautiful. I rose early, dressed myself in uniform – took a little breakfast & went down to the *Transit* to be conveyed to Brock's Monument with upwards of 200 Militia officers. The steamboat *Traveller* came up to take Sir George Arthur. The *Gore* & *Queen* also crossed, full of passengers. I unexpectedly met Papa on board the *Transit*, he had come in with Mr. Carthew – Mr. Boyd and John on board with all the Yonge Street people – spent one of the most delightful days that ever I remember – 9 boats forging abreast up the Niagara River[8] ...

Friday 31st. Drank tea last night with Bridgeford's friends the Trumbleys, pretty girl among them. Papa went back by *Gore*. I slept on the floor at Wynn's. All the vanguards alias X militia officers, very blue indeed. Up early this morning breakfasted at the marquee then walked about Queenston Heights with Spragge till time to pack up. We gave 3 cheers on striking tents & sang God Save the Queen before going on board the steamer *Queen*. Arrived in Toronto before 5 P.M.

Smith's account book for January 1841 shows that he finally paid (or scraped up) a 'subscription to Brock's Monument 8 shillings & 2 pence.'
Perpetually hard up, Smith nevertheless always seemed to have enough cash to indulge his musical tastes. In the winter of 1840 he began to take piano and singing lessons from a music teacher called Hyde. When they first met at a glee club, Smith was greatly impressed with Hyde's musical talent; the lessons went well until the middle of April when Hyde took a holiday, which continued until early May: 'I went to Hyde's house but he was too unwell to attend me – said he should not charge for piano.' Then, beginning 18 May, Hyde gave Smith a few singing lessons, but they did not last, perhaps because Hyde had moved his quarters: '*1st June* – No music lesson – Hyde's room in a mess – old woman sewing carpet but himself not at home. I waited till ½ past 6 ... *Monday 15th*. No music lesson – Hyde very hoarse altho' out boating. He promised me a ticket for Mr. Hill & Miss Reynold's soirée but behaved very shabbily about it. No ticket but he himself went to the concert.' On 7 July, Smith paid Hyde four pounds but says nothing more about him until Friday, 1st August: 'Hyde in Gaol – seduction ... *13th August* – Hyde Married.'
As Hyde the music teacher became more and more elusive and the music lessons more infrequent, his pupil turned to another pursuit, shooting. There were no game laws in Upper Canada at this time; anyone with a gun could kill a wild animal or a bird whenever he felt like it, even in the mating or nesting season.

Tuesday 13th May. After the office yesterday I went to the Island with Bill Jarvis in his boat. It was blowing too hard to fish so we did some shooting. Jarvis shot 2 Sand Pipers & I shot a duck & gave it to Henry Draper. Left the office very late & went shooting after dinner, missed a beautiful shot, ducks very shy. Later at home by myself, sat a hen on 7 duck's eggs.

Although wild ducks and other game birds were plentiful around Toronto Bay and the islands, the easiest prey of all were the great number of passenger pigeons that clouded the summer skies over Toronto and the surrounding country. In his journal for 15 June 1840, Smith described riding in the fields at Twickenham Farm and seeing flock after flock of these beautiful long-tailed birds flying northward towards Lake Simcoe. And in Toronto: 'Making preparations for morning pigeon campaign ...

tremendous pigeon shooting in every direction. John Bell shot his finger off pigeon shooting.'

In those early days, when Toronto was a garrison town, the officers and men of the British army stationed at the fort were an important part of the social life of the colony, and their comings and goings were watched with great interest.

Tuesday 2nd June 1840. The 93rd Regiment went off in toto yesterday. I dined late at 8 o'clock, then walked down to the wharf with Ned Hind to see if the 34th Regiment had come. It had not but 2 companies of it came in near midnight, and the 83rd touched here on the way to London. Went this afternoon to hear the band of the 32nd Regiment play in College Avenue for the first time.

Very hot weather, but despite heat the 43rd & 32nd Regiments were bridgading with the Lancers today on Garrison Common, and the 34th reviewed by Sir George Arthur. Then Sir Richard Jackson[9] arrived from Niagara per steamboat *Queen* at Government Wharf & went up & marched them past again. Heat ended by a violent thunderstorm. A man was struck by lightning & killed & the mast of the *St. George* struck as she lay at anchor in Toronto Bay. Torrents of rain – no marching today.

The new regimental bands soon took their places in St James' Church: 'I went to church twice today, the 32nd Regiment Band played in the morning & the 34th in the afternoon. Archdeacon Stuart preached in the afternoon (horrible).' This is George Okill Stuart (1776–1862), archdeacon of Kingston, Upper Canada. Dr Scadding wrote of him: 'He had a curious delivery characterized by unexpected elevations and depressions of the voice irrespective of the matter, accompanied by long closings of the eyes, and then a sudden reopening of the same ...'[10] With the exception of a certain elderly parishioner who always got up and walked out when Dr Stuart appeared in the pulpit, young Larratt Smith, the soldiers of the Queen, and the rest of the congregation – in thrall to custom – sat in passive endurance, theirs not to reason why.

JULY–AUGUST 1840

On Wednesday, 8 July, the attorney-general of Upper Canada, amiable William Henry Draper, gave his articled student time off to help with the haying at Twickenham Farm. Every able-bodied person in the countryside, armed with scythes and pitchforks, was trying to get the fodder in before the rains came. Young Smith pitched hay until Thursday the 16th.

A very fine hot day. I would have gone with Papa to Toronto yesterday but was too busy with the hay. Papa returned today bringing Mary & Adelaide from Mrs. Blake's school in the new drag,[11] one of the horses quite ill from the heat & fatigue, bled him. Aunt Boyd with Elizabeth & John & Miss Parsons came in the evening & drank tea with us. Mrs. Gapper was unable to come because of Mrs. Barwick's illness (confinement). It came on to rain so Miss Parsons could not go home & therefore slept at our house. I made a great fool of myself to amuse them.

The haying over, Smith went back to Toronto just in time to catch the circus: '*Friday 24th.* Found the National Circus here, went to it in the evening with Bridgeford, both of us very much pleased, many ladies there & a cram.'

The circus was followed by a travelling theatrical company. At that time Toronto had no proper theatre: plays and concerts were performed in the public rooms of taverns or in hotel ballrooms. Smith wrote: 'Went to the Theatre at the City Hotel where I saw acted *Hunter of the Alps* & *Perfection.* Very tolerable acting by an English Company.' He went to two more performances in the same week: 'Saw on Wednesday, *Soldier's Daughter* & *Blue Devils,* pretty well played, and to night, *Beacon of Death* & *Raising the Wind* admirably performed.'

When the players moved on to Montreal, the circus reappeared: 'Papa came in to town on horseback & we went together to the Circus. Ned Hind there in attendance on the Royal Family, alias Sir George Arthur, the lieutenant-governor, Lady Arthur & children. Circus very splendid indeed.'

SEPTEMBER 1840

The Happy Go Lucky Club was in its last stages. After a year in which scarcely a night went by without convivial friends dropping in to play cards, wine and dine, Smith and the Hind brothers could no longer afford to live in the cottage on Garrison Common.

Friday 4th September. Having given Thomas Kinnear due notice of our intention to leave his premises at the end of our year's lease, I paid him the sum of £7 and 10 shillings & gave the receipt to Tom Hind. Papa and

Mamma came in yesterday (bringing Mary to have 2 teeth extracted). Papa went with me to look at rooms in the house of Dodsworth, the shoemaker. We engaged quarters for me there, commencing on the 14th September & made arrangements to pay Dodsworth 4 dollars a week for the rooms & my board & ½ a dollar a month for cleaning shoes. I then drove up to Garrison Common with our man, Patrick in the waggon & fetched away my trunk, stove & bedding, & my spoons. Left the Happy Go Lucky Club for good & drove home to Richmond Hill.

While he was at Richmond Hill, Smith paid a visit to some friends who lived near the village of Newmarket on the Holland River.

Wednesday 9th September. Borrowed Papa's saddle-horse, Fop, & started for Mr. Edmund Carthew's farm at 11 in the morning. After a little difficulty in finding the road, arrived at the farm between 12 & 1 o'clock. Mrs. Carthew as usual without a servant. We took some luncheon and then drove in their carriage to call on Dr. & Mrs. Primrose at Newmarket and invited them to dinner. Mrs. Primrose came, but the Doctor did not arrive till after dinner. After dinner & later after evening tea, we had great singing & they made me dance the hornpipe. The party broke up at 1 A.M. Bitten by bugs all night & obliged to sleep on the floor.

Friday 11th. Showery all day yesterday. Walked to see the country with Mr. Carthew. After tea we put Fop with another horse into Carthew's waggon & drove in the rain, all of us into Newmarket to fetch a trunk, did not get home till 11 P.M. Left Mr. Carthew's after dinner today. Before leaving he gave me a pair of Spanish gaiters and I gave the little ones a yorker apiece for bull's eyes.[12] Rode home & on reaching Twickenham Farm found a card from Government House for *yesterday's* party!

Tuesday 15th. Left home for Toronto by stage-coach yesterday morning. Georgina Moodie also went in – pretty friendly. After staying at the office till ½ past 5, I procured a carter to bring my things & came to Dodsworth's for the first time, arranged everything & went to bed.

Wednesday 16th. Raining very hard. Hardly slept at all last night for fleas & bugs; killed 7 fleas & 1 bug – fleas on the whole pretty plentiful. Noise of Milk Men awakes me early, even so I was rather late to the office. After dinner I played the violin, then went to see Mary at Mrs. Blake's & took her the things I brought in for her. I came home & played the fiddle again after tea, read a little & went to bed. Rather slow here.

By 26 September, Smith's life became more lively.

Mr. Draper went off on the Eastern Circuit today. About 2 o'clock I left the office & went shooting with Jarvis. We sailed over to the point then walked over a great part of the island where we killed 2 brace of plover, then rowed back & came home about 8. When I got home I found Tom Hind, Ned Hind, Sampson, Breakenridge, & Alex McDonell quite comfortably ensconced in my parlor drinking brandy & water & eating the melons McDonell had brought me. They stayed till 11 P.M. then went away. I sent a 5 shilling order to Smith's for ½ a gallon of brandy.

Monday 28th. After church yesterday afternoon I read some Blackstone, took a walk to the toll gate in Lot Street [Queen], went to see Mary & gave her some crabapples. Studied Italian in the evening before I went to bed. Fine & cold today. Breakfast not being ready this morning, I went away without it & took it in the course of the day. Very hard at work all day copying declaration in Niagara Dock Company vs Hon. John Hamilton[13] in re Steamboat *Ontario*. At 6 o'clock Brough & I left the office & adjourned to this house where he dined with me & we wrote after dinner till 9 o'clock, when Brough left to serve the declaration. After tea I composed for the violin.

Wednesday 30th. Raining in squalls all day & blowing a gale from the East. I spent the greater part of the day writing letters for the Attorney-General & sending off writs. Mr. Boyd's manservant came in & brought me a letter from Papa enclosing £10 and a pair of stockings from Mamma. Bill Jarvis came to tea in the evening. I played the fiddle.

OCTOBER 1840

Friday 2nd October. I cashed Papa's cheque at the Bank of Upper Canada, paid Murcheson's bill of £2, 5 shillings, took receipt & bought a ready-made dress coat & a pair of cloth gaiters for 7$. Foggy & blowing great guns from the North East today. After the wind dropped I went sailing in Jarvis's boat, came home & found that Alex McDonell had left me 3 melons. After dinner took Mary a melon, then spent the rest of the time loafing about after calling on Hinds who were not at home at their new residence. I eat a whole large melon at tea; very uncomfortable.

Saturday 3rd. Cold & blowing tremendously hard from the South West, the steamboat *Transit* had to put back & the *Britannia* put back 3 times. Jarvis's boat was blown ashore, ditto Dalton's boat & many others. Aemilius Irving came in to-night & took up his quarters with me at Dodsworth's. Irving & I traded watches, I gave mine with 2 waistcoats, spurs, & a pair of gaiters, & bought a pair of corduroy trowsers for 5 shillings & lent Irving 5 shillings for his fare to Newmarket to see his father. Jarvis came to tea in the evening & Hinds looked in.

Wednesday 7th. Very fine & rather cold. Cattle Show in Toronto today. Papa & all the Yonge Street people came in. A letter came from Aemilius Irving with an invitation to go & see him at his father's farm. Met Captain Irving at the Cattle Show & agreed on a time for starting tomorrow, I then returned to the office & worked till ½ past 4. Papa came to my rooms in the evening & drank tea here & I gave him his papers sent in with his Petition for land (which was refused). After Papa left I packed up my things to go to Bonshaw.

This was young Larratt Smith's first visit to Captain Irving's farm, Bonshaw. Dr Scadding wrote of it and its owner: '... the conspicuous dwelling of Captain Jacob Aemilius Irving here on Yonge Street was known as Bonshaw, from some ancient family property in Dumfrieshire. Captain Irving had been an officer in His Majesty's 13th Light Dragoons and was wounded at the Battle of Waterloo. In addition to many strongly-marked English traits of character and physique, he possessed fine literary tastes, and histrionic skill of a high order, favoured by the possession of a grand barytone voice. He retained a professional liking for horses. A four-in-hand guided by himself issuing from the gates at Bonshaw and whirling along Yonge Street into town, was a common phenomenon.'[14]

Thursday 8th October very fine & intensely hot. Started from Toronto with Captain Irving & two servants in his four-in-hand about ½ past 9 A.M. Colonel Cotter of Newmarket went up with us. We reached Newmarket early in the afternoon. Bonshaw is a pretty farm 1¼ miles from Newmarket and the same distance from Holland Landing. I met Mrs. Irving who I am told is a daughter of Sir Jere Homfray of Landaff House, Glamorganshire, Wales, and found her to be a delightful woman & Miss Irving a nice girl. We had a very good dinner at 6 P.M., chatted in the evening & went to bed.

Saturday 10th. Yesterday went shooting with Aemilius & shot 1 snipe & a plover. After luncheon Aemilius, Miss Irving & I rode on horseback through Newmarket round by Primroses, first called on Colonel & Mrs. Cotter and then to George Hill's farm & back. Mrs. Primrose invited us to tea this evening, but the weather was so cold & unpleasant with drizzling rain & Captain Irving did not like us to use the horses on such a bad night, we stayed at home, chatted & went to bed.

Monday 12th. We all went to church in the carriage yesterday but did not arrive there till the singing before the Communion service. Bad roads & drizzling weather. Church thinly attended. It was still very cold today when I went out to shoot & killed an owl. After that I fiddled about until 2 o'clock in the afternoon when we dined. After dinner, Miss Irving, Aemilius & I sang until George Hill called about 5 when we all started in the light waggon to spend the evening at Colonel Cotter's farm. A rather pleasant evening, singing, & waltzing. The horses ran away with us coming home.

Tuesday 13th. A & I walked through the woods to George Hill's farm to invite them to dinner, shot nothing on the way. After luncheon I walked with Mrs. Irving & Miss I. to see their new house, & while in the woods we gathered some fungus on which to draw. In the evening, played cards with Miss Irving.

Thursday 15th. Went in the cart with Aemilius yesterday morning to Holland Landing to see some friends but they were not at home. After luncheon we walked into Newmarket & called at Mrs. Primroses & apologized for not going there on Saturday last. Today was the opening of the Newmarket Cattle Show, Captain Irving offered me a horse to go to it & when I refused Aemilius was very angry with me. In the end Aemilius walked to Newmarket alone & I went shooting & shot 1 couple of snipe. After dinner, played dominoes with Miss Irving.

Saturday 17th. Left Bonshaw Farm yesterday morning with Captain Irving in his four-in-hand at 11 A.M. On the way down we stopped at Barwick's where we took a glass of wine, greased the wheels of the vehicle & baited the horses. A beautiful morning but dreadfully cold & the roads were very rough. We did not reach the Black Swan Inn till $\frac{1}{2}$ past 4. I got down there & went straight to the office, but there was no one there. After dinner went to see Mary, then to bed very early. The fire bell at St. James' Church rang just after I got into bed. Spent most of this morning at the office Answering Questions[15] given by Mr. Draper on his arrival home from the Circuit. Later in the day I took a note for Mrs. Irving & some Statutes to Captain Irving at the Black Swan.

The Black Swan Tavern stood at 211 King Street East and was run by a Mr

John Baker. Baker was said to be a good landlord and his hostelry, although unpretentious, was noted for the reliable care given to the guests' horses. When Smith first knew him, Captain Irving always put up at the Black Swan.

Although Aemilius Irving was now living at Dodsworth's in a room next to Larratt Smith, Smith did not visit Bonshaw or see the Irving girl again until after the new year. As the autumn of 1840 progressed, young Smith's responsibilities increased. He was still a sort of human quill pen: 'Up until 11 P.M. last night writing affidavit & a letter to Scott Burns & Benson which I put in the post office at a ¼ past 11. Up early again this morning & walked over to see Brough to be sworn in affidavit in Simpson & Mittelberger. Wrote the affdt & then a letter which I took down to the *William IV* at the wharf & put in the mail bag on board.'

When he was not writing letters or copying legal documents with his quill pen, Smith was studying the law at its source.

Monday 19th. After dinner I attended Court & heard the case of Bethune vs Hamilton. Verdict for the plaintiff & £575 damages ...

Thursday 29th. Raining all day. Last Day of Assizes. In Court & heard the case of Mrs. Skulin accused of Infanticide. Hume Blake[16] defended her. The Jury retired about 4 o'clock & did not give the Verdict till 9 the next morning. Not guilty, altho' proof positive.

Sunday 25th. Before Papa left town last week he gave me £5 on account. Went at once to Rowsell's[17] library & got *Nicholas Nickleby* by Charles Dickens which I have been reading every evening this week. Frightfully cold & snowing this morning. Read *Nickleby* all morning. Went to church in the afternoon & was to have sat in Jarvis's pew, but Mr. Draper beckoned me to come into his. Went to see Mary after church, came home to find no fire in my room, & none all evening. No wood cut. Saw lost. I therefore lit my candle & read *Nickleby* with my great coat & cap on all evening.

Saturday 31st October. Raining & cold. I spent the day alone in the office writing a Deed, Brough away, Jarvis absent, & Mr. Draper at the Rackets Club to see the match between William Boulton with a racket & De Winton of the Artillery with a breakfast plate. Mr. Draper came back to the office & told me that William Boulton had won the match & the £5 stake ... I was to have been at Sam Jarvis's party but as George Jarvis forgot to give me the invitation, spent the evening playing the fiddle.

NOVEMBER 1840

Monday 2 Nov. First Day of Hilary Term,[18] kept it. Very busy all day, dined with Mr. Draper, then worked in the office with him till ½ past 9.

In the course of this legal work Smith met Bishop John Strachan (1778–1867), first Anglican bishop of Toronto. A Scot who had attended the universities of Aberdeen and St Andrews, Strachan came to Canada in 1799 on the invitation of Governor Simcoe. When Simcoe's proposed college failed to materialize, Strachan started a school for boys at Cornwall which became famous. In 1803 he took orders in the Church of England and in 1812 became rector of York; during the American invasion of York in the War of 1812 he played a prominent role. Later he became a member of the Executive Council and then the Legislative Council of Upper Canada. When Smith wrote of him in 1840, Strachan had been ordained as the bishop of Toronto for about a year. 'John Toronto' was said to have been a formidable, but most fascinating, man.

Thursday 12th. Very fine, easterly wind. After Witnessing Execution of Deed appointing new Trustees to the Hospital & releasing old ones, I attend John Toronto, first in his house, 2nd on the bench, & 3rd by myself at his house again in the evening ...

Wednesday 18th. I was very busy all day drawing an assignment between Bishop John Strachan & Sir Allan McNab[19] (by Clarke Gamble) from the latter to the former. No dinner today. Dodsworth avers I had told them to dress no meat.

Smith went home only once in November, but he made a record trip.

Saturday 7th. Left the office before 1 P.M. for home, reached the corner of King and Yonge Streets at exactly 1 P.M. & walked to Finch's in 2 hours & 18 minutes. Stopped at Finch's exactly ½ an hour by 3 minutes, and arrived home at ½ 6 P.M., performing the distance in 4 hours & a ¼, the shortest trip yet. Found all well at home. The Road is now Macadamized to Corbould's gate, & they are just putting up the 4th turnpike at Cook's ...

Monday 9th. Raining all day Sunday & today. Prayers at home yesterday. Mamma's Sunday School Class came. Left home about 11 A.M. this morning. Papa gave me a dollar & Patrick drove me just beyond Corbould's gate where I met Bill Jarvis & party coming from Coldwater. He offered me a seat in their waggon, but I declined as they were going to stop 1 hour longer at Bingham's to breakfast. Walked the rest of the way, roads horribly muddy, reached Toronto at 3 o'clock & went straight to the office where I found only Acland,[20] as Mr. Draper & Brough were in Court. Found a letter for Papa from George in England brought by Rowsell to the office. Read Blackstone & spilt ink in the evening.

As November drew to a close, and the weather became inclement, the Toronto social season warmed up.

Tuesday 17th. Very fine & a hard frost, the soldiers at the garrison put on their winter uniforms for the first time today. I was invited to Mrs. Draper's party this evening, got there very early at ½ past 9. The 32nd Regiment Band played. I spent a pleasant evening & came home at 2 A.M. An invitation came from Mrs. John Beverley Robinson[21] for Thursday next.

Thursday 26th. Very fine & colder. Went to Stanton's party last evening, very crowded but very pleasant. The 34th Band played quadrilles for the first time. I left at 3 A.M. rather squibby. Felt very unwell this morning. Walked before dinner & bought a pair of gloves – 2 shillings – & went to Mrs. Robinson's in the evening. The 32nd band was there with violins etc. Introduced to Miss Foster by John Robinson, & to Miss Turquand by Miss Robinson. I also danced with Miss Heath and the third Robinson daughter. Came home at ½ past 2 after a very pleasant evening indeed. Mrs. Robinson paid me great attention.

There were other kinds of entertainment: '*Saturday 28th.* After the office I called with Irving at the Chief Justice's house by leaving our cards. Spent the evening at Hinds with Irving, when I lost 9 pence at cards with Irving, but won $10 in a bet with him. Did not get to bed till ¼ to 1.

Monday 30th November, St. Andrew's Day: Very cold indeed & blowing a hurricane from the South West, the West, & later the North West. The steamboat *Transit* caught it & had to put back. I never saw Toronto Bay in such trouble before. It snowed during the day which made the walking very difficult for the St. Andrew's procession. Won a bet of $5 from Irving about cards.

DECEMBER 1840

Tuesday 1st Decr. Dreadfully cold. Irving compromised bets by giving me his watch, a satin waistcoat & a small gold pin for the $10 I won from him. I later went with George Jarvis to leave cards at Mrs. Collyers & ended by spending the evening at Collyers where I won 3 shillings & 9 pence at Whist. Came home at ½ past 10. Beautiful night & freezing hard.

Thursday 3rd. It blew very hard from the South West yesterday. After the office I went down to Garrison Wharf to have a look at the lake & found the seas very high indeed. Papa drove in from Richmond Hill in the evening, bringing Mamma & Adelaide. Irving & I went down to see them & stayed about an hour, then went to Dunlop's Restaurant where I treated Irving, 1 shilling & 1 penny. Papa came to my rooms after breakfast this morning & was measured by Dodsworth for a pair of long stocking shoes. Afterwards I walked about town with the family until ½ past 11 when they went out of town. Much colder, the bay froze over this evening.

Sunday 6th. Montague Stowe & Fred Kelly spent last evening with me walking about the town & playing some tricks, mixing up gate signs & door knockers on Beverley Street. We then came back here. Irving & Ruttan looked in & we smoked & drank. Went to church twice today & sat in Mr. Draper's pew. The 32nd Regiment band played in the morning, the 34th in the afternoon played beautifully Luther's hymn, *& dying Christian to his soul*. It was snowing so hard neither of the bands could play their instruments as they marched to church. In the evening Ruttan called & we went to Richey's Methodist Chapel. As I walked home from the Meeting with Ruttan, found someone had set fire to the steps of the English church. Put out the fire & got a policeman to ascertain the cause. After I came home I read Byron & Blackstone till ½ past 2 in the morning.

Thursday 10th. Very mild sloppy weather & very little to do in the office this week. Sat reading Richard Bentley's *Miscellany* all day on Monday. On Tuesday I drew a Lease, then, after the office walked with Irving. Later in the evening Irving won 38 York Shillings from me which I won back at double or quits. Yesterday after writing a letter to a client ... & posting it, I walked to the racket court to see some play. Bought some pills at Becket's on the way home. After dinner the Hinds came in with Frank Boyd. In the course of playing cards Irving threw his up, or rather towards me, supposing I had called him a liar. Took him to task for it, but nothing further unpleasant occurred. I took 2 pills & went to bed.

Friday 11th. Medicine called me out of bed early. After breakfast & before going to the office I walked in front of the Bay. Mild no wind, one of the loveliest days for a long time. After the office I walked up Front Street to the new Gaol. No one with us in the evening, so spent it reading *Jack Sheppard,* Ainsworth's novel about the robber who was hanged at Tyburn in 1774. Took another pill & went to bed.

By 17 December, Smith had postponed taking any more cathartics (the favourite nostrum of his time), and the weather had changed: 'Frightfully cold, the streets all ice, making walking very difficult. Left the office early & skated to the Island where I sailed in Jarvis's ice boat, & finally helped to drag her back, very little wind. F. Stowe, C. Fitzgibbon & Sawyers here in the evening, gulled the latter. George Jarvis raffled his poney at Ontario House.'

Monday 21st. Very cold & beautiful ice all over the Bay. Before I left the office Mr. Draper gave me leave for 2 weeks holiday at Xmas. Went skating on the Bay at 3 o'clock & continued at it till much past 5. After dinner I went down to Mrs. Collins' house en deshabille & met to my surprise, a little party. Mrs. Primrose & Miss Black, Mr. & Mrs. H. Heward, Mrs. Cockburn & Daughter – introduced to the latter & to some others – dancing & singing all the evening, got home at $\frac{1}{2}$ past 11. Snowing hard & drifting. Scarlet fever in the Dodsworth house.

Thursday 24th. Very cold indeed. Got up before Irving, obliged to clean my teeth with coffee as there was no clean drinking water. Capt. Irving drove in yesterday, & Aemilius went home with him this morning. Papa having driven himself in the cutter, followed by Patrick in the large sleigh, stayed the night at Ontario House. I paid Dodsworth's 3 months Bill £4.2.6. Papa at the same time paid him for his long stocking shoes. I left the office at 12, met Papa at Ontario House, Mary came from Mrs Blake's & we took her to luncheon at Dunlop's then Mary went home with Papa in the cutter while I waited at Dodsworth's until called for by Patrick in the large sleigh.

Christmas 1840 at Twickenham Farm was quiet as usual. On Christmas day the entire Smith family drove in the cutter, with a second horse harnessed to an outrigger, through the deep snow to the church at Thornhill; they received the sacrament, met the Boyds, and all dined together. The last days of 1840 they spent visiting friends: '*30th December:* Papa driving the large sleigh took me as far as Mrs. Carthew's, then he & Mamma, with Mary & Adelaide, drove about the countryside calling on people & inviting them to come to the party we are giving after the New Year.'

6: Parties, politics, pretty girls 1841

JANUARY 1841

Young Larratt Smith, having got a lift in his parents' sleigh as far as Newmarket, saw the New Year in at the Carthew farm, and spent the next few days visiting friends.

Sunday, 3rd January 1841. The Carthews & I spent last evening at the Primroses, very good singing & an oyster supper. After church today old Henderson drove the 2 Miss Cockburns, Miss Sarah Henderson & myself back to his house at Davidtown where we found the Heaths, Murray & Mr. & Mrs. D'Arcy Boulton. We had a very good dinner at which I carved & did the agreeable. After dinner James Cockburn drove Geo Jarvis & myself into Newmarket. A tremendously cold night & snowing fast ... We had a venison supper at the Newmarket Inn & slept there. George Jarvis played his violin.

Wednesday 6th. I left the Newmarket Inn on Monday morning & walked out to the Carthews' who were busy getting ready for their party. I spent the entire morning cutting ham then went to bed at midday. The Carthews' party in the evening a very pleasant one. I danced the hornpipe. Papa came up for the party & Miss Irving came down from Bonshaw to go home with us. We left the Carthews after dinner yesterday & reached Twickenham Farm at $\frac{1}{2}$ past 5. In the evening I played drafts & chess with Miss Irving & today drove her in the little sleigh to the Hill where I bought her some bull's-eyes.

Friday 8th. Raining & snowing all day yesterday. I fetched things we needed from the Boyd's. Elizabeth Boyd came, & all hands busy preparing for the party – I washing bottles & decanting wine. Took Elizabeth back after dinner then played Backgammon with Miss Irving. This morning I hitched up the mare & Fop & drove Miss Irving tandem into Markham to get champagne branches[1] (£10) at McKechnies. Our party in the evening rather large, among others, were Sam Jarvis & Aemilius Irving who came from Toronto.

Sunday 10th. Went to church today in the big sleigh, all of us except Mamma, who stayed at home to receive Captain Irving. Captain Irving came after church & took Miss Irving away with him. I drank tea at the Boyd's & arranged with Mr. Boyd for a lift in his sleigh to Toronto in the morning.

Smith was no sooner back in Toronto than he began to look about for new lodgings: four months of bad meals, fireless rooms, and slovenly service had made him dissatisfied with Dodsworth's place. By 25 January he was ready to move: 'Got up early, packed up my things, gave the servant boy 1 shilling & 3 pence, & the carter the same & left Dodsworth's bag & baggage for Mrs. Duffill's boarding house. I got there in time for breakfast & found my friends Dyett & Tarbutt there too. Came home after the office to a good dinner. Irving came up in the evening to see the place, and immediately decided to join us at Duffill's.'

FEBRUARY 1841

Irving's sister remained at Newmarket with her parents, but Larratt Smith contrived to see her from time to time. On 4 February he got leave from Mr Draper to go to the Boyds' party at Richmond Hill. He walked there, met Miss Irving at the party, danced till four in the morning when he left for Toronto in Jarvis's cutter, had a snooze, and was back in the office before noon. On 7 February Smith wangled an invitation from the Carthews to spend Saturday night and go to church with them on Sunday.

Went to the office early on Friday & staid there till 2 P.M. when I left & started home on foot, arriving there about 6 o'clock. The next day I took the grey horse, Kate, to be shod, & after dinner, about 10 minutes to 4, I started on Kate to Newmarket & arrived at the Carthews' by a little after 6. Found all well. Went to church on Sunday in the Carthews' large sleigh & found Aemilius Irving & George Jarvis in the Irving pew. Miss Irving there with her Papa & Mamma, had a little chat with them after church, feeling very shabby being obliged to appear in Papa's old great coat!!! I went back with the Carthews & after dinner rode home again. In the morning Papa drove me in the cutter to the 1st toll-gate at Cook's & I walked from thence to Toronto, taking the College Avenue, the roads in swamp & muddy from the thaw. Hinds looked in for a little time in the evening & drank tea.

Wednesday 10th. Cold & snowing. Boys snowballing at the street corners. A meeting was held in the Executive Council Chamber yesterday at which a Proclamation was made by the lieutenant-governor Sir George Arthur, of the Union of Upper and Lower Canada into the PROVINCE OF CANADA. Sir George Arthur resigned at 4 P.M.[2] The Union was officially proclaimed today at 12 o'clock when the Artillery fired 21 rounds. Mr. Boyd in town for a public dinner given to Sir George Arthur at Ontario House. I sent a copy of the newspaper *Patriot* containing the events, to George in England. Went to see Mary who gave me a letter from Miss Irving.

Mary answered the Irving girl's letter, but the answer was, of course, dictated by Mary's brother. Young ladies in 1841 did not write or receive letters from young gentlemen without their parents' permission; they could, however, correspond with their own sex as much as they pleased. Mary Smith's quill pen was kept quite busy for a time.

Another way to a maiden's heart was through her mother.

Saturday 13th. Walked into town with Irving last evening & bought 2 pieces of music for Mrs. Irving – 'Thou art Gone' & 'My Boyhood's Home,' both from the opera of 'Amelie.' I paid 4 shillings & 8 pence & gave Irving 8 pence for turnpike tolls. He left for Bonshaw this afternoon with Stowe. Miss Irving's sixteenth birthday today, oyster patés & port wine.

Although he was not invited to partake of the oyster pâtés, Smith saw the young lady a few days later.

Thursday 18th. Captain Irving & family came into town on Tuesday – Miss I & brother called to see Mary at Mrs. Blake's. After dinner I went down with Irving to the Black Swan to help him take the horses & sleigh to the stables at the North American Hotel.[3] The Irving family then went to a party at Mr. Baldwin's. Yesterday afternoon I left my card for Mrs. Irving at the North American, but was told they were driving about the town & had also gone to see the fox hunt on the ice. I was busy in the office today till 1 o'clock, then went to call on Mrs. Irving. I saw both Mrs. & Miss I & went down to luncheon with them. Afterwards I walked out with them to Laurie's, shopping. We then returned & went to see the artillery practising ball firing on the ice of the Bay. The Court Martial was actually adjourned to see it!!!

A few days later Captain Irving took his wife and daughter back to Newmarket, and the young law student was given an important assignment.

Wednesday 24th, Ash Wednesday. Freezing again & no pancakes on *Shrove Tuesday.* Mr. Draper has just given me leave to carry Writ of the Election to Niagara.

Thursday 25th. Very fine & rather cold with a South West wind. Harrington met me, gave me £10 in advance which started me off on my journey at ½ past 12. Rode in an open waggon for Hamilton. Stopped at Cooksville for a wretched dinner & arrived at Hamilton about 10 o'clock P.M. Supped at Benley's and then went on to Stony Creek where we stopped to water the horses.

Friday 26th. Still travelling in the open waggon to the Forty Mile Creek.[4] There I got into a stage-coach & found myself in very select company – *6 Yankees & a whore as fellow passengers*!! I arrived at St. Catherines about 8 o'clock & after breakfasting there, delivered 1 Writ to B. McKyrs who lives hard by the hotel & took a receipt. After changing horses we went on to Queenston, arrived there at noon & I delivered a Writ to McMicken, the returning officer, who found a mistake in the Writ. Went on to Niagara where I stopped at Barrington's Hotel. Then about ½ past 3 I delivered my Writ to Alma Esq. the returning officer for Niagara. After dining at the hotel I walked about the town & met Brock, Stevenson, & Nichol, the latter took me to see Niagara Harbour & the Dock Company Works. There I wrote a letter to Mr. Draper about the mistake in the Writ & left it in the mail bag for Toronto. Went with Nichol to his house where I drank tea & met an *on dit* pretty girl named Arnold. Left early as I could not keep my eyes open.

Saturday 27th. The Queenston stage coach brought me from Niagara to Drummondville for seven shillings & sixpence. I arrived at the little village of Drummondville about 3 o'clock, after first being thrown into the mud &

breaking my stick, not to mention losing my ring. In Drummondville I put up at Fralick's Inn. After dinner walked the quarter mile down to the Falls & Table Rock, & then up under the bank to Mr. Street's house. Ran into Tom Street who very kindly took me into the house & introduced me to his mother, Mrs. Street. Neither the old gentleman nor the young ladies & their governess were at home. I had however, the pleasure of drinking tea with Tom & Mrs. Street. Two old farmers also took tea there. Left the Streets at ½ past 8 and walked back to Drummondville. Saw great numbers of the 93rd Regiment drunk & dancing in the village street. Not to be outdone I took a glass of brandy & water & went to bed.

Sunday 28th. The driver I had engaged to take me to Cayuga woke me at ½ past 6. A very fine day & the roads hard frozen. On leaving Drummondville, passed Captain Irving's old house. We drove on, then stopped at the top of Short Hills where a fine vista of Lakes Ontario & Erie & an immense tract of country lay before my eyes. We eventually arrived at Mrs. Horton's Tavern, having driven in all, 17 miles. After a tolerable breakfast we drove on thro' the village of Narrows to Sansiban's Tavern where we took a very welcome glass of ginger beer. Thus fortified we went on to Canboro having covered 37 miles since morning. Having stayed at Canboro & rested the horses for about an hour, we then drove along the 10-mile piece of road made by the black regiment[5] reaching Cayuga where we stopped at De Coo's[6] Tavern. At De Coo's I met Mr. Thomson, candidate for the riding of Haldimand and Harry Powell subaltern of the black regt. We pushed on along the banks of the Grand River to Indiana. Mr. Thomson who took a lift as far as his own house, also invited me to take a glass of grog & dinner with him on my return from the village of York. I then drove the 7 miles to York. Delivered the Writ of Warner Nelles who lives in a beautiful cottage on the Grand River. To satisfy himself, Nelles opened the Writ which was a mistake. I therefore took a certificate of his having opened it & took away the Writ. Returned very late to Indiana, dined & slept at Mr. Thomson's house, having travelled 57 miles today.

MARCH 1841

Monday March 1st. After leaving Mr. Thomson's at daybreak, I stopped at Canboro where I tore down a placard of Hincks[7] in the bar room. Reached Mrs. Horton's having travelled 35 miles through Sansiban & the village of Narrows. Pushed on over the Short Hills to Allenburg where I found the Writ for Queenston altered to Port Robinson. Finally arrived at Drummondville about 3. Dressed myself as well as I could & went on to Mr. Street's residence where I found the old gentleman & Tom at home, as well as his sisters the Miss Streets & Miss Grant, the governess. After tea we had some singing & playing from the Miss Streets, Caroline, Cornelia, & Elizabeth. They are very nice girls & good performers on the pianoforte. The Streets were very kind, they gave such a nice room & a delightful bed.

Tuesday 2nd March. My driver was so late in coming this morning, Tom Street very kindly ordered out his horse & waggon to drive me to Drummondville, but whilst getting ready, the man came. Left Street's hospitable house at 10 o'clock & arrived at Queenston at noon, where I found the stage-coach had been detained to bring a passenger from Lewiston, so did not leave till 1. I dined at St. Catherines & arrived at Forty Mile Creek about ten o'clock – not in time to deliver the Writ & take the stage on – so left the stage & walked about 1 & ¾ miles on the Lake Shore to Nelles' house where I delivered the Writ & took a receipt, then walked back to Dayfoot's Tavern, supped & slept there all night.

Thursday 4th. Breakfasted at Dayfoot's yesterday then took the extra stage-coach to Hamilton with the same drunken passenger of Tuesday's stage. Arrived about 2 o'clock, dined & walked all about Hamilton & saw the place where the fire was. Went to bed after tea but was roused up about ½ past 1 in the morning & left Hamilton in an open waggon. Signor Lyman Blitz, the well-known conjuror, my fellow passenger. After a change of horses at 12 Mile Creek, we arrived at a tremendous hill covered with ice, the horses were thrown down, & the stage nearly went over the steep bank. However with God's help we arrived safely at the bottom. We breakfasted & changed horses at Cooksville & reached Toronto about 12 o'clock. Changed my clothes & went over to see Papa & Mamma who had come in yesterday to dine with the Radenhursts. Found them at Paterson's Hotel waiting for the stage to take them to Richmond Hill. Saw them off, then after going to the office & reporting myself to Harrington, went to my quarters at Duffill's & to bed at ½ past 7.

Friday 12th March. Last Monday was the first day of Elections for country places. Robert Baldwin the Reformer, returned in Hastings County.

Robert Baldwin, who was the eldest son of Dr William Warren Baldwin, had been born at York in 1804. His father had come to America on a sailing ship from Cork, Ireland, in the late eighteenth century. I was told by my father that Dr Baldwin had not only walked from New York to the Town of York, but he had swum the Credit and the Humber rivers in order to arrive there. Once at York, he began the practice of medicine and later combined this with law. It was said that Dr Baldwin not only brought his medical instruments with him to Canada, he also brought the idea of responsible government. This he passed on to his brilliant son Robert. When elected in 1841, Robert Baldwin was already solicitor-general for Canada West. In 1848 (after resigning in the crisis of 1843) this sagacious, far-sighted politician formed the second Baldwin-Lafontaine government and saw to it that the principle of responsible government was finally and firmly established in Canada.

When the twenty-year-old Larratt Smith recorded Robert Baldwin's victory in March 1841, he thought of himself as a dyed-in-the-wool Conservative who had borne arms for the Family Compact, and of Baldwin as the arch-villain of Reform. Smith little knew that within a few years he would leave William Draper's office and go to work in the office of this great statesman. In 1841 Smith was more taken up by the exciting events during the election than with the candidates themselves.

Friday 12th continued. News of a riot at Gamble & Price's Election at Thornhill has resulted in a company of soldiers being sent up Yonge Street today. Having obtained leave to go home, & after seeing Mary & getting letters from Mamma, I borrowed a horse from Wesley's Livery Stables & started for home. Met Mr. Carthew on the road looking for his lost horses, man, waggon wheel etc. When I reached Thornhill I saw Papa, Mr. Boyd & many others at the Election. James Hervey Price, the Reformer was returned by a large majority in that riding.

Monday 15th. Very fine, snow 3 feet deep. I left home in our cutter on Saturday for Mr. Carthew's place at Newmarket. Mr. Carthew, driving his own sleigh took Papa and Captain Armstrong. Aemilius Irving followed driving Carthew's cutter. I slept with Papa that night in the Carthews' Spare Room. Mrs. Carthew's children all ill with the measles. In the morning, Papa, Mr. Carthew & Capt. Armstrong started for Barrie in the big sleigh. I rode to church on one of Carthew's tall horses. Very stormy & drifting snow ... Met Miss Irving, Aemilius, & Edward Hind in the church. Captain Irving gone to Barrie. After church, I stabled the horse, then drove the cutter down to Irving's to dinner. A good dinner & a pleasant time. Left there at ½ past 7, overtook Hind, Irving & Stowe on the road & reached our house about 11. The servants & Adelaide in bed. Woke them up, & after some kind of supper, the entire party slept there, Irving on the floor before the fire. Hind in the Spare Room, Stowe in Papa's bed, & I in my own bed. We all came down to Toronto this morning in Mr. Boyd's big sleigh. A letter has just come for me from Mr. Draper to say that he is elected to Russell Township. The Toronto Elections begin today.

More than a year later, following Charles Dickens' visit to Canada in 1842, the *Toronto Herald* published a furious rebuttal to the English writer's scathing remarks on political violence in Toronto. In spite of the *Herald*'s emphatic denial, young Smith's diaries record that the elections were indeed violent. One might think that the closure of the polls at 10:30 P.M., Saturday, 20 March, would have been too close to the Sabbath to leave room for any unlawful and heated display of emotion, but this timing did not prevent a doughty club-wielding supporter of the newly elected Conservative candidate, Henry Sherwood, from striking at Smith's friend, Dyett, while the latter was on his way to meet Smith at Stewart's Tavern: 'Dyett unhurt, arrived at the restaurant where I settled my election bets by treating him & Tom Street to a good supper.'
Monday, 22 March, was another story.

A large body of persons processed through the town to celebrate the outcome of the Elections. The successful candidates, Dunn & Buchanan chaired through the streets. But, on the return of the procession great rioting broke out; one man was killed & 3 were wounded from shots fired from the tavern below the church. The Riot Act was read & the soldiers of the 34th Regiment & the Artillery were called out. The soldiers dispersed the mob & then took possession of the public house. All is quiet this evening.

Thursday 25th. The soldiers are still in town, consequently the streets are very quiet. Dined with Irving last night at Stewart's Tavern, his birthday. Dyett, the Hind brothers, Tarbutt, & self of the company. Excellent dinner; ducks, beaf, ham, veal pie, fruit, wine etc. Adjourned at 12 o'clock for Hinds' quarters where we kept it up till past 3 in the morning. The Reverend Henry Grasett's son, Bayley was there & singing too! Everyone was pretty squibby.

Monday 30th. Very fine & cold. A great deal of snow on the ground & there are still some sleighs on the streets. At Papa's request I attended the Auction Sale of Staff Officers & mess furniture at Osgoode Hall, also things

1841 / 59

left by Sir George Arthur who sailed for England on the 18th inst. Captain Irving there & bought a tandem cart, harness, cutter robes, whips, & a sofa. I bought a saddle for 12½$ & a harness (double) for 19½$, both belonging to Captain Byron who leaves soon for England with the 34th Regiment. Sent the bill for these things & a copy of the *Colonist*[8] to Papa. Little Edmund Carthew died of the measles at Newmarket last Thursday.

APRIL 1841

Tuesday 6th April. Although it has been cold & blowing for the past week & the ice only about 200 yards below Tinning's Wharf, the first Lake steamboat, the *Gore* managed to make her way in on Saturday & the steamer *Gildersleeve* went out the same day. I walked before breakfast on Front Street today, the streets in Toronto in frightful condition from the wet weather. After the office I went out with William Jarvis in his boat, the lake very rough & we shipped a good deal of water. Walked into town after dinner to Irving's lodgings & left a letter to Miss Irving from Mary. *Ice Out as Far as Mc Donald's Wharf.*

Thursday 8th. Rose earlier than usual yesterday & went into the Quarter Sessions Court. Mr. Boyd & Captain Irving the justices of the peace on the Bench. I then went to Mrs. Blake's school to fetch Mary & take her to Mrs. Radenhurst's where she met Miss Radenhurst & Miss Ridout & they all left for Twickenham Farm in Radenhurst's carriage. I followed with Patrick in our waggon bringing the luggage. Picked up the young ladies at Parsons' farm (Mrs. R staying there) & drove to our house thro' Miles' fields, the Macadamized roads were so frightful. Spent the evening singing & waltzing. Deep snow on the ground. GOOD FRIDAY. Prayers in the morning at home followed by hot cross buns. In the afternoon I put up a swing for the ladies & swung them.

Tuesday 13th. I woke up too late for breakfast on Easter Sunday, had it in my bedroom, then rode to church with John Boyd, he on his father's horse, I on Fop. Sacrament Sunday & a quiet evening. On Monday morning I transferred the ladies swing to the barn & made a very good one there. After dinner I drove them in a sleigh to the woods for a swing on a tree. John Boyd came over & we spent the evening waltzing & singing. Mr. Boyd very kindly brought me into Toronto this morning in time for the office. In the evening Irving came up & brought me an invitation to Mrs. Stowe's party – walked home with him to Mrs. Howe's. The ice is slowly leaving the Bay in one immense sheet & went out almost entirely in the night.

Friday 16th. Yesterday after breakfast I walked down town to the Bank of Upper Canada to see Irving & tell him of his being sent to Montreal next week. Whilst there, Irving gave me the latest gossip, which is that McCormack (who blew himself up about a week ago) is being superseded in the Bank by a son of Dr. Short with a salary of £150 Per Annum which is causing great discontent. In the evening Irving & I went to Mrs. Stowe's party, a very nice one & the first time I heard the 'Sleigh Bell Waltz,' played by the 34th Regiment Band. Dined with Irving today & we both called on Mrs. Stowe. Jane, Duffill's servant, turned away, drunk. Mr. Draper spoke to me about going to Kingston.

Here Smith is referring to the removal of the seat of government of the new Province of Canada from Toronto to Kingston.[9] William Henry Draper, as attorney-general, had no choice but to leave with it.

Wednesday 21st. Mr. Draper & Staff left for Kingston this morning per steamboat *City of Toronto.*

Sunday 25th. The steamboat *Gore* went off to Kingston last Thursday without most of her passengers, but taking with her Colonel Avery's child & servant who happened to be on board when she pulled out. The lake boat *Commissioner Barrie,* carrying the abandoned passengers, was sent after the *Gore,* overtook her at Cobourg, transferred the passengers & brought Colonel Avery's child & nurse back to Toronto on Friday. Very lovely weather for the last 4 days. Although the flies buzzing around the wharves & the post office, are troublesome, the frogs are croaking & I saw the first swallows this morning – all of which betokens the arrival of spring. Left off my flannel drawers today. Papa came into town & I told him of my having to go to Kingston.

MAY 1841

In the end Smith did not go to Kingston with Draper's entourage, but stayed out his time in the Toronto law office. Smith's diaries give no reason for Draper's change of mind; indeed he rambles on much as usual.

Tuesday 4th. Saturday was such a warm fine day, I put on my cotton socks, but when little clouds full of snow fell on Sunday, I was obliged to put on my worsted stockings again. Miss Augusta Jarvis died & was buried this evening. As I did not receive an invitation to her funeral, I did not go. After dinner I went down to Irving's rooms & from thence to Stewart's Tavern

1841 / 61

where they were playing 9 pin pool. Irving & I had coffee & watched the game till midnight.

Saturday 8th. Papa rode into town again on Thursday to attend a special meeting of the directors of the Bank of Upper Canada (the Commissariat Department of the Army about to leave the Bank). Papa's horse, Fop, lame & swollen in the hind leg. Papa bought a cannister of salve at Bernard's for Fop's leg, paid 6 shillings & 3 pence for it & left town at ½ past 1. Irving came up last night & asked me to come to his house for the weekend. I went to bed early but was wakened at ½ past 2 this morning by the fire bell. I got quickly out of bed & went down to find a great fire had broken out in the Foundry of Shelden & Deutcher and had spread to the dwellings on Yonge & Newgate [now Adelaide] Streets. I assisted with Mackenzie & Street in taking furniture & things out of people's houses, but there was little we could do, in the end, the flames had consumed some 22 houses. After the fire was out we all went to Watson's quarters at Mansion House[10] where we took a well-earned glass of grog, came home at ½ past 5 A.M. Got some sleep, breakfasted with Irving, had my hair cut, then at 3 o'clock we started on horseback for Bonshaw, Irving had a horse from Capreol, & I, one from Wesley. We got to our house about 6 o'clock. Mamma & Adelaide were walking in the woods, & Papa was out in the fields. After having something to eat, I took Fop (as Wesley's horse unfit to go on) then Irving & I left at 7 P.M. & arrived at Captain Irving's house Bonshaw at ½ past 8. Found Miss Irving & the family all well. I brought 2 pieces of music to Mrs. Irving, 'Long long ago' & 'The Merry Days.' We had tea, a little chat & went to bed.

Sunday 5th. Threatening to rain all day. After church I walked about with Mrs., Miss & Captain Irving looking at some new houses. Left the Irvings at ½ past 9 & got to our house about 10. While at the Irvings I slept in the same bed that Robert Baldwin & Francis Hincks had slept in!!!

In the days before the telephone and the telegraph, life often held little surprises.

Saturday 15th. I worked in earnest every day this week making up Record in Queen vs Chas Sheriff etc. This morning being fine & warm I walked about town & spoke to several merchants in order to ascertain if certain notes of Maitland were good. I then went down to the wharf to see the steamboat *Niagara* arrive from Kingston as I knew the soldiers of the 34th Regiment were on board. The ship docked, and lo & behold who should step forth but Mr. Draper who was not expected till the 25th. He came back to the office with me & I made up Bills of Costs till past 5. After dinner, I walked up Yonge Street with Tom Street, crossed at the Toll Gate & came down College Avenue where, trying to walk with my eyes shut, I sprained my ankle very severely. It made a loud crack & I roared with pain. Somehow with Street's kind assistance I managed to hobble home, had tea & went to bed. Street then kindly went down to Lyman Fair's & got a bottle of Opodeldoc[11] (10 pence). After putting it on my foot I read in bed till past 12 A.M.

Wednesday 19th. Arthur Acland, Tom Galt, Brought, Tom Hind, & Aemilius Irving all called to see me last night. Irving brought me 2 oranges (5 pence) the first this season. Tarbutt looked in. He had brought some elderberry wine & insisted on bringing the sofa upstairs. My foot very much better today, but I wakened with a most excruciating pain in my shoulder. Put a poor man's plaster & some opodeldoc on it this morning with little effect. However, Dyett came & rubbed some of Captain Creighton's counter irritant on it & the 2nd application took away my pain.

Saturday 22nd. Felt well enough yesterday to hobble down on 2 sticks to the lake to see the 34th Regiment off to England on the steamer *City of Toronto*, the 32nd Regiment Band played them off. I followed them down to Brown's Wharf where I saw poor Miss Billings (Captain Byron) & Miss Rogers (Lieutenant Norman) en laisses on the wharf in floods of tears.

In those days, sad farewell scenes like this were not uncommon. The dashing young British army officers quartered at the garrison, who kept Toronto society so alive, were under orders not to enter into matrimony while on colonial service. These instructions were almost always obeyed, and when the girls eventually discovered that dancing and flirting did not lead to marriage, there were some broken hearts. My father told me about two granddaughters of an early attorney-general of Upper Canada who were swept off their feet by a pair of handsome young British captains. The inevitable happened: the young men's regiment was recalled to England, the young ladies never heard from their cavaliers again, and they remained spinsters all their lives. 'You see,' my father added solemnly, 'they allowed themselves to be monopolized.'

JUNE 1841

The departure of the 34th Regiment in May 1841 was as nothing compared to the hectic removal of the government offices to Kingston which

1841 / 63

dragged on into June. Business was brisk at the Toronto wharves as the Court of Chancery, Colonel Fitzgibbon's office, the Surveyor-General's office, and the Department of Indian Affairs all took their departure. With them went a good many of Larratt Smith's friends, including the Hind brothers. Early in June, Smith, who had been helping with the spring planting at Twickenham Farm, came back to Toronto to find himself homeless: *'Wednesday 3rd.* Got into town yesterday about 12 & found that the Duffills were going away to Kingston this morning. Brought all my things here to Ontario House until I can find other lodgings. Everything is quite all right except that when the Duffills cleared out, they took away a pair of my sheets.'

About the middle of the month Smith's friend Tarbutt also went off to Kingston: 'I went down to see Tarbutt off to Kingston this morning. The Indian Department & Baines office – the last office to leave – also went, and a great many of the Members, among them Sir Allan MacNab who evidently attracted by my look, came up & spoke to me.'

When Tarbutt left for Kingston he arranged for Smith to take over his lodgings: 'Having arranged with Mr. Benje to board with him at £4 per month, am now occupying Tarbutt's old room. A fine salmon from the lake for dinner to night. Played the violin in the evening, but on going to bed met a bug travelling up the wall of Tarbutt's room. After killing him I moved into the parlor to sleep on chairs but had barely lain down 15 minutes when I was obliged to rise & kill another.'

Wednesday 16th. Watched the 32nd Regiment take their Departure in the steamboat *St. George* on Saturday. The *St. George* had a damaged nose due to her running foul of the *Niagara* at Kingston on Monday and breaking in the latter's wing & paddle box. Despite this, the *Niagara* brought up part of the 67th Regiment for Drummondville, with Drafts for some of the other regiments. Monday was very cold with an East wind all day but coming off the land at night. The first day of Trinity Term. I kept it; then worked very hard in the office all day on the Revenue. Still working at it on Tuesday & sending off Writs by the steamboats. Irving came in to Benje's after dinner wanting to borrow money again, he stayed on in the evening kicking up a great row & took the door knocker off.

News has just come in today by the Kingston boat that Civilian Speaker, Robert Baldwin, has resigned!!!!! The House is now adjourned till Monday next. It is said that Baldwin resigned because Governor Poulett Thomson refused to reconstruct the administration in accordance with Baldwin's party views. Who knows, this may well be true. After dinner today I walked down town & bought a chip net from Wightman for 1 shilling & 3 pence, also 13 pike hooks on a trapwire which I took down to Commissariat Wharf & gave to George Crookshank in return for letting me use his boat.

Thursday 24th. After the office Jarvis & I rowed to the Island where we picked wild strawberries & bathed. Later Irving came up to Benje's & dined with us. Bad roast mutton, sent it out, otherwise the dinner was good. Mrs. Draper went off to visit Mr. Draper in Kingston on the morning boat, she took the children with her & intends to stop the night at Cobourg & resume her journey on Friday.

JULY 1841

Larratt Smith spent the first weekend in July at Twickenham farm.

Monday 4th. After working late in the office on Thursday & until 3 o'clock on Friday, I left town with Papa, Mary, & Adelaide in the carriage. Stopped at Finch's for cake & ginger beer & got home about 7. Miss Irving at our house. Had a little fun with the girls in the verandah till late. On Saturday, Mary, Adelaide, & Miss Irving went in the woods & swung all morning on the tree while I mended the leaky water puncheon, helped to plant brocoli & picked gooseberries. After dinner I saddled Fop but Adelaide tumbled off & Miss Irving would not ride. Music in the evening & singing. After church on Sunday we walked in the fields to see the horses & I played the fool with the girls. Elizabeth Boyd came over on Monday morning, I put up the tent & had great fun all morning. Then after dinner I harnessed Fop & Mask and we all piled into the lumber waggon & drove down to a party at Parsons' farm where we sang songs & danced. I waltzed with Miss Irving to the music of 'Forget me Not' & 'Have Yesterday' till 1 in the morning.

Tuesday 6th. Raining hard all morning. I was having such great fun fooling with the girls on the verandah I nearly missed the stage coach which came by at 10 o'clock, the stage was so full I was obliged to ride outside. Got into town about 2 P.M., & knowing the Benjes were moving, went straight to the office where I found a letter & a parcel from Mr. Draper. After the office I walked with Street back to my old quarters, moved out all my things & brought away my hat box. Last of all I unscrewed the doorknocker & threw it down the privy! We then had tea at my quarters in Benje's new house. Irving came up in the evening but I left him & went to bed. Bitten by a bug in the night which I killed.

For the most part – and in spite of bedbugs – life at almost twenty-one was a light-hearted affair. But the summer of 1841 also included a serious episode. While I was working on the journals, a cousin told me that our grandfather had been a combatant in the last duel fought in Toronto. Larratt Smith's opponent was his best friend, Aemilius Irving, who, I was told, had made a derogatory remark about Smith's mother, Mary Violett. What he said I do not know. Smith's account, which was probably written up several days after the incident, is bald and reticent. It leaves no doubt, however, that he and Irving had a bitter quarrel. But did they actually fire pistols at each other? Smith wrote:

10th July, 1841. On Wednesday I went to the race course & saw the first 2 races & the last. After dinner I walked up to the course again & fired pistol etc. In the evening I went to the chief Justice's ball but did not dance. Next day Mackenzie received an insolent letter from Irving respecting me, enclosing the sum of 7 shillings & 6 pence. After dinner I went up to the Race Ground to see Irving. He was insolent again. I left, & went to consult Arthur Acland who kindly volunteered his services. I came home & wrote Irving a letter & took a copy of it. Acland came up in the evening. I borrowed a little whisky from Benje, gave Acland a drink then walked home with him & left the letter at Irving's rooms. Yesterday after the office, I called on Mr. Kent & laid the affair with Irving before him. He had already heard of it through Mackenzie & had written to Irving about it, but Mackenzie reasoned with him [this 'him' must refer to Irving] beforehand & did not deliver the letter. While I was at dinner, Irving left a satisfactory letter here for me which I answered after dinner. Street took my letter down to Irving this morning. I worked in the office all morning, then about 3 o'clock went up to the Race Ground, where I met Irving, shook hands & spoke to him. Later that evening I drank wine with Radenhurst & had some singing & music.

To judge by this account, a duel was threatened but no pistols were actually fired. That was the end of the affair; the two hot-tempered young men gradually cooled down and their friendship continued as before.

Young Smith found his lodgings in Mr Benje's new house just as vermin-ridden as those in the old house: his entries describe bedbugs in his bedroom and even in the parlour. His efforts to exterminate the insects led to a dalliance: 'Went down town & bought some bug poison from Beckett's, then Ellen, Benje's servant girl, & I laid on the poison & killed 2 bugs on the wall. Romped with Ellen & came very near kissing her ... Ellen took my sheets out & hung them on the line to rid them of bugs ... frolicked with Ellen, wore kilts for her amusement ... Tom Street larking with Ellen tonight. *August 4.* Ellen went away and Catharine came.'

Towards the middle of the summer the weather became very unsettled.

Saturday 24th. The day opened with a tremendous thunderstorm, the rain came down in such torrents it wetted my room & soon the streets were running like rivers with water. After the office, Mackenzie & I rowed to the Island intending to bathe, but instead we got caught in another terrific storm & 1 awful clap of thunder. The Benjes who had gone out in their sailboat for a pic-nic got caught in the storm & did not get home till 1 A.M. I went to bed about 9 but was awakened by a noisy party of loafers coming home with the Benjes. I stopped their noise & attempts to sing by coughing down the stairwell – they in a great rage.

AUGUST 1841

Tuesday 10th August. Early last week there was a fire; I had stayed up till near 1 A.M. reading *Mary of Burgundy* & had fallen fast asleep when I was wakened by the ringing of the fire bell. I rose at once, wakened Street & we walked up town as far as Judge Sherwood's but as no one could tell us where the fire was, we came home. It later turned out to be Sheriff's distillery. I spent the last weekend at Twickenham Farm. It rained hard most of the time & I got soaked driving Wesley's gig back to Toronto. It was still raining today when General Clitheroe[12] was to have reviewed the 93rd Regiment. By the time they had marched to the parade ground the men were wet through & therefore obliged to turn back. The General went up in the rain & was most annoyed to learn they had gone home. I myself got caught in the rain & was obliged to take shelter in a sentry box. Whilst in there I talked to the sentry whose name was George Grassie of the 43rd Regiment & who turned out to be from Compton Bishop in Somersetshire. He knew my uncle, William Violett & also Uncle Pursley. What a small world!

Monday 16th. Bought a fishing rod for 3 shillings at Regny's last week &, after the weather cleared, went fishing in the Don River where I caught 2 dozen perch. Kept the last day of Michaelmas on Saturday morning. I now have Mr. Draper's consent to my having the agency at the Niagara Commission to examine the state of public affairs, etc. There was a little fuss over my being appointed Clerk for the Commission vis à vis Boomer declined the honor, but now all is well. I worked all day in the office on Saturday & came back after dinner to complete the Memorandum & to arrange with Scadding to cover in my absence. Finished my packing after church yesterday & paid Mackenzie what I owe him for 1 quart of raspberries. Left

Toronto by the steamboat *City of Toronto* at ½ past 7 this morning. Paid John, Benje's servant boy, 1 shilling & 3 pence for taking my things down to the wharf on the wheelbarrow & paid wharfage 7 pence halfpenny. On going on board the ship, I saw Bishop Strachan, Mr. Henry John Boulton, the member for Niagara and a Chief Commissioner, and Mary Jane Moffatt whose father owns the Neptune Inn at Niagara. The ship also brought away to the Falls 650 psalm singers. On arrival at Niagara, I dined with the other clerks at Ducat's Crouch & Press Tavern; the man there lied to us about his wine. Left there & came to Moffatt's Neptune Inn where I took Colonel Thorne's usual room. The Commission opened at 4 P.M., when the Commissioners & myself as official Clerk were sworn in. The other fellows, meanwhile, played cards.

The official clerk spent his days copying the documents and minutes of the royal commission, and his night eluding bedbugs at the Neptune Inn. 'I was copying till near 12 last night while the others amused themselves playing vingt un & Lanterloo.[13] Bridgeford had lost 30$ when I went to bed. I was so eaten up by bugs in the night that in the end I slept on two chairs with the carpet rolled up under me.'

SEPTEMBER 1841

Towards the end of August the commission adjourned, then reconvened early in September.

Monday 6th September. I came back to Niagara last week by the steamer *City of Toronto*. We had an exciting crossing as the *City* with all sails set & engines going full steam ahead driving her mighty paddle-wheels beat the old lake vessel *Transit* by near an hour! The *Transit* was carrying Judge Hagerman, Lord Prudhoe & Sir Henry Hart to the Falls. The commission commenced sitting on Tuesday & I have been copying 50 to 60 folios[14] a day. After church on Sunday I was introduced to a very nice girl, Miss Deborah Muirhead, who is staying with Captain & Mrs. Downs. After dinner Debbie & I walked with some other young people up to Claus[15] & Lyon's gardens & eat peaches there. As the commission did not sit today, I took the Ferry over to Lewiston in New York State and there for the first time in my life saw the locomotives & the cars. In the cars were some soldiers of the 4th Regiment, United States Army, the first American soldiers I had ever seen. I got in the cars & when I arrived at Manchester, left them & walked over to have a look at the Falls from a point of rock hanging over them. When I got back to the town saw the soldiers again but the locomotives & cars had gone. I started to walk to Lewiston & on my road down saw a great number of Militia training, and in Lewiston the whole town in arms marching up & down with fife & drum. As it was too late for the steamers I crossed in the Ferry at Lewiston, then walked back to Niagara in less than 3½ hours.

Tuesday 7th. Up at 6 this morning, worked hard all day, then at 4 o'clock – although the weather was threatening – started on a pic-nic. After McCormack & I got the ale & the boats ready we waited until at last the ladies came down & we started in 2 boats with Debbie Muirhead & 6 other ladies, as well as 8 men. We rowed to a place about a mile below the American fort where we had been on a former occasion. A tremendous wind was blowing up the lake, white-capped waves broke over the boat & we had to get into the water to land the ladies, even so they also got wet. Once ashore we picked crab-apples & eat them after supper which turned out to be a pretty good spread. We left there at dusk. I got wet up to the middle trying to launch the boat in the heavy seas, but eventually we all arrived safely back at Niagara by 8 o'clock, although the ladies seemed a little cross. After changing our clothes, some of the pic-nic party met at Captin Downs' house where we sang till past 10. A fine night. Picked up a little black kitten that followed me all the way home to the Neptune Inn. I soon went to bed, but was wakened by Colonel Thorne who had just returned from St. Catharines & wanted a light. I lit his candle for him & went back to sleep.

Friday 10th. Since there was very little copying to do yesterday I walked up the Queenston road where I overtook une femme et sa fille, and by the simple artifice of dropping a letter, had a great talk with them which only ended when they went into a house by the roadside. I walked on until I came to the tree where Tom Moore the famous Irish poet composed the 'Woodpecker' nearly forty years ago. I picked some mushrooms under that very same tree before walking home to the Neptune Inn. We got all ready for a pic-nic today but the ladies broke it up, saying it was too rough. So I took a walk with Colonel Thorne on the plains by Fort George. We picked some mushrooms, then walked back to Barr's shop where we each bought a spy glass for 3 shillings & a penny halfpenny. A most terrific storm of rain & wind over the lake wakened me in the night.

The Niagara commission broke up at 8 P.M. on Saturday, 11 September. Smith, however, did not finish copying until nearly midnight. He was paid off by Henry Boulton before church time on Sunday and left for Toronto on Monday, 13 September: 'After church yesterday I talked a little with Debbie Muirhead at the steps of Captain Downs' house while the band played. We met again in the evening at Bridgeford's where I had been invited to drink tea. She was with Lieutenant Patterson. I wished her farewell. Saw her again at Downs' window this morning as I walked down to the Toronto boat.'

Smith was hardly back to Toronto before news of the governor's riding accident came from Kingston: 'Lord Sydenham is in very serious condition due to a fall from his horse. Dr. Widmer went off to Kingston in great haste on Friday to attend him. Parliament prorogued by General Clitheroe at 10 o'clock A.M. on Saturday, as the Governor is much worse.' To his entry for Sunday, 19 September, Smith added: 'Lord Sydenham died at $7\frac{1}{2}$ A.M. today. A Proclamation of a general holiday on Friday 24th September has been served on account of the Governor's funeral. Weather cold & raining, fire in the parlor first time this season.'

Thursday 30th. Am now back from a pleasant few days at Twickenham Farm & am writing up my journal for the week. Papa was driving Mamma & Adelaide into town last Thursday to see Dr. O'Brien, when Fop shyed at a calf & the buggy upset into the ditch on Yonge Street. Fortunately, except for a few bruises no one was hurt. As Friday was a holiday, I got into the buggy with them & drove home. I had intended to return to Toronto on Saturday, but missed the stage coach, heard the horn at our gate, but when I ran down it had gone. I was therefore obliged to come down on the crowded Sunday stage. Mr. Draper has been in & out of the office this week, but has now left for Cobourg & Kingston. I drew £8.15 shillings out of People's Bank with Papa's check on Bank of Upper Canada, then after Dinner, walked up to the Races. The Race Ground swarming with pugnacious Orangemen, saw plenty of fighting & was made to say 'To Hell with the Pope.'

OCTOBER 1841

Sunday, 10th October. Very fine lovely weather ever since the first of the month. Papa brought my sister Mary & Elizabeth Boyd into town last week to hear John Braham the celebrated English tenor. I left the office late, dressed, met Papa & the girls at Ontario House & all four of us went to Braham's concert. Among other songs he sang his own popular composition, 'The Death of Nelson.' We were all highly pleased. Mr. Draper came up from Kingston on Friday bringing a Shetland Poney for his sons. I went to a party at Mrs. Draper's where I had the pleasure of meeting Braham & his wife. Mrs. Draper had another party last night in honor of Arthur Acland & his bride to be. I danced & waltzed all evening, did not get home till 1 in the morning. Put some Wedding cake under my pillow to dream on.

Whether or not the cake had an effect, a dream was coming his way.

Thursday 14th. Met Miss Irving in town & walked to Mrs. Hagerman's with her, she also called on Mrs. Draper but forgot her calling cards so was obliged to use two of mine. Walked back to the North American Hotel with her. After dinner, I went out & bought 2 songs for Mrs. Irving: 'Bygone Hours,' and 'Gondolier Row,' for which I paid 2 shillings & 10 pence halfpenny, I then went back to the North American where I found Miss Irving alone, I had barely given the music to her when her Papa came in. Talked with him for some time, then left. Miss Irving & father went back to Newmarket today in his tandem cart.

Tuesday 26th. Spent last Saturday morning running all over the town trying to find Irving & make arrangements for going to Richmond Hill. Irving & I finally left town at ½ past 3 in Crew's waggon driven by Roberts. Terrible weather – raining & snowing all the way! Too much for Irving who got off & returned home when we reached the first toll gate. The driver & I had some beafsteak at Finch's & I reached home at ½ past 9 at night. Dreadfully cold snowing all day on Sunday – prayers at home. Elizabeth Boyd came over in the afternoon, she & Mary measured me for a pair of slippers to be made by Mary. Left home yesterday a little before 10, having managed to get a ride on top of Robert's team hauling cedar fence rails into town. Went to the office and after dinner to sing at Mrs. Gilkison's.

Sunday 31st. Very fine & warm all week; Indian Summer. The blacksmith's shop behind Upper Canada College caught fire last night, got out of bed & assisted in putting it out. Bishop Strachan went to Thornhill today to consecrate the Reverend Mr. Townley's church in Vaughan.

NOVEMBER 1841

Sunday 7th November. Weather very fine. Slept with my window open by mistake last night, but seem to have suffered no ill effects. Papa came in town on Friday & we went together to Wakefield's Book Auction. I bought

2 prayer books at 2 shillings, 2 testaments for 1 shilling & 9 pence, & 2 French Testaments at 6d & 8d. I also bought Samuel Butler's *Hudibras* as well as copies of Milton & Gilpin. Gave Mr. Draper the *Hudibras*. Today was Sacrament Sunday, we sang the Anthem *I will wash my hands*, nice music & pretty good singing. Mrs. Gilkison went out of church with a cough per usual. I went to bed early & read *Amelia*, a novel by Henry Fielding.

Sunday 14th. Mrs. Draper gave a small party last Thursday. I went to Perrin's in the morning & bought a pair of gloves. Wilgress & I slung our boots around us & took brushes & a looking glass & went into the office & dressed for the party. A pleasant evening, I danced a little & waltzed & came home in the pouring rain at 2 o'clock in the morning. Acland & his wife arrived by the *Transit* to visit Mr. Draper. Acland is now quite the buck, but has been refused admission this Law Term as he has not been under Articles 5 years. The singing in church today only tolerable. George Jarvis sat in Miss Crombie's pew playing the fool with her all the service. In the evening I read *The King's Own*, by Captain Marryat, washed my feet in warm water & went to bed.

Sunday 21st. Mrs. Gilkison held a meeting on Friday & formed a Committee of ways & means to collect money to buy a Monte organ for St. James' Church. The meeting went on till very late. On my way home saw a very beautiful Aurora in the sky. Very busy copying music for Mrs. Draper every night. Went over yesterday & gave it to her, also called on Mr. Draper & gave him the book he wanted & took the correct time from him. In the evening I treated Acland at Mr. Scott's restaurant where we eat oysters & drank Mint Juleps & came home squibby at 12 o'clock. Sat in Mrs. Draper's pew at church this afternoon. The choir sang the beautiful Anthem 'Great is the Lord' very well. It came on to rain like blazes & I got wet through seeing Mrs. Draper home. Invited to dine there but declined as I was too wet.

Monday 29th November 1841. A beautiful day. 21 YEARS OF AGE TODAY.
Up pretty early, called for Kent who borrowed Rowsell's sleigh & we drove to Twickenham Farm where we spent a happy evening, champagne and songs.

Thursday 30th. St. Andrew's Day, beautiful weather. Drove Kent into town, then did business in the office. Dined with Acland & his wife – they gave me a capital dinner & some mulled port wine before I came away.

DECEMBER 1841

About two weeks before Christmas a disturbing rumour reached Toronto.

Yesterday after church we were told that some Yankee Regular Soldiers had licked a company of the 68th Regiment on Disputed Territory. This was most alarming news, if true. However, today thank God the story has turned out to be nothing but a pack of lies & the news from England is good. My own prospects are equally good as Mrs. Draper has just returned from Kingston & put in my hands a most gratifying letter from Mr. Draper in which he promises me professional advancement. I immediately wrote to Papa & gave him an extract of the letter. Took Papa's letter to the post office, then sat down & spent the evening reading law.

Young Larratt Smith spent Christmas with the Irvings at Bonshaw, apparently with the understanding that the Irving girl would come to Twickenham Farm at the New Year, to visit Smith's sister Mary, of course.

Friday, Christmas Eve. After two days of pouring rain it is now very fine & freezing hard. Did a little business in the office this morning, then started at 12 with Aemilius Irving, a man-servant, & young Henderson of Newmarket, in Captain Irving's light waggon with a pair of horses. After a frightful drive in which the horses were thrown down twice on the icy roads, we reached our house at 3 & the Irving's at ½ past 6. They had already commenced dinner. Mrs. Irving was downstairs for the 3rd time since her accouchement. This was the first time I had been in their new house, a very handsome one.

Monday 27th. Captain Irving drove Aemilius, Miss I & self to church on Sunday as well as on Xmas Day, but as the Irvings do not have breakfast until after 11 A.M. we were late for church both days. Dinner was not until after 6 o'clock and Captain Irving brought out his champagne both nights. We left on Monday about 11 with Captain Irving's 4-in-hand in the brake. We had only proceeded 2 miles when Capt I broke his whip & had to return to Bonshaw for a fresh one. We reached our farm in an hour & a half. Finding that Papa had gone to Toronto with Mr. Barrie, Captain Irving left Miss Irving & self & drove home again. Mary & I & Miss Irving spent the evening with singing & fun. Papa came in late from Toronto. He had a nasty cut on his head due to Barrie's sleigh upsetting into the ditch on

Yonge Street. Mamma bathed Papa's head, then while he dined, the rest of us went into the Drawing-room where I beat Miss Irving at Drafts then waltzed for the rest of the evening. Papa brought the news that Gas has just been introduced in Toronto.

Wednesday 29th. Fine with little snow showers. This morning I drove Miss Irving over to Boyd's farm to borrow a few things for our party tomorrow. Coming home I took us on a sleigh ride through the field but just as we neared our gate, the mare was thrown down & the sleigh upset in a snow bank. Miss Irving a little cross this evening, no waltzing. I went out & skated on Mr. Boyd's pond with John Boyd.

Friday, December 31st. Our party last night was not as large as usual, as the Thornes, Barries, & Parsons were all unwell with bad colds, Acland's wife had hurt her hand, & Mrs. Cockburn could not be prevailed upon to let the girls come. However the Gappers, Sharpes, Boyds, Pollywog Stewart & his wife, all came, everyone danced & all seemed satisfied with the supper. The party broke up soon after 1 as it began to snow very hard. It was still snowing & drifting from the West when I woke up this morning. However, in spite of the weather I drove Miss Irving & Mary in the large sleigh to Richmond Hill where I bought them bull's-eyes. Came home in a dreadful snow storm which no one minded. Miss I in a much better mood, waltzed & danced all evening. Mary has been invited to stay with the Irvings at Bonshaw.

7: 'Myself the most lively'
1842

JANUARY 1842

Larratt Smith came back to Toronto with his head full of romantic thoughts about the fascinating Miss Irving.

Monday was a melancholy day; while I was in the middle of a game of Drafts with Miss Irving, Captain Irving's man arrived with the sleigh to take her & Mary back to Bonshaw. I rode in the sleigh with them as far as Boyd's farm where I saw them off. Came home feeling damned miserable, packed my things & left home with Papa in the cutter for Toronto & went straight to the office, then after dinner walked with Papa to see the great Gas Illumination which commenced at 7 & ended at 9. Very poor indeed. I became so dreadfully fatigued & tired with walking, I went home early. After tea I tried to read Samuel Warren's new novel *10,000 a Year*, but went to bed very miserable.

Friday, 28th. Went to Clarke Gamble's party on Tuesday, a magnificent affair, Miss Irving there & quite a belle. I came home with her brother at 5 in the morning. I met her on the street yesterday walking with Boulton, she bowed to me rather stiffly. Why? This morning I was in the Court House when I heard the sound of carriage wheels, and looking out of the window, saw Irving, Stowe, Mackenzie, & Miss Irving in a carriage evidently on their way out of town. Irving waved but his sister was looking in the other direction.

FEBRUARY—MARCH 1842

Smith's infatuation went on for some time: '*Saturday 12th February,*

1842. Got to bed just as the new Town Clock in St. James' Church was striking 12, and as I counted the strokes I thought of the morrow & Miss D Irving's 17th Birthday & seriously too. Mary has already written a note at my dictation to D.I. at Newmarket, which I hope she will receive in time for this most important anniversary.'

Letters from Larratt Smith (written by his sister Mary) continued to find their way to Miss D. Irving at Newmarket. There were few replies. But Smith, undaunted, wangled an invitation to Bonshaw at Easter.

Thursday 24th March. Cold & rainy. Did a little business in the office this morning, then discovering Boyd's light waggon in town, found out John Boyd who had come down from Richmond Hill to fetch his little brother from Upper Canada College. John very kindly offered me a lift & we started off about 3. The roads were so villainous that when we reached Richmond Hill we were obliged to get out & walk. Everyone at home rather surprised to see me as I was not expected, slept in the spare-room. This afternoon I waited at our gate till Aemilius Irving & Hind, driving tandem, came by & I gave them my carpet bag to take to Bonshaw.

Saturday 26th. Started for Irving's house this morning on Papa's mare, Kate. The roads were in such a fearful state it took me 3 hours hard riding & I arrived at Bonshaw covered with mud. I was kindly received by Captain & Mrs. Irving who were alone as Aemilius & his sister had gone off on horseback with Tom Hind & did not return till 5 o'clock. After dinner we had a little singing before going to bed.

Sunday 27th. We did not sit down to breakfast till near 12. A shower prevented us from going to church although the drag was got ready. Aemilius Irving & Hind fooled about, betting on walking blindfolded & hopping on the Verandah. Then some kind of prayers. Then Captain Irving, Aemilius & sister, Hind & self, mounted our horses & rode through Newmarket & went on to visit David's Temple,[1] returned, dined, tea, & went to bed. (Rather cool riding – I do not mean the weather.)

Miss Irving seems to have remained cool towards her would-be suitor for the rest of the weekend, but he does not appear to have been unduly upset: 'Spent all Monday morning with Aemilius firing at a target & his hat for York Shillings. We lunched, then left Captain Irving's house at ½ past 4. Aemilius & Hind, driving tandem, upset just inside Bonshaw gate in full view of the family. After helping them right their vehicle, I followed on Kate & was joined by Capt. Irving & Parson Street who were also on horseback & rode with me as far as the second turning to Newmarket. I then caught up with Aemilius & Hind. We reached our house about 7, then after a kind of tea dinner, they left for Toronto at 9. A pitch dark night, very cold, roads terrible.'

For how long after that Easter visit to Bonshaw did Larratt Smith fancy himself in love with the Irving girl? My father used to laugh about a family story which suggests that grandfather could be impatient when snubbed in his wooing. According to the story he was courting a girl, said to be very attractive, who lived on a farm near Newmarket. One fine day Smith rode over to see his love and found the maiden swinging on her father's front gate. He greeted her, she made some reply, but remained perched on the gate. He said something else; she did not answer and continued to swing on the gate. Whereupon he wheeled his horse and galloped home. Is this a glimpse of the fascinating Miss Irving? In the end she married his friend William Jarvis, but not until 1851 when Larratt Smith was already happily married.

APRIL 1842

On 21 April the new governor, Sir Charles Bagot,[2] visited Toronto for the first time: 'The Governor arrived today in the steamboat *Traveller*. He was met at the City Wharf by a Coach & Four and driven under the newly erected Triumphal Arches to a splendid reception at Government House, where he made an excellent speech. After the ceremony he was driven to Mr. Draper's house for a quiet evening.'

Saturday 23rd. A great Ball was given last night in honor of Sir Charles Bagot. As his coach passed by on King Street, Rockets were let off in great profusion. The Ball itself was said to be one of the most splendid affairs every given in Canada. The weather was lovely & intensely hot all day. Before going to bed last night I washed myself de tout in preparation for my role in the St. George's Day Procession today. A fine morning altho' nothing like so warm. Having paid Savigny, the Treasurer 4$, I was admitted a member of St. George's Society. The Procession formed at Upper Canada College with myself carrying the Wells gonfalon at the head. We proceeded to the University ground by College Avenue where the Governor passed through us. The Procession then returned to the College where he spoke prettily. After the parade I went down to the Radenhursts' where I spent the evening waltzing. The Governor dined with Bishop Strachan.

1842 / 77

Monday 25th. The Governor went at noon today to Boulton's race course to see the Steeple chase. Charley Boulton's horse was killed. Charley himself nearly killed & Irving thrown. In the end the race was won by Jas. Stanton. In the afternoon His Excellency went to fix the site of the Lunatic Asylum. He left Toronto at 6 P.M. on board the *Traveller.* Mr. Draper also on board. Papa is in town with Mr. Boyd on the Grand Jury. I went down to the Court after dinner & staid till past 11 P.M. when the Grand Jury was dismissed & the Court closed. McDonough acquitted of peeping & the Earnests of burglary.

About this time Captain Smith sold his grey horses, bought another pair, and instructed his son to buy a carriage: 'Bought a light carriage at O'Neill's Coach Factory & wrote to Papa for £17. I went back to O'Neill 2 or 3 times to see if the carriage was ready. It was not. Told him he was humbugging me. The Carriage is now ready. I paid him, then took the carriage lamps to Mills Livery Stable to make holders for them & gave Mills Papa's crest for the carriage door. Read Dickens' *Old Curiosity Shop* before going to bed.'

St James' Church, which had depended since 1807 on the military bands from the garrison for its music, had now, through private subscription, acquired a Monte organ. The choir, because of the retirement of Mrs Draper due to illness, was under the direction of well-known singing teacher, Mrs David Gilkison: 'Went to choir practise at St. James' last evening, there was a rumpus & a remonstrance about the bellows blower. Today at morning service Mrs. Gilkison fainted after the Te Deum & could not be restored until after the 1st Psalm, when she was carried out.'

The cause of Mrs Gilkison's indisposition is unknown, but Mrs Draper's illness turned out to be a baby: *'Thursday 4th May,* Mrs. Draper had a little girl, her 4th daughter, making her family number 7. The child is to be baptised Caroline Martha, after Mrs. Moffatt & Mrs. Cozens, Godmothers.'

MAY 1842

On the first Friday in May 1842, Charles Dickens visited Toronto: 'Having just received an invitation from the Chief Justice, Sir John Beverley Robinson to a reception for Mr. Charles Dickens who arrived here yesterday, I hastily dressed & went to the Chief's small party where I met Boz and his lady.' This meagre description, coming from a young man who had sat up night after night reading *Nicholas Nickleby* and *The Old Curiosity*

Shop by candlelight, is disappointing. Perhaps Smith was so overcome by meeting the celebrated author that he could write nothing except this brief record of the event.

JUNE 1842

Friday 3rd. Papa, Mamma, & Adelaide came into town in the Stage Coach, they stopped overnight at the North American Hotel. Patrick our man, brought the horses in, then we all started for home in the new carriage. I drove, with Patrick beside me in the box. It began to rain near noon & continued so all day. The roads became miry & the carriage very heavy so that one of the horses, Joe, became knocked up. It rained so hard that by the time we stopped at Finch's for something to eat, my hat was ruined. We got home in time for evening tea & singing.

Sunday 5th. Raining all Saturday morning. I just clapped on my uniform over my dirty trowsers, did not even bother to shave, but went straight over to the training ground for the inspection of my regiment – the 4th North York Militia. Found a pretty good muster in my Company, about 40 men present. Treated the men then lunched with the other officers at Mr. Boyd's expense. Unfortunately I drank a little too much brandy in wine; as after I came home, shaved, cleaned my boots & changed my epaulets preparatory to going to Mr. Boyd's, I fell sound asleep on the bed & so missed the party. It was too wet to go to church this morning; we had prayers at home & Mr. Kent read the sermon. After dinner when it became fine, I rode Joe in the fields, the passenger pigeons flying very thick. After dinner the Boyds came over & the evening was spent Larking with the damsels. Papa is allowing me to ride Fop back to town tomorrow.

Friday 10th June. It has been raining just as heavily in town as in the country. Yesterday being the 2nd day of the races, a tremendous thunderstorm came up, drenched the riders & left Boulton's Race Ground in horrid state. The weather then turned cold & a hard frost covered the ground, killing everything in the gardens.

On 23 June young Mr Smith traded his leghorn hat[3] for Aemilius Irving's white shooting jacket, bought himself a new hat at MacCormack's for fifteen shillings, bought Bulwer Lytton's latest novel, *Zanoni*, at Scobie's for a shilling and sixpence; he then spent five shillings to have his head examined by a famous London phrenologist named Fletcher. Mr Fletcher stayed in Toronto for more than a week giving lectures in this popular science. Captain Smith came in from Richmond Hill and attended at least one of them, but what diagnosis his son Larratt received for his five shillings is not recorded. The weather was showery: '*Thursday 30th*. On the whole, June has been a very wet month; it has been rainy ever since the anniversary of the Battle of Waterloo & was still thundery this evening when Wilgress, Baker, & I left Mr. Benje's rooms & moved into Mrs. Howe's Boarding House on George Street. Mrs. Howe's lodgings seem tolerably comfortable, although I was tormented by bed bug in the night.'

JULY 1842

Monday 11th. Papa rode into town on Friday on his saddle-horse, Fop. After leaving Fop at Howcutt's Livery Stable to be sent out to grass, Papa spent the day in my office writing to Uncle George in England. I wrote ½ a sheet to my brother George & enclosed it. In the evening Papa & I went to the theatre where we saw *Golden Farmer* & *The Sailor's Return*, we were both very much pleased. Papa went home by Stage on Saturday. Aemilius Irving, Father & sister in town, invited me to go with them to Newmarket, but I refused. On Sunday morning I took little Miss Georgina Ridout to church, went boating in the afternoon, & spent the evening at Mr. & Mrs. Heward's. While I was there, Mr. Heward took Dr. Telfer down to his farm to see a sick woman there. After the office today, I walked down to Front Street with Mrs. Heward & helped her pick strawberries in Caer Howell[4] gardens. On our way we saw the 93rd Regiment marching into Osgoode Hall Barracks.

Thursday 14th. Although it has been intensely hot all week, the Orangemen paraded through the town on the 12th, as usual. Fortunately all was quiet. Last evening Dr. Sewell[5] & Jacob Hirschfelder[6] came here & we had a great fiddling contest; Sewell & I played our violins & Hirschfelder the flute. Afterwards we prowled down to a small party at the Radenhursts' where we had a merry time, myself the most lively.

Friday 29th. Having been very busy at the office most of the month, I did not work myself to death this week. Nicholl's Circus here. Saw *Timon the Tartar* & *The 40 Thieves*, both capital performances. Got nearly drunk with Norman Bethune[7] & Saxon on 2 bottles of port in the middle of the day today, after dinner we all had a bathe off the old derelict boat, *Chief Justice*. The *Chicago Erickson* propeller boat came in & went out again – first time I ever saw a propeller boat. Spent the evening at the Primroses, played the fiddle & had a great fun with the Cockburn girls – they put custard in my pocket.

AUGUST 1842

Tuesday 9th August. Having assumed my share in Wilgress & Baker's boat & paid them 8$ for it, I now find it has horrid oars & on the whole am displeased with it. However, I invited Mrs. Heward & Georgy Ridout to go out with me in it, but they excused themselves. Last night, Baker, Wilgress & I went boating, but a thunderstorm came on which obliged us to put in at Yonge Street Wharf where we staid for nearly an hour before going up to Cull's place to spend the evening. While there F. Stowe came in in a great state to tell us that 9 fellows were drowning in Toronto Bay. We rushed out into the pouring rain & although it was very dark managed to find their boat which had upset, brought it in & picked them all up, 2 of the fellows very drunk.

Saturday 27th. Lovely & hot. I left the office early yesterday & went to Mrs. Widder's[8] pic-nic at the Bend of the Island. Some of the party crossed the Bay in Cull's galley the *Wave*, & the others in Irving's & Stowe's boats. The pic-nic was a very large fashionable affair. Saw Miss Irving there but we did not speak. After a very pleasant party, I drank tea at Mrs. Stowe's & finished off at Culls. Called at Lyndhurst this morning & left 2 cards for Mr. & Mrs. Widder.

SEPTEMBER 1842

Friday 2nd September. After work today, Borthwick & I took our boat over to the old derelict steamboat *Chief Justice* where we pulled her up & scrubbed her thoroughly before entering her for the Toronto Regatta to take place on Monday.

Monday 5th. Fine but blowing very hard & squally from the North West. Papa came in at 11 o'clock this morning driving Dick, his new poney, in the light waggon. After giving Papa a ticket for the Regatta, I left the office early to get dressed. At 12 o'clock sharp, Augustus Heward & his brother with Borthwick & myself got into our boat. We had dressed ourselves in blue striped guernseys, white trowsers, blue striped shirts, black belts & black neckerchiefs, and on our heads we wore blue striped night-caps. It was a capital Regatta; two or three boats upset & there was plenty of excitement. After the races were over we sent our boat home & went on board the steamboat *City of Toronto* where we waltzed & quadrilled to the music of the 83rd Regimental Band. After cruising about the Bay, the ship made a short trip to Garrison Wharf before landing the passengers. I saw Miss Shaw & Miss Boyes home, then came back to my lodgings & went to bed. Papa slept here in Baker's room. (I lost a bet on the boat race, of a pair of white kid gloves to Miss Shaw.)

Towards the end of September Dean & Forest's theatrical company arrived in Toronto.

After working day & night in the office, I treated myself to a seat in the Pit at the Theatre on Yonge Street, where I saw *Lady of Lyons* & *Family Jars*. The Theatre then moved to the North American Hotel Ball Room. Went with William Heward, sat in the Pit & saw *Soldier's Daughter* & *John Bull in France*. Tonight, after tossing a coin with Saxon – in which I lost, I bought Pit tickets for *London Assurance* & the farce, *Pleasant Neighbour*. Both very excellent, especially the latter in which the Ciacovienne was very nicely danced in full character with brass heels.

Thursday 29th. Weather fine & warm. Spent last evening at the Radenhursts. The old cock was still in Kingston so we had a merry musical evening. Mrs. Draper is very kindly lending me her little poney to ride home on the weekend. Am reading *Charles O'Malley the Irish Dragoon* by Charles Lever.

OCTOBER 1842

Tuesday 4th October. Spent a pleasant weekend at Twickenham Farm, but had a trying time getting there & back as Mrs. Draper's poney turned out to be dead lame on all fours as well as broken-winded. On the road back to Toronto it came down once or twice on its nose, so I was obliged to have it shod on one leg, it went so lame. Having no money with me, I did not pay the blacksmith & there was no charge at the Thorn Hill Toll Gate.

Monday 10th. Papa came into town last Thursday & put up at the North American Hotel where I dined with him, then afterwards he treated me to a box seat at the Theatre where we saw *Love Chase* & *Joan of Arc*. Mrs. Draper has given me a task to make 2 copies of a song called *Beautiful Venice* for the Bazaar on Wednesday next. I finished the second copy today then went to the Theatre Pit to see the last half of *King Lear* & the dancing of *Fortune's Frolic or the Ploughboy turned Lord*. Johnson's brass band played very well indeed. I got a sharp note from Mrs. Draper scolding me for giving 'her little Frank' tobacco & making him sick.

Thursday 20th. Since the defeat of the Government last month & the formation of the Baldwin-Lafontaine Government, Mr. Draper is now back in Toronto & I have been going through my Crown Revenue Docket with him previous to handing it over to Mr. Baldwin. The office is in a great litter as Mr. Draper has masons, carpenters, & stove pipe fixers swarming all over the place making holes in the wall & the floor to admit a pipe & dumb stove[9] which will make us more comfortable. The Drapers' house is also being renovated, a fatigue party of the 93rd Regiment removed Mrs. Draper's piano from the Drawing-Room to the Library today.

Sunday 23rd. I went home last weekend & while there Aemilius Irving called on horseback & invited me to his house. I saddled Dick, the poney & went with him. We arrived at Bonshaw in time for dinner at 7. I was well received by the Irvings who had bad colds, especially Miss I. Breakfast this morning was at 10 A.M., no talk of going to church. After prowling about the farm, Irving & I rode on horseback, I on Sydenham, he on Poulett, to Holland Landing. We had a look at the steamboat there, & then rode back to Hunter's field where we put up some snipe & jumped some logs in his woods. On the road home we met Minny of the Bank notoriety. Irving kept back & talked to her. He then came back with me to spend the night at our house before leaving for Toronto in the morning. I am staying on in order to help put up the stoves, clean the stove pipes & get Twickenham Cottage ready for the winter. It is still Indian Summer & beautiful weather.

NOVEMBER 1842

Thursday 10th November. A very hard frost. I got up at 5 A.M. & left the farm with 30 bushels of potatoes in the waggon & old Patrick[10] beside me on the box. The new horse baulked at first & would not go. Licked him till he started, he afterwards pulled willingly. We reached Toronto about 10 A.M. Mr. Howe allowed 3 shillings & 9 pence per bushel for the potatoes. Patrick drove out again. I finished my commissions for Papa & went to the office. Paid 10 shillings for a years subscription to the *City Observer* for Papa, which I will send by whoever is riding or driving to Richmond Hill. This evening I read a novel, *Lottery of Life,* then read a little of Stephen on *Pleading.* Have now come to a determination to give up novels and read Law in earnest.

Saturday 19th. It blew a hurricane from the North West yesterday, several schooners were pitching about off the bar & no steamboats would venture out of Toronto Bay until today. Having orders to go to Hamilton re Maitland's Mortgage, I left at 8 this morning on the steamboat *Gore,* she was loaded with goods & carrying about 100 passengers. Unfortunately the ship ran aground in front of Hamilton so we could not go ashore till 4 P.M.

Wednesday 23rd. Went to church on Sunday, a very pretty church, sweet toned organ, but very poor voices. On Monday, hired a horse & rode up the mountain to see about the Mortgage at the Registry office in the lodge of the castle. Went thro' the property, a Mr. Greening living in the house. Yesterday I rode over to the Registry office at Dundas, finished my business, wined, cidered & dined at Bamberger's Tavern, then rode into Hamilton by 8 P.M. It was snowing rather fast when I went on board the *Gore* today. However the weather soon cleared & we had a fine voyage down the lake. I played the fiddle all the way to Toronto on a capital violin belonging to Bray the Purser.

Saturday 26th. Cold & snowing, excellent sleighing on Yonge Street – none in town. The last of the schooners wrecked on the bar in the storm, got off today. Our man Starker came into town on horseback early today with a letter from Papa enclosing papers from Christie's mother regarding her petition for Land.

Mr. L. Smith Junr
at Mrs. Howe's Boarding House
George Street   Richmond Hill
Toronto   Friday Evening
My dear Larratt:
I take advantage of Starker's going to the city to enclose you a dispatch from Christie's mother on the subject of applying for Land. I know nothing of its contents, it was left here to be forwarded ... You can write to the Bearer who will bring the Observers or any other little thing you may have to send. He leaves here at a very early hour tomorrow morning and he returns at night – Very good Sleighing between here and Finch's – beyond which I hear there is no snow, I wish we could send a little of ours down that way, we have too much. It is so dark I cannot see to write any more, So Adieu –

                                Your Affectionate parent,
                                L. Smith

Christie was one of the maids at Twickenham Farm. The letter, a single folded sheet of paper, its red wax seal imprinted with a dolphin, is of no importance save that it was written at dusk (before candle-lighting time) the evening before; was carried by a horseman who must have left for his destination at dawn; and reached its recipient in shorter time than it would have taken a hundred years or so later.

Young Larratt Smith acted at once: 'Answered Papa's letter & drafted Christie's mother's Petition to the Governor & sent the letter home by two niggers who are chopping wood for us. Papa will show Christie's mother how to revise & sign the papers which I will then send on to Kingston.'

About this time a system called Mesmerism, more popularly known as 'Animal Magnetism,' reached Toronto. Anton Mesmer's idea of the curative power of hypnosis had been introduced into England in 1785 and it flourished there until well into the nineteenth century. In Toronto its first practitioner was a Mr Cavendish: '*Thursday 29th November.* I went to Mrs. Gilkison's usual choir practise & to my astonishment found a large party assembled of such eminent persons as Judge Jonas Jones, Mr. Macaulay, Clarke Gamble etc. & Mrs. Gilkison being magnetized by Mr. Cavendish.'

Mr Cavendish became all the rage, especially with Mrs Gilkison who allowed herself to be magnetized at least four times and gave magnetizing parties: 'I went to a party in the evening & saw Mrs. Gilkison & Mrs. Mainguy being magnetized by Mr. Cavendish, walked home with him at 1 A.M., he seems a nice person & is going to the Asylum to magnetize the Lunatics. I called on him & left my card & asked him to let Papa see Mrs. Mainguy magnetized, but Mr. Cavendish would not take Papa to see the magnetizing.'

DECEMBER 1842

Mr. Cavendish did a brisk business in Toronto, mesmerizing several important persons. What his charges were, I do not know, as the diarist apparently did not allow himself to be magnetized. Smith had more amusing things to do: '*Wednesday 14th December.* Mr. Brough having very kindly paid my subscription of $5 to the Assemblies, I bought myself a white satin stock & a pair of white kid gloves & went last evening to the 1st Assembly at Stowe's Hotel. Danced only twice, my coat tails, I fear, are too broad, so went today to Russell the tailor & ordered a new coat with a promise to pay him 12 or 14 dollars for it in January.'

8: 'All my spare time... writing Briefs' 1843

JANUARY 1843

Young Smith spent Christmas and New Year's in Toronto.

January 2nd 1843. After church on Christmas Day, I dined with Dr. Sewell & his mother, came home early, read Dickens *Pickwick Papers*, then went to bed but was wakened at midnight by Borthwick & Frank Stowe bringing grog into my room. We adjourned to the dining room where I played the violin & we sang & drank till 2 A.M. I have had a very bad cold all week so stayed at home from the office. Some of the fellows looked in on New Year's Eve & we played Brag poker & Lanterloo. Mrs. Howe very kindly sent up 7 different kinds of cake, mince pies & elderberry wine.

On Thursday, 19 January 1843, the Smiths of Twickenham Farm gave their yearly dance (the last they would give in Canada, but they were unaware of this fact).

Sunday 22nd. Papa came into town in the cutter on Wednesday, I lunched with him at the Toronto Club, then loaded the cutter with the Confectionary & drove home. Beautiful sleighing all the way & the new poney as lively as ever. Our party was not as large as usual; Mrs. Widder's Ball kept a great many away. However, out of 67 people invited, 40 came & we kept it up till past 3 on Friday morning. We intended to have some sleighriding on Friday & Saturday, but the mizzling weather prevented us, so we played drafts & backgammon, fluted & sang. We were joined on Saturday by William Jarvis & Captain Buchanan of the 93rd Regiment who were en route to Bond Lake, but had had a smash on the road. They spent the night here and we all went to church in the lumber waggon, Parson Townley,[1] in his sermon, gave us a blowing up for so much gaiety.

Tuesday 24th. I came back to Toronto with Papa & Patrick in the lumber waggon. We brought in some butter, fowls, & pork for Mrs. Gilkison who is ill in bed. In the evening we called on Mrs. Thomson, took her a basket of butter & eggs & thanked her for the apples she sent Mamma.

Tuesday 31st. The Toronto Debating Club met on Thursday night with Mr. Draper in the Chair. The Debate 'Ought Capital Punishment to be Abolished?' was offered by Haggarty & opposed by Tom Moore. The Majority was *for* Capital Punishment. After the office yesterday, I called on Mrs. Gilkison & made arrangements to live at her house. In the evening, Papa & I went to the Theatre in the North American Hotel. The plays, *Charles II*, & *Bombastes Furioso*, were miserable affairs; none of the officers could act but Captain D'Alton. I am now resolved to commence some Civilian Theatricals & Papa has promised to bring in some of his play-books next week. Freezing rain today has made the streets icy but the sleighing, however, is good. Moved all my books & things into Mrs. Gilkison's to-night.

FEBRUARY 1843

Friday 17th February. On Captain D'Alton's invitation I played Waldeck in *The Miller & His Men* with the Garrison Players last night. After the play was over, spent a jovial time with the officers, going round the town serenading, & did not get to bed till ½ past 5 this morning. Papa walked into my bedroom before I was out of bed. He brought me some of his play-books.

Thursday 23rd. Mr. Baldwin has very kindly given me the Crown business. With it and my other work in Mr. Draper's office, I am very busy in the daytime. However, last evening I met Captain D'Alton & the Thespians at Deering's house & we cast the characters for *John Bull*, & a farce, *The Unfinished Gentleman*. Deering had printed my name in flaming characters as singing in the farce, made him alter it before I went home.

Tuesday 28th February. Fine weather & pretty mild. I was busy in the office all day. The Theatre opened this evening with the farce of *The Unfinished Gentleman*. I played Charles Danvers & sang, 'Oh this heart it is thine love.' Mrs. Gilkison had 4 seats given her by Deering, she took Street & Miss Boyes, but became unwell just as the farce was finishing & was obliged to go home.

1843 / 87

Mrs Gilkison, Larratt Smith's new landlady, seems to have suffered from chronic ill-health: terrible bouts of coughing in public places, fainting spells in church, and taking to her bed for weeks at a time were only a few of her misfortunes. Her boarder had barely settled in when she fell ill in the night: 'Mrs. Gilkison very ill with inflammation of the throat & delirious.' The lady, however, never quite succumbed (in fact she outlived her husband). The Gilkisons had children; Smith writes of one of them: 'Little Frances Gilkison opened the parlor door by herself in the house in Richmond Street today for the first time.' The Richmond Street house sounds comfortable enough, except for an occasion when a certain stiffness occurs with Mr Gilkison (who has not been mentioned before). 'After Rehearsal I came home late to dinner, Gilkison rather sharp about late hours.' Despite this slight difficulty, Smith stayed on at the Gilkisons' until he entered King's College in June of that year.

SPRING–SUMMER 1843

Meanwhile he continued to act with the Toronto Civilians Theatrical Company which was making good use of Captain Smith's play-books. By the time the season closed, young Smith had played Lampedo, the apothecary in *Honey Moon*, Charles Courtly in *London Assurance*, and Captain Canter in *The Mummy*. He refused a part in the farce, *Rumfustian Inamorata*, but played David Dulcet in *Amateurs & Actors* and, as spring drew near, took the part of Jeffrey in *Animal Magnetism*. The season closed with Larratt Smith as Henry Popkins in a play entitled *Frank Fox Phipps*. After that the company broke up for the summer. Smith's own last performance was on 12 May when, after weeks of vocal and instrumental practice, the amateur musicians and singers of Toronto gave a grand concert: 'Fetched my little sister Adelaide from Mrs. Rankin's school & got her a seat at the Concert in the City Hall. The evening went off admirably. I sang a duett "of Stars the Fault" with Miss Hocken. The whole town at the concert.'

By this time, young Larratt Smith had his father's permission to enter the University of King's College which was about to open under the auspices of Bishop Strachan: 'Having been examined in Horace & Homer & passed by Dr. McCaul in April, I paid my entrance fee to Dr. Boyes & ordered my Cap, gown, & surplice from Preston's, using the cheque given me by Papa.'

King's College, a small edifice of Palladian design, stood at the top of College Avenue (now University Avenue) almost where the Ontario Parliament Buildings are today. Since the building contained no living quarters for the students, they were assigned to certain nearby boarding houses appointed by the governors of the college. Smith was placed in a rooming-house run by a man called King.

Thursday 8th June, 1843. having paid Mrs. Gilkison for last month's room & board and given her a dress length of a handsome pattern from Miss Vandermission's shop, I hired a carter & moved all my things into Mr. King's house. Carter very drunk & King's lodgings not impressive. I then got a ticket from the Bursar & went today to the opening ceremony of the University of King's College conducted by Bishop Strachan. The Bishop made a most inspiring speech. He was followed by Dr. McCaul, Chief Justice Robinson, & Judge Hagerman,[2] all of whom spoke on the occasion. Later in the course of the proceedings, I Matriculated. The day was somewhat marred however, by a letter from my brother George in England, containing the melancholy news of Uncle George's death by his own hand on the 7th of May last. Mr. John Kent, my old schoolmaster, has sent me by the same post, a copy of the *Evening Standard* giving details of Uncle George's suicide by hanging, & the Inquest. I made haste to post George's letter & the English newspaper to Papa at Richmond Hill.

Tuesday 20th of June marked the beginning of Trinity Term & University work in earnest. I have attended all lectures but Chemistry, dined at Hall & attended both Chapels. I have also given notice of my intention to seek admission as a Barrister next Term & have stuck up a notice for myself as Attorney. I am working very hard at Virgil, Homer, & the Bible, also Euclid, Algebra, Literature, & Natural Theology.[3] Besides my studies, I have today moved the Crown Docket[4] into Mr. Baldwin's office & occupied the study there. Had my likeness taken in Daguerrotype by Dessaur.

AUTUMN 1843

When Larratt Smith entered King's College, he assumed his articles with William Draper had expired, and that his only outside work would be the charge of the Crown Docket in Robert Baldwin's office. However, after learning that his articles had not ended, he continued to work in both offices as well as attending lectures at the university.

Monday 11th September. As I spent all my spare time last week, writing Briefs in Mr. Draper's office, I was obliged to stay from church yesterday to work in Mr. Baldwin's office preparing Judgement Roll[5] in Her Majesty the Queen, versus the schooner, *Dolphin*. A long letter came in today from Mr.

Baldwin allowing me an increase in salary. Papa came in town & I took him to Potter's Exhibition of Magic Lantern at the College.

Mr King and the other lodging-house keepers were appointed to provide adequate living quarters for the students of King's College, but Larratt Smith was unlucky in his first choice.

Thursday 18th November. All the fellows boarding with Mr. King have complained about the state of his establishment; a student named Lyons has even threatened to Petition the Council but King will not listen. I myself sent in a petition to the Council about King's charges & the filthy condition of his house but received an unsatisfactory reply from Dr. McCaul, so was obliged to get rid of King's vermin-ridden blanket & buy myself a new one. When the cold weather came in November, I had to hook wood from the College for my bedroom fire as King had none cut, nor does he ever have his chimneys swept. Finally I applied to Dr. McCaul for permission to leave King's place, & have today temporarily moved into Bell's boarding-house which is clean & comfortable.

Young Larratt's stay at Bell's lodgings was brief: his father had left for England rather suddenly only a few weeks before, and his mother and sisters were about to move into a rented cottage in Toronto. Captain Smith's earlier decision to take his family back to England had abruptly come to a head in late September 1843.

Thursday 21st. Papa came into town yesterday & took me to have a look at Lyon's cottage with a view to renting it for the winter. Then, first thing after breakfast this morning, I went with him & Rankin to measure off one Lot he owns in Toronto (next to Hepburn's). After College Hall, Papa & Carruthers called for me in a cab & took me with them up to the agent, Brown, to talk over the purchase of Twickenham Farm, Brown promising to take Carruthers up to see the farm tomorrow. Papa will meet them there. In the evening I went with Papa to the concert of the Master Hughes, a most horribly trumpery affair.

Saturday 14th October. Very fine & cold. I kept no Lectures, Chapels, or Hall today as Papa came into town for the last time. He sat with me in the office arranging his affairs. Papa has given me Power of Attorney to execute Conveyances & sell his property in his absence. I drew up Articles of agreement between him & Mr. Brown for the purchase & conveyance of the

Lot in Toronto & the farm in Yonge Street. We also arranged about my receiving his Commercial Bank Dividends & I executed a Bond to the Law Society. Then, since Mamma & I & the girls will be residing in Lyon's cottage in Toronto, I gave Mrs. Rankin notice that Adelaide will be a day scholar next quarter. I then dined with Papa & Adelaide at Mrs. Thomson's & rode down to the Wharf & saw him off at 7 P.M. on board the *Admiral* to sail to Rochester, from thence he will travel to New York where he will embark for England.

Why Captain Smith left Canada in such a rush no one knows. Perhaps the sudden death of his brother George, the wine merchant, hastened his departure. Many years later my father was told that his grandfather's fortunes had changed when the latter had come into money in England. Be that as it may, Captain Larratt Hillary Smith bought a house in Southampton, sent for his wife and daughters in the spring of 1844, and, except for a visit to Canada in 1847, lived in Southampton for the rest of his life.

When Smith, senior, sailed away on that October night of 1843, all his unresolved Canadian affairs fell on the shoulders of twenty-two-year-old Larratt who passed his bar examinations on 6 November, was called to the bar 13 November, but had never tried his wings as a lawyer.

Thursday 23 November 1843. I went up to see old Brown at his house after dinner today & had a couple of glasses of wine with him. He told me that Bernard & Thomson have bought our farm, lock, stock, and barrel. Old Brown then gave me £450 in addition to his deposit of £550 & his promissary note for £550 payable with Legal interest on or before 1st of May 1844, & left the Deed of his house as security. The Deeds of Twickenham Farm were signed, sealed, & registered today. Brown also gave me £7.2.6 for the wheat. I have lodged the cheque to Papa's credit in the Bank of Upper Canada to bear interest at 3%. Now that all is finished, Patrick will drive Mamma & Mary in to town in the cutter next week. Two loads of things & the dogs, Isabella & Major, have arrived in the waggon, & I myself, driving the carriage & blowing the horn all the way, brought in the guns & pistols last night.

When young Smith wrote this entry he did not know that there would be a hitch in the sale of the farm due to a dispute over some blankets and a clock. This was not settled until just before Mary Violett and her daughters left for England.

Saturday 13th April 1844. Met Bernard in his own house in the presence of Brown & gave him the Tent, the Comforter, 12 shillings & sixpence, & the Time piece, in lieu of all claims & demands whatsoever relating to the Yonge Street affair.

DECEMBER 1843

Friday 1st December 1843. Yesterday was St. Andrew's Day. A great bonfire was lighted opposite the University on confirmation of the news of the resignation of Mr. Baldwin and his party. The boys at the College had a whole holiday with all Lectures allowed. And instead of the usual St. Andrew's dinner, a great Ball was held at Stowe's Hotel, tickets $5.

These festivities celebrated the defeat of the Baldwin-Lafontaine administration four days earlier, when nine out of ten ministers had resigned after a disagreement with Sir Charles Metcalfe, the new governor of Canada. William Henry Draper was again sworn in to the Executive Council as Metcalfe's chief adviser. This affected the Crown Docket and its keeper: '*Saturday 16th December.* A letter has come from Mr. Draper in reply to mine, giving the Crown Docket into my charge. I have therefore moved the Docket into Mr. Draper's office.'

9: 'Great fun with Miss Thom' 1844

JANUARY 1844

By the New Year, Smith had left Bell's boarding-house and was living with his mother, Mary Violett, and his sisters, Mary and Adelaide, in Lyon's cottage in Toronto. 'Did little odd jobs of carpentering around the house today, then traded Papa's colt for McDonell's horse, "Jerry" & got in 15 bushels of oats at 11 pence a bushel for "Jerry." Horrid open weather has made for a great deal of sickness in the town; scarlet fever & Typhus fever are raging, there is no ice in the Bay & the roads are rascally. I made some calls with Mamma this morning, we called on Mr. H.J. Boulton & saw him & left cards on Mr. Colin Cameron & Mr. Jarvis. The Toronto streets are ankle-deep in mud & dreadful.'

Despite muddy streets and risk of catching the fever, people visited each other much as usual. Smith and his friend Henry Boulton made a record thirty-three social calls on New Year's Day, and another fifty-four the day after.

There were parties in Toronto throughout the entire winter. Smith went to them all. The most memorable was a dance on 28 December: 'Snowing, sleeting & raining all day. Went to the office as usual. In the evening I took Mary & Miss Thomson to a party at Mrs. Cozens. Wore my white neckcloth in public for the first time. It was a splendid evening, I danced with a good many ladies & had great fun with Miss Thom.' This is the first time young Larratt Smith has taken notice of Eliza Thom, the girl destined to become his first wife.

Eliza was one of the daughters of Dr Alexander Thom, medical superintendent of the military settlements of the Rideau District. Just how long Dr Thom resided in the area is not known; he does, however, turn up as one of the principals in a passage of arms sometime after the War of 1812: 'Duel – On Friday the 11th instant. Alexander McMillan, Esquire, and Alexander Thom, Esquire, met in a field on the Brockville Road to decide an affair of honor – the former attended by Mr. Radenhurst, and the latter by Mr. Cumming. After exchanging shots, the seconds intervened, and on mutual explanations being made, the matter terminated. Dr. Thom received a contusion on the leg.'[1]

Dr Thom survived his leg wound and married twice, two sisters, the daughters of Patrick Smythe, justice of the peace at Niagara. The first Mrs Thom, Harriet Smythe, by whom he had several children, died young. On her death Dr Thom married her sister Betsy, who bore him three more children: Alexander, Eliza, and Caroline.

The Thoms lived on a farm by the River Tay on the outskirts of Perth, an isolated town in the Bathurst District about seven miles from the Rideau Canal and about forty from Bytown (Ottawa).[2] Although Perth was the principal town of the district with a population of eighteen hundred people, it could be reached from the main centres by water only, for there was no road fit to travel between Kingston and Perth. There could not have been very much going on in Perth to amuse a girl of eighteen, nor could there have been very many eligible young men to ask for her hand in marriage; therefore Eliza Thom went on long visits to her married half-sister, Catherine Spragge, in Toronto. On one of these visits Eliza met Larratt Smith.

Like all lovers they seized every opportunity to see each other. In early January Larratt wrote: 'Miss Thom spending the day at Mrs. Radenhurst's, I went down in the evening & had great fun there & also coming home in the cab ... I declined Mrs. McCaul's invitation of last Tuesday & instead spent a merry evening at Mrs. Barrie's, Miss Thom there. *Friday 2nd February.* Drove Miss Thom & Mary in the cutter with "Jerry" to the Island & about the town.' By the end of February Larratt Smith was calling Eliza 'Tommy.' In early March he wrote: 'Walked with "Tommy" & gave her a nosegay, missed my dinner because I *preferred* the walk.'

APRIL 1844

Just as the courtship was becoming more serious, the Smiths received a long-expected message from England.

Wednesday 3rd April. A letter has come from Papa to tell Mamma & the girls to come home immediately. He has taken a house, Number 3 Bellevue

Place, Southampton, & has arranged for Adelaide to go to Miss Evill's School at Bath, therefore all is now in readiness. I wrote back to Papa by way of New York, telling him that Mamma & Mary & Adelaide will leave Toronto on the steamboat *Gore* at 9 A.M. Monday 15th April. I have also given Papa the approximate dates of their itinerary to New York from whence they will embark for England.

Mary Violett Smith began at once to pack and there was a flurry of notes and calls.

Sunday 14th April. Having had an accident & smashed our waggon all to pieces, I harnessed 'Jerry' into a carriage borrowed from Howarth & drove Mamma to call on Mr. & Mrs. Hume Blake & Sheriff & Mrs. Jarvis. I then took 'Jerry' back to Alex McDonell, as after Mamma's departure I will no longer be able to afford a horse. Apart from seeing the Boyds & other friends who have come in from the country to take leave of her, Mamma has been completely engrossed all week in writing P.P.C. cards.[3] I went to church alone today & sat in Mr. Baldwin's pew, Miss Thom there. Mamma & girls staid at home, the better to rest for the long journey that lies ahead of them tomorrow.

After his entry of 14 April 1844, Smith's journals break off; whether he stopped writing them, or they were mislaid or destroyed by accident, may never be known. The available material shows a gap of eighteen months and one can only conjecture what happened during that time.

10: 'Our long cold winter journey' 1845

NOVEMBER–DECEMBER 1845

The journals start again on 1 November 1845. Young Smith, who has just moved out of lodgings in the house of Wallis, a grocer, is still attending King's College, studying for his doctorate in common law. He is also practising law, having bought a partnership in a firm called Smith, Crooks & Smith,[1] in which he is the last-named Smith. To do this he has borrowed five hundred pounds from an aunt in England, the widow of his uncle George Smith who committed suicide. This loan is shown in a special account book in which Smith has written: 'By amount drawn by me on Aunt George to pay towards premium on joining Shuter Smith, & Robert Crooks the same to be returned without interest in five years.'

The same account book shows the payment of forty pounds a year rent for a cottage on Front Street belonging to Dr. Christopher Widmer. Dr Widmer was a well-known Toronto surgeon, a veteran of the Peninsular War, who for his services to his country had been granted certain parcels of land in the Toronto area. The cottage young Smith was renting from him stood on the old natural shoreline of Lake Ontario just about where the Toronto Union Station is today. (In 1848 Smith wrote: 'Took a man out of the water in front of the house this morning – drowned.') The property itself comprised enough land for a vegetable garden, a flower garden, a paddock, and a cowshed (Smith soon acquired a cow), and there were other outbuildings. There was a well on the property for which he bought new wooden buckets but spring water for drinking was brought in in puncheons from time to time. The cottage contained a cellar and a root cellar which were soon filled. Smith's accounts for November 1845 show the laying-in of a large amount of apples, potatoes, and winter vegetables, as well as nearly a hundred pounds of salt butter in large tubs. His accounts also show the engagement of a housekeeper with a bad cough: 'Paid Mrs. Currie her wages of 1 sovereign for November & bought her a plaster & a bottle of cough medicine at Beckett's chemist.'

The Smith family Bible records the private wedding of Larratt William Violett Smith to Eliza Caroline Thom at Perth, Bathurst District, Upper Canada, on 23 December 1845. But when his journals open in November 1845 there are few signs of an imminent marriage: the bridegroom is living alone in the cottage in Toronto, the bride-to-be is two hundred and forty miles away in Perth, the weather is stormy, the roads impassable, and the steamboats constantly delayed. '*No boat from Kingston since last Saturday & consequently no Mail,*' wrote Larratt Smith.

Surprisingly, despite the bad weather, Eliza's mother, Mrs Thom, is in Toronto staying with her son-in-law John Godfrey Spragge. Although Larratt Smith notes dining at the Spragge house, escorting Mrs Thom to church, and being generally attentive to her, he makes no mention of Dr Thom. Then, on 21 November, Smith wrote: 'The steamer *Princess Royal* came in today at last. It brought a letter from Eliza & also a letter from John Jackson regarding the late Dr. Thom's Will. I sent a letter to Eliza & also sent Mrs. Thom's Papers to the Military Secretary by Gillespie.'

Monday 24th. It has been snowing in gusts all weekend, freezing & blowing great guns from the North West. However, so far the snow is not laying. I gave Mrs. Thom a Mourning ring on Saturday & bought Eliza's Wedding ring. Took Mrs. Thom to church yesterday and after pleading with her again & again, she finally gave her consent to our Union, the wedding to take place immediately. I wrote at once to Eliza & Papa to inform her & him of our marriage, then went shopping with Mrs. Thom & ordered some furniture for our cottage from Jacques & Hay.

Four days later the two of them set off for Perth. Since the miry road between Toronto and Kingston was impassable, they went by water to Kingston on what was probably the last boat of the season.

Saturday 29th November. Left town with Mrs. Thom by the steamboat *Princess Royal* at 2 P.M. yesterday. It was freezing hard at Toronto but with little snow on the ground. There was no wind of any consequence on the lake & very few passengers on board the ship. We docked at Kingston at $\frac{1}{2}$ past 8 on this very snowy Saturday morning. After first taking Mrs. Thom to visit her friend Mrs. Murney, I hired a sleigh from Minto, called for Mrs.

Thom, & we proceeded to drive as best we could over the rough country trails, our destination, Perth. We had barely driven the 6 miles to Kingston Mills when the sleigh struck something, broke a runner, & we were thrown into a snow bank. I hired another sleigh & we left Kingston Mills at 2 o'clock, but just as we were getting close to Rideau Lake at Brewer's Mills, the horses balked & we were detained some time on the road & only reached Dulmage's Tavern, 25 miles from Kingston, at ½ past 7. Snowing heavily all day and nothing to eat from 8 in the morning to 8 at night. I managed to find a room for Mrs. Thom at Dulmage's, but I myself was obliged to lie all night on buffalo skins on the floor. Entered my 25th year today.

Sunday 30th. Still snowing. We left Dulmage's at ½ past 7 A.M., reached the village of Beverley about 20 to 10 A.M., breakfasted at Hastwell's Tavern, then drove on & arrived at Perth at 6 P.M. Took them all by surprise as they were about setting out for church.

Out of respect for the memory of the late Dr Alexander Thom, the marriage was to be a small private affair, and one would have expected the ceremony to take place without delay. But such was not the case: the wedding date was set for 31 December, the bridegroom spent long dull weeks waiting for the banns to be read in the church and the sewing and the baking to be finished in the Thom house. His diaries reflect his ennui: 'After spending all day in the house doing nothing, I took a walk to Captain Adam's Hill, & later watched a bee of 150 sleighs drawing stone for the new R.C. church ... Too tired to go to Holmes's house to play cards – went to bed early instead.' Smith wrote letters, went to church twice on Sundays, helped Mrs Thom with her business papers, and generally managed to fit himself into the household except for a small incident: *'Tuesday 9th December.* Black puddings for supper – could not eat them.' His reprieve came sooner than he expected.

Monday 15th December. A letter has come from my senior partner, Robert Crooks, in Toronto informing me that I must go home immediately as my presence is required at the office. In consequence I have altered the date of our marriage to the 23rd instead of the 31st inst.

Friday 26th December, 1845. Tuesday the 23rd was Our Wedding Day. I rose at 7 A.M. it was 18 degrees below zero & a very fine day. My dear Eliza & I were married by Parson Harris at 10 o'clock that morning. Eliza's bridesmaids were her sister Caroline & Susan Harris. After the wedding breakfast, I gave Parson Harris £2, tipped Mrs. Thom's servants 15 shillings, & having rented a sleigh to take us to Kingston, left Perth at ½ past 12. We reached Beverley at 5 P.M. & after spending the night at Hastwell's Inn, left at 9 A.M. and reached Daley's Hotel at Kingston by 4 P.M. In the evening we called on Mrs. Murney. We left Kingston at ½ past 7 on Thursday morning in a covered stage sleigh, stormy weather & most bitter cold. After travelling all day & night we changed the sleigh for the stage coach from Bowmanville & reached Toronto at 5 P.M. and went to the Spragge's house where we were most kindly received by Eliza's sister and her husband Godfrey. As I write up my journal this evening by candlelight, I give thanks that we are safely home after our long cold winter journey.

11: 'At Home' on Front Street 1846

WINTER 1846

Eliza's sister Kate, wife of Godfrey Spragge (who was soon to become vice-chancellor of Upper Canada), lived in a spacious wooden house close to the lake and within walking distance of the Smiths' cottage. Larratt and Eliza stayed with the Spragges until after the New Year.

Monday 5th January 1846. Eliza & I left the Spragges for our own house on Friday. While I was at the office on Saturday, Anna Fortye spent the day here helping Eliza put the house to rights. Our housekeeper, Mrs. Currie, is handy, but slow. I have therefore engaged a servant boy, John, to help with the rough work. Mrs. Currie did not give us breakfast yesterday until 12 o'clock, consequently Eliza & I did not get to church. We have, however, commenced reading prayers morning & evening. I went to the office as usual today. Crooks is a little better & came in for a short time this morning.

The junior partner in the law firm of Smith, Crooks & Smith attended the office every day including Saturdays. His diaries show that the peremptory order he had received from his senior partner Robert Crooks, to advance his wedding date and return immediately to Toronto, was sent because Crooks had fallen ill. Although Smith's entries do not reveal the nature of this illness, Crooks seems to have been unwell for most of the winter of 1846. The other senior partner, John Shuter Smith, is a shadowy figure who appears in Larratt Smith's journals only occasionally; he too is frequently at home indisposed, or gone to Port Hope to see his father. He is rarely in the office. Under these circumstances most of the work of the law practice was left to young Larratt Smith.

He seems to have accepted the extra work with equanimity and even to have found time to play an occasional role at the theatre. This was quite agreeable to Eliza who entertained her friends while her husband was rehearsing, and was always in the audience when he was playing. '*Monday 16th January*. Eliza's 21st Birthday today. After the office, in the evening, I took her & some friends to the theatre to see *Honey Moon*, the comedy by George Coleman & the farce *Love à la Mode*. I played Volante in the former to an overflowing house.'

As a newly married woman in the tight little circle of Toronto society, Eliza had her own part to play.

Friday 20th February. Eliza spent two days last week sitting at home receiving visitors. Her sister Mrs. Spragge & her friend Rose Cameron sat with her. Many people came to call on Eliza, including the entire Boyd family from Richmond Hill. On Monday, I took time off from the office, borrowed Mrs. Spragge's carriage & drove Eliza to return her calls. In all we made 29 visits. Yesterday, having written Mrs. Boyd that we were coming, I again borrowed Spragge's horses & sleigh & drove Eliza to Richmond Hill. We spent a most delightful afternoon with the Boyds, then drove back to town in a violent storm of drifting snow. It was still snowing & drifting this morning, the drifts in some places 8 feet in depth; too deep to go to the office. Paid a man 3 shillings & 9 pence to clear the snow around our house. In the evening, finding that a path had been cleared on Front Street, Eliza & I walked over to the old City Hall to hear the concert.

Friday 27th February. Very cold again. It was snowing & drifting on Shrove Tuesday. The steamboats may not get out of Toronto Bay for at least a fortnight as the ice extends as far as Humber Bay. I stayed home from the office on Ash Wednesday & took medicine for my sore throat & cold, making myself useful in addition by hanging the beaf we bought in the Market up the kitchen chimney in order to smoke it. Although my cold is still bad I attended the office all day today. Eliza went to church in the afternoon, then called for me on her way back & we walked home together. The Fortyes & Jane Harvey here in the evening, playing cards & tippling.

Early Toronto with its wooden buildings, wood-burning stoves, and open fireplaces was constantly exposed to the hazard of fire. The tolling of the fire bell echoes through young Smith's diaries. It rang on the night of the card game, this time for the law firm of Smith, Crooks & Smith: '*Saturday 28th February*. A great fire broke out last night in Webb & Barwick's premises & spread next door to our office. Webb & Barwick are completely burnt out & our office very nearly so. I went down there at once & began to repair the damage.'

SPRING 1846

Smith could not, however, restore the papers and documents lost in the fire, or foresee the other effects of the catastrophe.

Tuesday 24th March. I have just returned from a long day at the office. Affairs there are desperate. Gillespie our Chancery Clerk has left us & gone off to Montreal. Some funds appear to be missing. Crooks talks of leaving the firm, & Shuter Smith went off in the steamer *American* to Port Hope to see his father. I shall have to put all my efforts into saving the firm therefore I have written to Dr. McCaul resigning all my offices & declining to act further at the Philharmonic meetings & Concerts, also wrote to Irving to the same effect regarding the Theatre.

These resolutions were easily made, since it was the middle of Lent when public entertainments were considered wicked. Toronto society played cards and drank wine; they went to 'sacred' concerts of church music; but, from Ash Wednesday until after Easter Sunday, there was no theatre. 'On the evening of Easter Monday, Eliza & I went to the Theatre. I played Dr. Ollapod, the eccentric apothecary in the comedy *The Poor Gentleman*. Later during the farce, *Irish Lion*, a fight broke out in the Pit.'

Larratt Smith showed his long fascination with the theatre when he bought Summer Hill and called one of its many rooms 'the Green Room.' Therefore it is not surprising to find this entry written on a stormy day in May 1846: 'A terrible gale blowing great guns from the East brought such torrents of rain that we could not go to the Market this morning. Fortunately the weather cleared by evening when the Hamilton Amateurs performed. I gave our Julia & the Spragges' servants tickets to the Pit to see the Scottish tragedy *Douglas* & the comedy *Married Rake*. I staid at home with Eliza. Later in the evening I sloped down to see some scenes from *Julius Caesar*.'

The season ended with the Toronto Amateurs playing *High life below Stairs;* for theatrical variety *The Irish Lion* was replaced by *The Irish Tutor;* and a rousing finale was provided by *Charles II* in which Larratt Smith played the king.

The theatre-going Julia was the Smiths' current cook, the third in a line of succession that continued throughout the summer of 1846. Despite the shaky condition of the law firm, the Smiths kept servants: '*Monday 2nd March 1846.* Mrs. Currie & John went away & Mary Ward & Tom Rooster came.' Mary only lasted a month; Larratt Smith evidently liked Tom for he had a coat and vest made for him. But on 4 May: 'Tom left us to go to Niagara, disappointed in the new boy.' The household accounts for April show that when Julia came Smith bought three bake pans and a kneading trough, an indication that she knew how to bake bread. But on 2 June he wrote: 'Paid Julia her wages of £1 in full and sent her off. We then hired a new girl, Jane & a new boy, Robert ... Robert behaved very ill by absenting himself all day without leave ... Jane was sent off in disgrace ...' Smith's accounts show the purchase of a new kitchen teapot and the replacement of broken kitchen crockery from Norris the 'crockery man,' as well as the payment of a shilling to Rowsell for mending the spout of the 'Good Teapot.' A procession of servants came and went, until early September when the Smiths hired a girl called Rose and a young man, William Bellmore, both of whom stayed until after the birth of Eliza's first child in November.

A small part of the Smith income was derived from the legacy Eliza had inherited from her father, Dr Alexander Thom. This legacy provided her with such necessities as a thimble, a brush and comb, hair oil, and a tooth brush (both Larratt and Eliza brushed their teeth, a practice not observed by everyone in Upper Canada), as well as dresses and bonnets and a card case for her visiting cards. Larratt also indulged her in frivolities: a powder puff, Eau de Cologne, sugared almonds, lollypops, and a fan. The accounts also show that he gave her small sums of money: five shillings here, ten shillings there.

The diaries inevitably record an endless procession of confinements and infant deaths: '*Thursday 9th April.* Eliza's sister Mrs. Spragge was confined of twins last Monday morning. Unfortunately, the boy died. Eliza, who I am happy to say is expecting, was not up this morning – too sick.'

On a warm April afternoon when Larratt took Eliza to call on her sister Kate, he found his brother-in-law, Godfrey Spragge, in the garden sowing radishes in the hot bed. Two days later we find Smith sowing radishes, spinach, and parsley in *his* hot bed. By the end of the month he had sown six other varieties of vegetables as well as melons and nasturtiums, and given Eliza a shilling to buy some flower seeds. The accounts show the purchase of a 'little fire engine' to water the garden, and the hiring of a gardener at a dollar a day: '*Friday 8th May.* The Gardener went home at 12 o'clock today with the Ague.'

Smith also kept chickens: '*Saturday 16th May.* Yesterday was the 3rd day of the Assizes. Having spent most of the day in Court, I came home & set the grey hen without a comb on 15 eggs. I then set my yellow hen on the eggs upon which the grey hen had sat before. When I came home from a rehearsal of *Rob Roy* late this afternoon, I discovered a hen sitting on 21 eggs hidden away behind our little orchard. She must have been sitting at least a week!'

As well as the hen house there was a loft for the pigeons Smith's friends gave him from time to time: 'As Crookshanks has just given us another pair, I cleaned the roosts & spent 3 pence on a looking glass for the pigeons.'

Late in May Smith bought a cow for four pounds. To go with the cow, he bought a milk pail, three earthenware milk pans, a skimmer, a butter ladle, and, of course, a dasher for the churn. Their servant boy took the cow to Denison's bull at a cost of two shillings.

SUMMER 1846

As the weather grew warmer Smith let the fires out in the parlour and hall stoves and took down the stove-pipe that heated his and Eliza's bedroom upstairs. The kitchen fireplace was let go out, and a small iron cooking stove, a luxury at that time, was carried into the outer, or summer, kitchen. An iceman was paid twelve shillings and sixpence for the season, and spring water for drinking was delivered by a man called Goulard at seven pence halfpenny a puncheon. Every other drop of water had to be carried into the house from either the rain barrel or the well: the rainwater was used for washing, the well water for cooking. Since there was no sewage system, the ordinary slops and the dishwater were thrown somewhere in the back yard and the chamber pots were emptied into the outside privy; Smith referred to the latter as the 'little house' when he hired masons to repair its foundations while Eliza was in Perth in the summer of 1847.

On 10 June, Eliza left to visit her mother at Perth. Larratt hired a cab and saw her off on the *Princess Royal* giving her fifty shillings for the expenses of the journey. He joined her two weeks later and spent an idyllic nine days at his mother-in-law's farm: reading, playing cricket, taking Eliza out in the canoe and walking with her in the fields in the cool of the evening. He went fishing with his brother-in-law: 'Fished at Otter Lake with Alex Thom. Despite the heat of the day, caught 110 bass, some of them very large. Cooler today. Spent the afternoon canoeing with Eliza, and the evening singing.'

104 / Young Mr Smith in Upper Canada

Thursday 9th July. Eliza & I left Perth in a great rush at 7 o'clock last Monday morning with her brother Alex driving the waggon. Had hoped to cover the 7 miles to Oliver's Ferry on Rideau Lake in time to catch a boat for Kingston. Arrived at the Ferry in very good time, but no sign of a boat. Therefore obliged to wait at the tavern on the wharf till ½ past 2 P.M., when the *Prince Albert* finally came by towing 8 barges & took us on board. The *Prince Albert* went so slowly we did not reach Kingston till 11 o'clock Tuesday night. Put up at Patterson's (late Daley's Hotel) till Wednesday night. Then left by the steamer, *City of Toronto.* The weather very fine all the way till we got near Toronto when it rained hard.

Smith's early summer journals, written just before he left for Perth, hint of a gathering storm in the firm of Smith, Crooks & Smith. The diarist had barely returned to Toronto when the storm broke: Shuter Smith, the senior partner, and a client called Macara came to Larratt Smith in a fury about Robert Crooks. On 13 August Smith wrote: 'At Shuter Smith's behest, the firm of Smith, Crooks, Smith was dissolved today after a duration of 18 months. The partnership henceforward will be known as Crooks & Smith. Wrote to Papa & gave the letter to Norman Bethune to take to England.'

Larratt Smith and Robert Crooks remained partners for some two years. At first all seemed well: they visited each other's houses; their wives were friends; on one occasion Crooks gave Smith a dog, on another Smith gave Crooks some fresh perch he had caught in Toronto Bay; other civilities were exchanged. But by December 1847 there is a note of uneasiness in Larratt Smith's journals. 'Boulton made application to the Vice Chancellor to strip Crooks of his gown ... Capreol fined £1 & costs for assaulting Crooks. I was subpoenaed as a witness. Crooks has since gone to visit his father at West Flamboro & has not been in the office for a week.' Not surprisingly, a coolness developed between the two men; they finally parted company in the winter of 1849.

As to their former client Macara, he was last seen in Toronto on 20 July 1847: 'Macara taken thro' King Street drunk in a cart.'

OCTOBER–DECEMBER 1846

In the same week in late July, after the Spragges had spent a pleasant evening of boating and drinking tea with the Smiths, their house caught fire. Larratt Smith was up all night helping to drag out furniture. The damage was repaired by 31 October, when the Spragges moved back into the house. One piece of their furniture, however, seems to have found its way into the Smiths' cottage: *'Tuesday 29th October.* Eliza & I gave a party to the Crookshanks this evening. 16 people came & we danced to the music of Mrs. Spragge's pianoforte.'

That was the last party for a while because Eliza was about to give birth. Her husband had already engaged the services of a surgeon, Dr Edward Mulberry Hodder, an Englishman who had practised in France and at Niagara before coming to Toronto.

Sunday 8th November, 1846. On Friday Eliza's pains started. I sent for Mrs. Spragge, Nurse Owen, & Dr. Hodder. On this stormy Sunday morning at 2 A.M. the baby, a boy, was born. I went to church & received the sacrament. Eliza & the baby seem pretty well.

Friday 25th December. Last Wednesday was the anniversary of our wedding day, but it was a sad day for Eliza and me as our poor baby was taken much worse with the hooping cough and inflammation of the lungs, which Dr. Hodder tells us was contracted almost from birth. Late in the evening I had him baptised Larratt by the Reverend Mr. Mackenzie. The poor little dear lingered until 3 A.M. on Christmas Eve, then died. He was placed today in the vault of Thomas Harris pro tem, until I am able to buy my own plot in St. James' Cemetery.

12: 'Not such a wilderness as some imagine' 1847

WINTER 1847

Eliza Smith's twenty-second birthday occurred on 16 January 1847. She had been married a little over a year, had borne and lost a child, and was in poor health with a bad cough and painfully swollen breasts. This condition continued until 10 February: 'Dr. Hodder's prescription of leeches & poultices has not alleviated Eliza's suffering one whit; I was up with her most of the night, lighting fires & trying to comfort her. Dr. Hodder then returned today & lanced Eliza's breast. I spent a quiet evening with her & she is already much relieved.'

Larratt had already written to tell his parents in Southampton of the baby's death. His first extant letter of this period was written to his father on 18 February 1847.

My dear Papa:
Your letter of the 2nd of January I rec^d in due course, but too late to answer by the last Mail, and both Eliza & myself feel obliged for your kind congratulations on the birth of our poor little boy. He was admitted a member of Christ's flock, as Mamma imagined, on the 23rd December last, but it was a melancholy occasion for me, and but the prelude of his reception into the hand of Him who gave him to us.

Poor Eliza has had a hard time of it since her confinement with her breasts. The right one has been lanced, she is now much better and if I could only remove her for a change of air, would soon be well but the Toronto weather is against her.

There has been hardly any sleighing this winter ... the cutter would not sell for this reason last winter, it has not sold yet. Wakefield put it up today but could get no bidders, and I am afraid it will not sell at all, although I have told him to get whatever it will fetch.

Edmund Carthew's uncle is at length no more & has left Carthew an immense fortune of about £2000, a year. He will go home to England soon and the family will follow later. In the meantime he has taken old Wm. Campbell's house which, if you recollect, is opposite to Howard the Postmaster's house. But Mrs. Carthew will not on any account come into Town to live. I have not seen Carthew since his good fortune.

Poor Judge Hagerman is I fear on his deathbed,[1] his liver is in a bad state, there is a danger now of it being ulcerated, and he has a dreadful cough which is settling on his lungs. Draper will of course succeed him if his party is in power when this sad event happens. I should be afraid that another fortnight will not find him alive.

Provisions are rising here tremendously & one half the population of this country are without potatoes. I fortunately laid in a supply at 2 shillings a bushel which has lasted me well ...

I have been obliged to write to Aunt George by this mail to tell her that it will be impossible for me to send her an installment as I had expected. Indeed if I can scrape together the interest upon the balance I owe her, it will be as much as I can do. I have candidly told her the reasons and rely on her kind forbearance ...

The letter to Aunt George Smith at Greenwich was posted the same day.

My dear Aunt:
You will doubtless have heard from my parents of the loss of my poor little boy, one calamity out of many against which I have had to contend during the past year. I am truly sorry to be compelled to write you that it will be out of my power to send home, as I had anticipated, the second installment of your very generous loan. It is only fair to you to recapitulate as briefly as possible a few of the causes which have operated against my being able to fulfil my intentions.

At the commencement of the past year a fire consumed the premises adjoining our office and although we were providentially spared, still we suffered a good deal in the destruction of our papers & office furniture. We have lost by the rascality of some of our clients, about £300, one scoundrel owing us £200 of this, has been taken, & we have him in custody in the Gaol at Montreal, with what prospect of our recovering our money, I know not. Then Gillespie, our Chancery Clerk left us withdrawing £300 or £400 of our funds, aided & abetted by our senior partner, John Shuter Smith, who withdrew from the firm having overdrawn his account. I candidly assure you that in July last, I felt as if all I had embarked was lost forever.

I am free from Debt here thank God, and without one farthing of my own (having embarked all in my business), have furnished my house, not handsomely, but decently out of my office earnings. The preparation needful for Eliza's confinement and her continued illness since the death of our poor little boy have necessarily absorbed a great deal of money, and I trust that you will not think the worse of me because I have disappointed you. There is no danger but that I shall be able to pay you if the Almighty spares me, even to the last farthing – Time – time is all I require & if you will let me pay you interest on the amount owing you will confer a great obligation on me. Be kind enough to write and tell me if you will give me time. With my sincere thanks for your kindness to me at all times ...

Captain Smith's letter of condolence did not reach his son in Toronto until 18 March 1847. Larratt's answer was written two days later:

Your & Mamma's joint letter has just reached us and we thank you for your kind sympathy. I am happy to say that Eliza is now almost quite well again. I was much assured by your letter in regard to my installment due Aunt George. I shall be able shortly to make some remittance on account.

I put into a Lottery the other day for some Acre Lots on the Kingston Road, about $2\frac{1}{2}$ miles from town upon terms of paying £5 down & the balance in equal annual installments with Interest in 9 years, but having a Vote against the party for £50, which I could not realize, I gave it him for my throw, & took a Deed at once. I drew one of the best of the Lots, which, by the way, gives me a Vote in the County.

We settled some Costs of ours the other day by taking 400 acres of Land in the Township of St. Vincent on Nottawasaga Bay, which Ridley the Surveyer says is worth from 4 to 5 dollars an acre. Then again in a settlement we will get 50 to 100 acres at about 4 dollars an acre in the Western District of Doon.

Since I wrote you the Court of Directors of the Bank of British North America have confirmed our appointment as solicitors to the Bank here. In one of the British Colonist newspapers I am sending, you will see that I am appointed a *Notary Public*. I wrote Mr. Draper for it & the next Gazette contained the appointment. By the way, I think you will agree with me that the Toronto newspaper, *The British Colonist*, is without exception the best paper in this Province.

Mr. Draper has had £10,000 left him by a Mr. Bond in England. It was the merest chance it was not £50,000.

Heath's place, Deer Park, fetched by Lottery £100 an acre, or the sum of £3500 payable in 10 years. If you think it advisable, I may be able to sell 66 acres of your 132 acre Lot at $8 an acre on time. I have subscribed for you 100 shares in the Upper Canada Mining Company. Robert Crooks has 700 shares & New York merchants hold 15000 shares of this stock.

Thorne & Barwick have dissolved partnership; the latter was at his old tricks with a sister of their head clerk at Holland Landing, the clerk thereupon horsewhipped him soundly. Barwick seems to be a poor creature, for I am told that when he was being licked he begged the young man *on his knees* to let him off.

By mere accident in looking over Burke's Armoury the other day for the purpose of finding out someone's crest, I discovered our own, among the 259 (!) families of Smiths that were in it. The founder of our family is of Methven Castle, County of Perth, and was the *great apothecary* you represented him to be, but instead of the anvil as I thought, it appears the armourial bearings are a cup proper issuing flames between two chessrooks. I am having my seal cut with Eliza's arms impaled, but I should never thought of mounting the shield had I remained under the impression that they were anvils, as though our forbears had a smithy.

Lord Elgin,[2] the new governor-general of British North America, seems to give satisfaction thus far, but he has not yet met the wild beasts in their menageries, a treat yet in store for him.

The winter has been a long one, the Bay is fast locked up with ice, the Niagara boat (the *Admiral*) has been running all winter, & the *America* announces her trip tomorrow, but they cannot get nearer town than the Garrison Wharf.

Poor Judge Hagerman is still lingering on, so reduced that he may be said to be dying. His worthless son staggers drunk to his (father's) bedside in the daytime, whilst his nights are spent in the most abandoned company, resulting sometimes in his being hauled up before the Police Magistrates in the morning. The Chief Justice, Sir John Beverley Robinson has lectured him, but he still persists in his infamous conduct.

Immense subscriptions for the relief of the Scotch & Irish have been made in this country, the Home District has already given £5000. Besides subscribing 50 shillings, I am going to play Geribo in the *Illustrious Stranger* on Easter Monday for the benefit of the Relief Fund.

Macara, our former client, & Shuter Smith, our erstwhile senior partner, have now quarreled & don't speak! 'When Rogues fall out' – you have the rest.

I sincerely hope we may have a better account of my cousin, poor William Violett's health by the next Mail. I heard from George and his Mary by last mail, letters full of kindness and sympathy which I must answer. All here send their kindest love to Mamma, Adelaide, Mary & all enquiring friends & accept the same from your very affectionate son.

Larratt also wrote to his brother George, the wine merchant. Both letters went to England by the same hand. (An obliging traveller who would carry mail was always a lucky find; in a later letter Larratt explained: 'The reason why I have not written earlier is that the mail is so irregular no one knows when to be prepared for it.')

Thank you kindly for your sympathy on our behalf. Eliza is very much better I am happy to say & about completely recovered. I send this letter together with Papa's by

Mr. Beckett, the extensive & wealthy Druggist of this place who leaves for England by the next Packet. He has just taken George Boyd into partnership with him & they intend to increase their Wine business, so I have spoken to George Boyd for you & given him a list of your wines. He promises to give you a chance, but is afraid that your prices may be too high for him. George must have paid a large sum to Beckett on entering the firm.

I notice your very kind offer to allow me the profit for three years on any business I can get you here, & I feel much obliged to you for it. In declining it be assured that I shall not the less be alive to extend your connection & benefit you if possible although my profession would not allow me to participate in the benefit of such ... I wish that you would send me 2 or 3 dozen of your lists of juices by Mr. Beckett, or by first opportunity that I may send them to those who would thereby be induced to purchase from you. I have given George Boyd the only one I had.

My business is pretty good & steadily improving, if Aunt George were only paid off I should feel wealthy. It is very gratifying for me to learn that you are doing so well in your business & that every additional year may add to your comfort & independence. We have indeed an estimable friend in Aunt George. I have only time to write you these few lines & with my kindest love to Mary & my little nephew in which Eliza joins me.

SPRING 1847

In the late spring of 1847 Larratt Smith's cousin, William Violett, died in Bristol. Smith immediately, on 31 May, wrote to the young man's father, William Violett, senior, the uncle who had befriended him ten years before:

Little did I imagine that the first letter I should have occasion to write you from this remote corner of the globe, would be one of sympathy and condolence, and most heartily and sincerely do I grieve with you the calamity which has called it forth ...

I am now writing you in the midst of business and during our Assizes, but I cannot refrain from expressing myself in the language of sympathy and sorrow for one whom I knew as a playmate in youth and have since esteemed for his manly virtues. My sister Adelaide used frequently to speak of him in her letters to me, and, poor girl, she has written me some lines on the melancholy event, in which her goodness of heart is more to be appreciated, than the structures of the metre.

How much I should like to see you, come out here and stay with us, the change of air and scene would do both my Aunt & yourself the greatest possible good. You shall be welcome at my house as long as you like, & although but a beginner as it were in life, I think I have the wherewithal to make you comfortable. The voyage out in one of the steamers, inclusive of the inland travel, can be made, *I'll warrant it*, in less than 20 days from Bristol. Indeed you shall reach Toronto in 16 days from Liverpool! The expense for you is not very great at all event. Do think it over in your mind.

Canada is not such a wilderness as some imagine, and when you tread the gas lit streets of Toronto, and look into as many handsome shops with full length plate glass windows as there are in Bristol or London you will not look upon us as many of your countrymen do, when you see steamer after steamer entering our noble bay as comfortable as magnificent in their internal arrangements, the bay wharves, the thousands and thousands of passengers hourly arriving from the United States and all ports, the electric Telegraph almost from one end of the Province to the other every moment conveying intelligence with the rapidity of thought, you will have reason to be proud of your country and of her glorious dependencies, if you never were before, and to thank God that you were born an Englishman. Now I'm getting Grandiloquent, can't I induce you even without all this. Do consider it seriously, you need not be from home 3 months altogether if you cannot spare the time. Remember me kindly and affectionately to my Aunt and believe me always ...

SUMMER 1847

Despite these cajolements, William Violett never came to Canada. But even as his nephew was writing this letter in praise of ocean travel, ships other than the kind he mentions, filthy overcrowded immigrant vessels, laden with sick and penniless people, most of them victims of the Irish potato famine, were arriving at Toronto. In a letter to his father, written 23 June 1847, Larratt Smith described them:

Canada is not after all such a poor place inasmuch as it is doing an immense deal to keep from starvation not only your own destitute at home, but the thousands who survive to come to this country and swarm among us. The City has passed some very stringent regulations with regard to Immigrants and measures are adopted to keep them as much as possible from being a nuisance to us. They arrive here to the extent of about 300 or 600 by any steamer. The sick are immediately sent to the hospital which has been given up to them entirely and the healthy are fed and allowed to occupy the Immigrant Sheds for *24 hours*, at the expiration of this time, they are obliged to keep moving, their rations are stopped and if they are found begging, are imprisoned at once. Means of conveyance are provided by the Corporation to take them at once to the country, and they are accordingly carried off 'willy nilly' some 16 or 20 miles North, South, East, & West and quickly put down, leaving *the country* to support them by giving them employment. By this means added to the judicious &

restrictive measures adopted for landing them only in one place, we hardly know whether there is any immigration going on at all – woe betide anyone from friendly feelings advertising for labour! John Gamble advertised for 50 for the Vaughan plank road, and hardly were the placards out, than the Corporation bundled 500 out and set them down (at least so George Boyd says & he is to be married to one of John Gamble's daughters and of course goes out now & then!).

It is a great pity we have not some railroads going on, if only to give employment to these thousands of destitute Irish swarming among us. The hospitals contain over 600 & besides the sick & convalescent, we have hundreds of widows & orphans to provide for.

Mrs. Thom had a narrow escape from drowning on her way home to Perth, when the Ferry boat sank with them crossing the Rideau River & everything went to the bottom. They were fortunately rescued by two girls who came off shore in a boat & saved them. The horses were cut from the carriage & saved by swimming – the carriage & contents went down.

I have now a very nice piano for Eliza which I bought at Lewis's by auction for £30 & paid for into the bargain, so I am doing pretty well on the whole. Eliza is very much pleased with the Lady's Magazine you sent out once or twice to her. You haven't any more of that in hand, have you? I received by this mail an *Illustrated London News* & a *Punch*, but no letter ...

The summer of 1847 was a time of happiness and gaiety for the Toronto Smiths. Eliza had recovered her health and there was no lack of amusement in Toronto: Larratt's diaries and letters mention band concerts, picnics, parties, and plays. 'James William Wallach, the well known actor has been playing here with Skerrett's company, delighting everybody. He was himself not a little surprised at the general appearance of Canada after the account he had heard of it. So far Eliza & I have seen him as Don Felix in *The Wonder*, also in *Thumping Legacy*, & in *Hamlet*.' From the end of May until 2 July (when the company moved to Montreal), Skerrett put on eighteen plays. Larratt and Eliza went to them all.

After the theatre closed, Smith noted 'Van Amburg & his Menagerie here,' but he does not say whether he and Eliza went. Apart from taking her on a short boat trip to Port Credit, and to Niagara Falls on the Firemen's Excursion, they spent their evenings boating or listening to the 81st regimental band playing in the gardens of Government House.

Early in August the 81st Regiment was ordered back to England. For the Smiths, who had become great friends with some of the younger officers, especially a certain Lieutenant Woods, this was a sad parting: 'Woods dined with us, then having settled to take leave, he bade Eliza farewell. I walked with him to the Barracks & embarked on board the steamer *Cherokee* by means of a scow towed by the little puffer *Prince of Wales*. Stayed there with Woods & the others till near 12 o'clock when the ship was about to leave the harbour.'

Woods carried with him a letter to Captain Smith at Southampton dated 7 August:

The 81st Reg^t is leaving us & going to Portsmouth, I think I shall write by Mr. Woods a Lieut in that Reg^t, not a handsome man but an intelligent one, & one with whom I have been on the most intimate terms since the Reg^t has been stationed here. If he gets to Southampton I have begged him to call upon you & I am sure you will like him exceedingly. They are a nice set of young fellows, very quiet & not much 'tin' [that is, money].

Their band is a famous one & about one of the best in the service, Crozier the Band Master is a splendid musician & has written some exceedingly popular Polkas as 'Le songe de Crozier,' 'Les jolies filles de Canada,' 'Les belles de Toronto' – Mary & Adelaide must get them if possible, even if I have to send them home, but I should think that when the Reg^t gets to Portsmouth they can be had, I am certain that Crozier would give them if my name were mentioned. When the band plays here in the Govt grounds he always has a programme of the music for Eliza which he comes up with regularly and presents to her – and if you ever hear the band playing at Portsmouth all the favourite airs they play here for the lieges of Toronto, fancy yourself in the Govt grounds listening to them with us, and for a moment we may make a family party once more.

We are shortly going into a new office here, adjoining the Bank of British North America, a splendid building to be finished like the Bank 3 stories, attic, & basement, cut stone front with fire proof vaults for each story. Our rent is very high £80 per annum, we can however, let a portion of it we think, to reduce our rent to about £50. We are just appointed Solicitors to the 'Colonial Life Assurance Company' established in Edinburgh with a branch in London, it is now extending itself all through the British Possessions on this continent – our Governor General, Lord Elgin, is the Governor of the Company ...

Do you notice an advertisement in the newspaper *British Colonist* relative to the Taxes in the Simcoe District? They are so poor it appears that they have raised the Taxes on Wild Lands to a penny an acre, which runs up a tremendous sum annually on your Lots. I wish to goodness I could find a purchaser for them – the man who made the offer has backed out again – at least I have heard nothing more of him.

Mr. Draper is still in England, he has been gazetted Judge of the Court of the Queen's Bench since Judge Hagerman is now deceased.

John Beverley Robinson[3] has now been married to Mary Jane Hagerman the daughter of the late Judge, these last six weeks. She has been singing in the public assembly rooms at Saratoga Springs[4] – unfeeling creature! Everyone is talking about it.

Besides connecting Toronto to Hamilton, the Electric Telegraph is now in full operation with Montreal.

Eliza & I took a cheap trip to the Niagara Falls the other day with the Firemen for 15 shillings, meals included, back the same day. It did me a great deal of good; long confinement to town & close application to business from 9 in the morning till 7 at night & often later before I have my dinner, was making me a little the worse for wear.

With the proceeds of my Mining Stock, Eliza & I intend shortly to go hence to Montreal & Quebec, thence down to New York, Boston, Washington, Baltimore, & back by Rochester. This will last us for some time & do us both (ailing a little) a great deal of good. Everybody is travelling now that can, to get out of the typhus fever sickness.

AUTUMN 1847

Two weeks later Smith changed his mind about the eastern seaboard and took Eliza on a boat trip to Chicago. Eliza was pregnant again; just before they left he wrote: 'Eliza fancied she felt the young 'un.' Just how much the poor girl enjoyed the voyage to Chicago is not mentioned; her husband's journals show that she spent a good deal of the time lying in her berth. He himself had the time of his life, so much so that he wrote three different accounts of the excursion. The first, to his father, was written 9 September 1847:

On Monday evening last, Eliza & I returned from a long trip through the Upper Lakes, Erie, Huron, & Michigan, which we accomplished in one of the splendid steamers that leave daily from Buffalo to Chicago. You will find in the Newspapers I send you a card or two of the Boat *Empire* in which we sailed. She is about 1300 tons & 1000 horsepower – splendidly fitted up, an upper deck cabin 230 feet long containing 70 odd staterooms, ten feet in height. Windows of very handsome stained glass in the Gentlemen's Saloon where they played the carnival music which enabled the passengers to dance every night.

This boat, in the five days going to Chicago, burnt 500 cords of wood. We had 500 cabin passengers, rather a small number for her, as she generally accommodates 800 to 1000. She made in one trip last fall, 13000 dollars clear of expenses.

We ourselves lived like fighting cocks, upon every dainty that you could imagine and, being in the country of fish & game were abundantly supplied with prairie hens & Mackinac trout & white fish, the last being the finest fish that swims in our waters.

At Chicago are all the evidences of a community. Ten years ago it was one vast prairie without almost one settler, now it contains I suppose, from 15 to 20000 inhabitants. It has its foundaries, mills, shipyards etc., a nice Theatre & excellent hotels.

Enroute we bought several nice Indian curiosities for you, but the difficulty will be to get them home to you. I am enclosing a line for George which please forward to him.

Larratt Smith's note to his brother George emphasizes the cheapness of the Chicago excursion: was this with an eye to his letter being passed around the family and Aunt George reading it?

Eliza & I have just returned from a very delightful trip to the west on a steamer with every luxury the best hotel in the States could boast. The charge from Buffalo to Chicago being £20, about £30 of your money for nearly 1000 miles! Best this if you can.

I was able on the voyage to acquire some very handsome curiosities which I intend sending your dear Mary by the first opportunity that offers. I think that they will prove acceptable to her from being purchased at Fort Michillimackinac, the most northerly fort held by the United States on Lake Huron.

If Mary can procure the novel called *Wacousta or The Prophesy* by Major Richardson (it is rather an Historical Romance), she will have greater reason than ever to appreciate anything that came from so interesting a locality of Indian tribes & manners.

When you are again to be an uncle, I cannot say for certain – probably next March or April will tell a different story if all goes well till then. Eliza is anxious to make a few enquiries about her sister-in-law's prospects, now she finds you so inquisitive about hers – tell us?

A few weeks later, with the voyage to Chicago still fresh in his mind, Larratt Smith answered a letter from his friend Lieutenant Woods:

The very day your letter to us was penned some hundreds of miles below Quebec, we were on a pleasure excursion in the 'Far West.' Our trip lasted over three weeks during which time we navigated & circumnavigated Lakes Erie, Huron, & Michigan, witnessing every possible variety of scenery that the northern part of this continent can display; at one time rolling about on Lake Huron out of sight of land fancying ourselves on the ocean, at another calmly gliding in the beautiful waters of the River St. Clair. Now visiting the Indian in his wigwam & again wrapped in amazement on beholding the wonderful advancement of that 'City' of the West known to us hitherto but by name & imagined to be slumbering in the forest.

Chicago, some ten years ago had hardly a house in it; it now rivals Toronto in most particulars, & in many excels it. The Hotels 'American like' are far before ours – They have a gem of a theatre there & very tolerable acting indeed. You will see more shipping there in one day than in our Bay during the whole year. Chicago is situated on the borders of Lake Michigan, & on the edge of the boundless prairie, which may be seen stretching away as far as the eye can see without a solitary tree to interrupt the view – a friend of mine went out with his gun some 8 to 10 miles & in two days bagged 150 prairie grouse!!!

So much for Chicago! Here in Toronto there is a great outcry among the fair sex at the funereal appearance of the Rifle Brigade & they seem to be sighing for the red coats again. To add to our consolation we have just been strengthened with three more companies of *Canadian Rifles*! who have ensconsed themselves in the Old Fort. The band of this Rifle Brigade is a very good one & some prefer it to yours, for my own part I prefer yours to it. We do not see much of the officers, as only four show themselves at all, in fact there are but two universal party goers, Lord Maldon & Stuart. The former is very attentive to Caroline Stanton, your old flame, & this ought not to be ought it? The rest of the officers are very religious & hold prayer meetings in each other's quarters.

By this Mail I send you a *Herald* giving an account of our doings here on the occasion of Lord Elgin's visit.

By the same mail Larratt Smith wrote to his father in Southampton:

We have just received the parcel from England by the Wilcocks & are very happy to get it. The Wilcocks lost, for the Barries, a most valuable parcel containing Deeds & securities which is a really serious thing for them.

Eliza is delighted with your kind presents, and the shirt did indeed make me laugh – I was just dressing for the Govr Gen^{ls} levee, when the parcel was opened & Eliza proposed I should wear the shirt outside. Lord Elgin's reception & entertainment must have been gratifying especially as he said that he should much prefer having the seat of government here, to Montreal, and that he felt for the first time in Canada that he was in an English Town, surrounded by English & loyal hearts.

I have finished my education at last, having passed my Examination for B.C.L., which degree will be conferred on me next Thursday the 28th inst. I shall then take up my post as a Member of the Convocation of King's College, eligible for a seat in Parliament to represent the University whenever a Member is required.

On 24 November a traveller leaving for England was entrusted with a parcel and a letter for brother George in Greenwich:

By Mr. Hall, I send you these lines, also a small parcel of Indian work. The very handsome card case with a pincushion enclosed & one of the Mococks [Mohawks?] is for Aunt George and you will oblige me by handing them to her with our love. The other Mocock & the little 'baccy box' is for your Mary with our kindest love. They were brought by us from the Island of Michillimackinac.

Owing to some legal difficulty I have not got my Degree of B.C.L. yet, although I have passed my examination of 2 days in Law, compared my English & Latin Theses from Civil Law subjects & read them before the Convocation. But, owing to the resignation of Bishop Strachan as President no one can confer the Degree without special authority from the Governor General, the Chancellor, & he does not seem disposed to come up himself to confer them, & has not delegated his authority.

Typhus fever is very prevalent now among the citizens of Toronto; we have just lost Dr. Hamilton, the most eminent physician in Canada from it. We are all well through the mercy of God.

Just before the boats stopped running, Eliza Smith's sister, Caroline Thom, arrived from Perth to spend the winter with them. Eliza, well into her second pregnancy needed company. Caroline, who loved parties and dancing, needed no urging; *'Tuesday 30th November, St. Andrew's Day. I took Caroline & Eliza to the St. Andrew's Ball at the City Hall. A very large party indeed. We danced all night to the music of the Rifle Band & did not get home to bed till 5 A.M.'*

13: No lack of parties — or of travel 1848

WINTER 1848

In the winter of 1848 there was no lack of parties for the young fashionable set of Toronto. Larratt Smith described one of these affairs in a letter to Lieutenant Woods, written 16 January 1848; as it is a military ball given by the new and unsophisticated Rifle Brigade that had replaced Woods' own popular regiment, Smith is disparaging:

The Rifle Brigade broke out on the 31st inst by giving their first garrison ball. It was very kind of them to furnish highly decorated rooms, good music, and excellent grog for the townspeople to make merry with, because poor fellows, they are altogether too modest to partake themselves of any amusement, or to assist others in doing so. They adorned the 'exits & entrances' (to use theatrical parlance) of the different rooms for the greater part of the evening, looking as though they did not belong to 'the house' and as if they waited for an invitation to dance. Thanks to our own Juveniles we enjoyed ourselves very much. It was a dreadful night, rain pouring in torrents & the road to the barracks axle-deep in mud. Many were the mishaps that occurred; 'Shays' dismantled, shafts broken. However, no lives were lost; with the exception of a few heartbreaking sighs, no personal injuries of any consequence were inflicted.

Your old room was the lady's dressing room, which of course was 'got up' for the occasion by the classical arrangement of some 8 or 10 very large 'utensils,' which I learn were ranged very systematically in order behind a 'masked battery' of screens – all for the accommodation of the fair sex. This was certainly the most spicy thing done by the 'green Bobs.' I did not think they had so much pluck. I hear that this ball is to be followed by three others before spring. On the whole there have been more parties this winter than when you were here, as at least fifteen families including the

Spragges & the Stantons have let off their squibs, besides one or two public balls – not so bad either.

Am much obliged for the hint about dress etc – I took advantage of it at once, & appeared on the very night of the day I received your letter, in a correct 'Joinville' cravat, voting my fellows in a white choker as *Low bred, common* & *unclean.* Let the ladies alone, my dear fellow, for their fashions, 'Victorias'[1] have been all the rage long since. The 'Deux Temps' dance is all the rage, requiring only to be once started by a *real fine Viscount* to set the girls all mad about it. We have had vis-à-vis, dos-à-dos, long in vogue here, but from your accounts 'bussum-à-bussum' seems to be coming in – It is to be fervently hoped that it will end there.

The Elections are over & Baldwin & the Radicals are in again by overwhelming majorities – We shall have another revolution, & you will be ordered out here once more.

There has been no sleighing here at all this winter; nothing but rain & mild weather. If this continues we shall soon sell our sleighs with explanatory remarks as to their use & origin.

I send you by this mail a thorough Radical paper the *Globe.* It will give you some insight into the Elections, although you must not believe all it says.

Caroline Stanton is not flirting with Lord Maldon now, but is behaving very correctly.

Paddy Bernard is here again. His universal popularity & winning manners called for a Demonstration on the part of his creditors immediately on his return & a deputation headed by the Sheriff at once offered him a hearty welcome & reception in the stone jug at the other end of town, where he lay for three days until Mr. Bethune bailed him out.

A theatre will shortly be commenced on King Street to cost £5000, you'll have to come out & play your old part again 'in the order of the day.'

Captain Larratt Hillary Smith's sixty-sixth birthday was on 17 January 1848. His son Larratt wrote him a letter which he entrusted to a friend called Perrin who was leaving for England.

Many many happy returns of this day and may God grant you health and strength with every spiritual and temporal blessing for years to come is my earnest and fervent prayer. Eliza entered her 23rd year on Monday & George's birthday will not be overlooked by us on Wednesday. I am now several letters in your debt. The reason I have not written oftener is that the Mail is so irregular no one knows when to be prepared for it.

I have been looking for a fall in exchange to remit you your dividends – I only wish that all your funds were in England that I might loan them out here & employ them & I would only ask 5 years to double your capital – money never was so valuable. The Banks here doing nothing in the way of discount – panic & alarm on all sides. Fortunately I am about to make an exchange of some of your Oro land for ⅔ of ½ an acre in Town, this Lot is on the road to the right turning off the Yonge Street Toll Gate.[2] The Sheriff is getting £5 a foot frontage for land more out of the way – whereas this is on a most excellent road with the Church near at hand.

I have not had my B.C.L. Degree conferred on me yet. Dr. McCaul has purposely raised a difficulty, which he will not see fit to have removed until they make him President in place of Bishop Strachan who has resigned. This is all fudge. I feel greatly annoyed at Dr. McCaul's humbugging & have left King's College Chapel in consequence.

The Radicals are returned by overwhelming majority & will be enabled to form the strongest administration this country has *ever* seen. Baldwin, Price, Blake, & Morrison are returned by immense majorities for the Ridings & all are lawyers. I sent you Papineau's treasonable address to the electors of St. Maurice. He appears to be getting as bad as ever; Baldwin & his party disown him; – you see he is ranked among the doubtful ones.

If the American War with Mexico over the annexation of Texas is much longer protracted, the American Banks will be all broken. The States is suffering woefully from the continued drain of *specie* to pay their troops.

Eliza & her sister are sitting at the table where I am writing, pulling Latire molasses candy. Eliza says her hands are getting sore & that you once pulled the skin off your hands at this work, is this so?

My letters are intended for the whole family, although only addressed to you. Tell Mamma that I am much obliged for her note. I omitted to thank her for her slippers, I was much obliged to receive them. Eliza would most gladly write to Mamma, Mary, & Adelaide, but she is a poor sailor, & her time is much occupied in waiting for the young 'un thats on his road.

Eliza's second child, a healthy boy, was born in the cottage on Front Street, and lived for nearly twenty years. His short biography is in the Smith family Bible, written in his father's hand:

Larratt Alexander Smith, son of Larratt William Violett and Eliza Caroline, Smith. Born Monday 9½ A.M. 13th March 1848. Christened at Perth, Canada West, by the Rev. Michael Harris. Larratt Smith for Captain Larratt Hillary Smith, Alexander Thom and Mrs. Thom, Sponsors, on 23rd July 1848. Confirmed at Cobourg by Bishop Strachan 3rd July 1864. Died on Friday 10th January 1868 at 11:30 P.M. at Summer Hill, of consumption taken from privation & fatigue during the Ridgeway affair in June 1866, and buried with military honors by the Queen's Own Regiment and the 13th Battalion in St. James' Cemetery.

The Ridgeway affair was a clash between Canadian militia and American Fenians at Ridgeway near Fort Erie. Various members of the family told me that the boy's father always blamed the senior officers of the regiment and Sir John A. Macdonald in particular for his son's death. He claimed that the wounded had lain untended in the open while those in charge were carousing at Sir John's drinking party. It was a part of the Smith family tradition that my embittered grandfather never spoke to Macdonald again, cut him on the street, changed his own politics, and became a Liberal.

SPRING 1848

Larratt Alexander Smith's birth is also recorded in his father's journal: 'Routed up at ½ past 4 A.M. Dr. Hodder, nurse, & Mrs. Cameron sent for. Eliza confined 5 hours later. Wrote Mrs. Thom at Perth, then wrote Papa in time to catch the English Mail.' As these letters have been lost, we have no description of the child until 22 April 1848, when the father writes to the grandfather in Southampton:

Easter Monday evening. We had a letter from George lately, announcing the birth of a daughter & were glad to find that she had been too expeditious for her Mamma, for the sooner these matters are over, the better. My little boy is a fine little fellow, six weeks old today. He is remarkably good looking for a child. Mrs. Davies says that he has your head & is very like you. Don't be vain now, Eliza insists that he is to be called after you – adding her father's name, Alexander. All her folks are annoyed at it, they think that Alexander should come before Larratt, but she is fixed in her purpose. She is, I do not know why, very fond of you. She has seen you, but has never spoken to you. Your letters amuse her much – I really believe that her affection for all of you is even stronger than for her own family, but her antipathy for letter writing is insurmountable; she is so averse to it, that the few letters she has ever penned were all written by me, or nearly so. The reason she gives is that Mary George's letters are so expansive, you would think but little of hers, unless I touched them up for her. She has now been very busy for two or three hours writing Mamma, but I don't think has got through twelve sentences.

She is a dear affectionate girl, & saves me by her excellent management, thoughtfulness & hard work at her needle & otherwise, at least a hundred pounds a year. She is likewise very economical in her dress & household matters, always preferring solid unpretentious comfort to empty display.

We have only had *three nurses & two babies* in the house for the past weeks. Thank goodness, one baby & two nurses have left; now we have but one wet nurse, Jane Fitzpatrick & her baby. I pay Jane £2 per month, a high wage, but she is the source of life for my boy. I also keep a cook, a housemaid, & a servant boy, the three for little more than I pay the wet nurse.

Eliza has just cut off some of baby's hair, which I enclose for you.

I do not know how many *Illustrated* papers you send by each mail, but sometimes I get one, sometimes two, & frequently none at all. Eliza has not received a *Lady's* paper nor I a *Punch*, for these three or four months past. When they do come, the covers are invariably off & torn to rags.

Aemilius Irving has returned here via the West Indies. I saw him today. He says that the profiles you gave him of Mary & Adelaide were most carefully packed, but his trunk got in the water at Mobile, Alabama and everything was destroyed.

I don't think we shall long be part of the British Empire, everything tends to sever the connection & nothing more so than the suicidal policy of the Home Government in withdrawing protection which has thrown us & our business, altogether into the hands of the Americans. Indeed more business is done by us with New York now, than with England, or Quebec, or Montreal, which last, amounts to nothing at all ...

Young Smith had scarcely posted this letter when another one arrived from Captain Smith, informing his son that, owing to the high rate of exchange involved in sending his Canadian dividends back to England, he had decided to sell all his investments in Canada, but was unsure of how to get the money back to England. Larratt answered at once, pointing out the advantages of a visit to Canada.

5 May 1848

I am delighted to think that I have it in my power conscientiously to say to you that by coming out you will save your expenses. I do not speak on my own authority, but after consultation with Mr. Cassels the Manager of the Bank of British North America, a very warm friend of mine, & who has just told me that he will put you in the way 'to do it,' ... you had better come out by the next trip of the *Sarah Sand* – she is tolerably expeditious, & I learn the cheapest of all the vessels in her charge – I have been told that the first cabin fare is but £15.0.0 – Young Henry Boulton reached here by the *Sarah Sand* last Monday. You cannot think what pleasure, what delight it will give us to see you with us ... It just occurs to me what arrangement you could make to get your funds home at a great saving, & this is what Cassels has done with the banks. Dispose of your stock at the best price you can, then come upon the banks with specie, & as the amounts are very large, they will gladly give you exchange upon New York at 1 or $1\frac{1}{2}$ at farthest to get rid of you, where you can buy at a very reduced rate.

However Cassels can manage it for you, if you only come out, & will save you your expenses in the bargain which if left to me & I have to buy Bills here must all be sunk.

If you cannot manage by exchange, then get specie & take it with you. The banks will make you take American silver, as they do not keep gold & never pay large sums in gold ...

(When I read this I pictured great-grandfather staggering up the gangplank of the *Sarah Sand* weighed down by great sacks of American silver coins.)

... We have hardly given your European troubles a thought, & there is no danger whatever of an uprising here unless among a very few of the Lower Canadians led by the old cowardly Dotard Papineau, which would be easily quelled as raised – Loyalty to the Queen is uppermost here & if a separation is ever mooted it will be a very quiet one. The Papineaus in different parts of the Union have been told pretty plainly already that if they attempt to get up a demonstration or any disturbance they will be put down at once – It is a fortunate thing for us that Baldwin's Radicals are in power, as they can now have no cause to complain seeing that they run the Government de facto; the consequence is that they disclaim & disown all Papineau's rebels & are closely watching him to put him down the first chance they have ...

The lake steamboat *Admiral* which took you to Oswego on your way home has just commenced running again – The railroad to Oswego from Syracuse is just completed, & it will be the most direct route from New York to Toronto – The season has been very backward, although a cold spring commenced very early – We have now fully made up our minds to see you in July, & you must not disappoint us – Write & tell us when we are to expect you, & we will make a promise of being at home to receive you, as Eliza & the baby go to Perth next month for two or three weeks, & I join them for a week & bring them home, if I can get away ...

SUMMER 1848

Between 29 May, when Eliza left for Perth, and 6 July, when Larratt followed her, his diaries are dispirited. He lived the life of a summer bachelor: besides gardening, taking down winter stove-pipes, and setting hens, he picnicked, fished, and dined with his friends, but appears to have taken little pleasure out of anything. Although there is no record of any theatrical entertainment, the journals do mention the visit of a renowned personage, Charles Sherwood Stratton, better known as General Tom Thumb. This famous American dwarf, who was said to have been only two feet high when P.T. Barnum first exhibited him, had made a fortune entertaining the courts of Europe. 'Tom Thumb is here exhibiting himself – he can be seen daily in the streets of Toronto driving in his carriage given him by Queen Victoria.'

Larratt Smith answered another letter from his father just before he left for Perth. Since Captain Smith's letter has been lost, one can only assume the tone of it by his son's reply:

29th June, 1848

Your letter of the 1st instant reached me on the 20th ... I find it impossible under all circumstances to advise you to take the trip out. In the first place, I do not & should not recommend the sale of your stock at all, as I think you might do worse with your money than just get 7 per cent with it in Canada, without risk or trouble. However I should not presume to dictate to you in matters that do not concern myself, & if you decide upon removing your funds, my duty shall be to assist you to accomplish your object.

It is a great blow to our hopes, your not coming out. Eliza still expects you; she left here the latter end of last month with the baby & Mary Ann, the wet nurse, for Perth where she has been ever since. I hope to be able this day week to go for her, but first I intend going to Montreal & Quebec. I am to spend a few days at Brockville on my way down by invitation from Eliza's relative, the Hon. James Morris. I am to have letters from Walter Cassels, my friend in the Bank of British North America to several parties in Quebec, a Mr. John Thompson is one, do you know him? He is very rich. I will then go to Perth by the Ottawa & the Rideau the latter end of July & will bring Eliza home with me, first of all having christened my boy, which is fixed for Sunday the 23rd July. Alex Thom standing for his godfather and your humble servant standing for your worthy self. We call our boy 'Larratt Alexander.' He is thriving amazingly & is very intelligent already & *like myself* good looking! Before I see him again, I shall have been away from them 7 or 8 weeks, a long time indeed.

The time passed. Larratt Smith made a brief journey to Montreal and Quebec. The journals complain of broken-down machinery and bedbugs in the steamboats but say little of his first sight of the Plains of Abraham and the garrison his father had known so well. Perhaps young Smith's mind was intent on the joyful reunion that awaited him at Perth, which he reached by means of steamboats and stage-coaches on 15 July.

A leisurely interlude was spent at the Thom farm; then, the day before the Smiths left for Toronto, their infant son was duly baptised: '*Sunday 23rd July*. The christening party took place last Friday evening when we danced & sang till 2 o'clock in the morning. On coming into the church today, baby squalled lustily, but quieted on being nursed. After Morning Prayer he was baptised Larratt Alexander by Parson Harris.'

The following afternoon Larratt and Eliza, with their baby and nurse, left for Brockville by way of Oliver's Ferry and the steamboat *Rochester*. At

Brockville they embarked on another ship for a circuitous voyage to Toronto.

Saturday 29th July. A very fine day. We left Brockville at 10 A.M. in the American boat *Ontario.* Raced the vessel *Passport* and reached Kingston at 3 P.M. Left again at 5 P.M. for Sackets Harbour where we had time to walk about before the ship left for Oswego where it tied up for the night. We reached Rochester on Sunday afternoon, walked up to see the town and Mount Hope, then left at 7 P.M. for Lewiston. After rather a rough night we docked at Lewiston at 4 A.M. Changed to the Toronto boat *Magnet* at ½ past 9, & reached Toronto at 1 P.M., showery & very rough indeed all the way across the lake.

AUTUMN 1848

Nine days after the Smiths returned to Toronto they had an unexpected visitor; Larratt described the arrival in a letter to his friend Lieutenant Woods, dated 11 September 1848:

I was very agreeably surprised the other day to see my father walking in, having just come across the road from Southampton to pay us a visit – for want of something to do I suppose. We have been dodging about the country together a little. We were at Buffalo last week at a great exhibition where near 100,000 people had congregated so that the very steamboats at the wharf could not give accommodation to the stranded thousands. Papa & I put up at the Western Hotel which was so crowded we were obliged to sleep 4 in a room. The show was an Agricultural Fair which lasted for three days. I was glad to find that a very large number of the prizes, especially for cattle, were carried off by Canadians.

Whilst at Buffalo we went to the Theatre where we saw the 'Viennoise Children' perform. By the way, our new Theatre in Toronto which is being erected back of Macdonald's Hotel at the end of a Lane opening into King Street, is expected to be completed by the 1st of November, so that for the first time Toronto will have a proper Theatre, a legitimate one.

I must also tell you that six of the Brigade Band deserted here the other night. Taking their instruments valued at £50 with them, they crossed Lake Ontario in an open boat, but just as they were on the eve of giving a concert at Lockport, they were taken & handed over to the American authorities, subject to the demands of our Government under the Ashburton Treaty, for Larceny. They have completely ruined the Band, two or three were Corporals & fine players – I heard one of them at a concert last winter play remarkably well on the pianoforte. The present Band is at once to be broken up & a new one found increased in number to 40, who will all play a new instrument just invented & known as the Saxe horn.

Speaking of the Military, Mrs. Smith has for some time been relieving & indeed almost supporting a woman with two children, wife of a man who was probably in your Company at the garrison. An infant that she has is very ill & likely to die. I think the husband was Dr. Taylor's servant, do you know such a man?

Mrs. Smith & I thank you for your good wishes touching the 'Illustrious Stranger' who I am happy to say is a thriving little fellow.

We have frequently thought of you in the midst of the troubles at home, but from all I can discover from the papers, I do not see that your Regiment has yet been ordered to Ireland & shall therefore address this letter to Chester from whence you wrote me. The return of my father to England affords me a favourable opportunity of writing to you. This letter may not reach you for some little time as he intends overhauling the country a little more before he returns.

I do not think there is much more for me to say at present, so with kind regards in which Mrs. Smith & the 'Illustrious Stranger' join ...

This letter did not reach its recipient until late in October, but at that it did better than the Smiths' own correspondence through the regular mail. In his journal for 5 October Larratt stated: 'A letter came from Papa today. I wrote him at once at New York & enclosed letters etc.' But Captain Smith apparently embarked without receiving this correspondence. On 18 November he wrote to his son from Southampton:

I was disappointed at not hearing from you before leaving New York to embark for England. I am still more so at receiving no letter by the last Packet that left Boston on the 18th and arrived at Liverpool on the 31st October, bringing Toronto papers to the 6th of that month. My chief anxiety and fear is that you may have addressed a letter enclosing a remittance to me at the Astor House, which in the present uncertainty in the transportation of Mails between Canada & the States, may not have reached in time for me to have rec^d it on, or before the morning of the 11th when we sailed, and in that case may be still lying at the Bar of the Hotel before alluded to ... I should have written you by the last Mail, but was misled by thinking that the Fortnightly trips of the Steamers commenced in November.

I had a nice passage home, in something less than twelve days, only ill for about twenty four hours, when we had a bit of a blow. A highly respectable set of passengers, about a hundred, the majority Yankees, but of a superior description – smoking in moderation and *expectoration* at a low level.

Having nothing more to say at present ... and as Mammy gives you all the domestic news ... I must conclude with kindest love to Eliza, lots of kisses for

Alexander the *Small*, and kindest remembrances to old friends ... Tenez en, Your very affectionate parent. L. Smith.

NOVEMBER–DECEMBER 1848

This letter was forwarded by his daughter-in-law Eliza and received by his son Larratt at the Land Registry Office, Chatham, Upper Canada, on 7 December 1848. Larratt was on the last leg of a business trip which had begun on 8 November and taken him as far as Sandwich and Detroit.

It is almost a month since I left home on my cold rough voyage to Niagara. The vessel *Chief Justice* rolled & pitched in such a manner I was seasick most of the way. On reaching Niagara I caught the stage coach but the snow being over 2 feet deep at Black Rock was obliged to walk from thence into Buffalo. Put up at the Western Hotel & in the evening went to the Theatre. Left the next day in the lake vessel *America* for the voyage down Lake Erie to Detroit. About 300 passengers on board. Obliged to sleep on the cabin table as my berth too wet & steamy. Reached Detroit the following evening, put up at the National Hotel. Went twice to the Theatre & to church on Sunday. Left Detroit on Monday by the river boat *Brothers*[3] for Amherstburg & Malden. Very busy there, investigating property for clients. On riding out to look at a Lot in Malden, got spilt in the ditch. Roads in horrid condition.

Having finished my business in those parts I embarked for Sandwich on Thursday 16th November in the *Brothers*. Spent most of Friday searching Assessment Notes in the office of Charles Baby, Clerk of the Peace at Sandwich and dined with him in his house on the river. Spent a wretched night at Johnston's Hotel – kept awake by the noisy drinking brutes who frequent the place. Next day I crossed the river by skiff with my client Mr. Eberts, & slept at his house in Detroit. Thereafter, while doing my daily business in Sandwich, I spent my nights at Duncan's comfortable house, the Prince Albert Hotel,[4] in the quiet village of Windsor. Sandwich too noisy & filthy for me.

Whilst at Windsor, on the last night of November, I saw & heard from across the river at Detroit, the celebrations of Zachary Taylor's election as the 12th President of the United States. 100 cannon were fired at Sunset followed by rockets & other fireworks.

Next day the weather worsened with a blizzard of snow that turned to sleet & torrents of rain at night. On Saturday morning I drove to Sandwich expecting to leave for Chatham in the *Brothers*, but it was blowing such a hurricane from the South East the ship would not venture out. By evening the wind had fallen, the ship sailed, & I reached Chatham in the afternoon of Sunday the 3rd of December. Put up at the 'Royal Exchange Hotel' – another filthy house. However, I met a friend called Foote at the Registry Office, who very kindly invited me to dine & sleep at his house for the remainder of my stay at Chatham. Very comfortable there & within walking distance of the Registry Office. Whilst there I received Papa's letter enclosed in one from Eliza. Hers to tell me that her brother, poor Alex Thom, had died of brain fever at Perth on the 17th of November. Wrote her at once.

Larratt Smith did not finish the account of this journey until after his return to Toronto.

Wednesday 11th December. My stay at Chatham was marred by bad weather, rain & sleet all day every day until last Friday when I left for London in the 8 P.M. stage-coach. The weather turned fine, but the roads were so frightfully bad we made only 26 miles travelling all night & until 8 next morning. After driving all day on Saturday it came on to rain by 6 P.M. & poured in such torrents our coachman could barely keep the stage on the road, thus we did not reach London until ½ past 10 P.M. I was fortunate in finding a room at the Western Hotel, a most comfortable & excellent house.

On Sunday I attended St. Paul's Church, a most handsome edifice, the Reverend Benjamin Cronyn officiating. I spent the remainder of the day preparing my client's case. On Monday, after transacting my business with the Treasurer's Office, I had plenty of time to walk about the town as the Mail coach did not leave till ½ past 1 P.M. This fast coach covered the 81 miles to Hamilton by ½ past 4 in the morning, having stayed on the road only some 3 hours! I waited about, then left Hamilton at ½ past 7 in the steamer *Eclipse* & reached Toronto at 12 noon. Found Eliza still staying with Rose Cameron. Dined there & then drove Eliza home.

Rose Cameron's husband, John, was the cashier or general manager of the Commercial Bank, a neo-classical edifice on Wellington Street. He was a business acquaintance of Larratt's, his wife Rose was Eliza's closest friend. The Camerons lived in the elegant suite of rooms provided for the manager above the bank. '*Sunday 31st December, 1848.* Eliza & I attended St. George's Church twice today, then in the evening went to Cameron's Chambers in the Bank & saw the New Year in. Oyster supper & champagne accompanied by great romping & skylarking.'

14: 'Sowed my early peas... made my Will' 1849

On the last day of January 1849, after months of uncertainty, Larratt Smith finally forced his partner Robert Crooks to sign the dissolution of their law firm. The unsatisfactory partnership was already disintegrating when Larratt wrote this letter to his father in the spring of that year:

I have had occasion to require an explanation from my partner Robert Crooks on the course he has been running & have written him a letter of 10 sheets in order to show him the injury he has been inflicting on me, with the result that he has stopped drawing on the firm, but has not as yet been able to pay back the amount he has drawn, although he has been full of promises for some time back. He has several thousand pounds in freehold property in the heart of the City of Toronto, yet, he cannot for his life raise a hundred pounds on it. The lawyers in Toronto are without exception the most greedy of men. I am happy to say that in the midst of my troubles my character stands unimpeached & I am growing in popularity here, to the extent that I would care but little if Crooks left the firm tomorrow.

I believe I have the goodwill of all the clients worth having & what is more, I'll keep it. Our business never was better than this present, since the beginning of the year ought to be worth £200 a month, & hard, very hard have I slaved at it night & day – never taking a meal to eat from breakfast time till dinner at 7. However I certainly feel 'au fait' at the work & ready for anything almost.

The day after the signing of the dissolution, he wrote again:

You will doubtless be rejoiced to hear that I am now in a fair way of getting rid of my partner Mr. Crooks. His irregularities of late have been so atrocious & caused such injury to the business & my clients that I could endure it no longer. And when threatened by the loss of the Bank of British North America solicitorship, for his misconduct, I at once resolved to have done with him. I offered him £1000 for the business. He refused to answer my letter, whereupon I pitched into him for his outrageous conduct. He then agreed to refer the matter to our good friend John Cameron, the Cashier of the Commercial Bank. Cameron consulted Walter Cassels of the Bank of British North America, but Crooks would not sign, & so it went on from day to day until yesterday when Cameron insisted & Crooks signed. I am now free to act for myself on the 1st of March & I owe Crooks nothing.

Meanwhile, I found a connection with Adam Wilson,[1] Mr. Robert Baldwin's late partner. Wilson, of course wrote Mr. Baldwin to consult him as to taking me into partnership, knowing that Mr. Baldwin had left me in charge of the Attorney's General's office when he was Minister in the Legislature. Mr. Baldwin has very kindly sent me a copy of his letter to Wilson in which he writes of me in most flattering terms & completely unsolicited on my part. I shall enclose a copy of it in this letter.

We have had a very sickly winter here, many deaths from Scarlet Fever & influenza. The Scarlet Fever is very malignant indeed & almost always proves fatal. Botts of the Rifle Brigade died of it today & one of Frederick Widder's daughters cannot last the night out. Although Eliza has been rather poorly & my little boy has had a severe cold, they are both well again. It is getting rather late & I am very tired. God bless you ...

Even after he joined Adam Wilson, Larratt Smith was endeavouring to clear up the muddled affairs of the late firm of Crooks & Smith. His letter book is full of explanations to creditors and entreaties to ex-clients for money. As late as the spring of 1850 he was still corresponding with a rather unsatisfactory client in Pennsylvania: '... I took your note in March 1849, when I could have insisted upon the money ... In your letter of October last, you write that by the 15th January your brother expected to be with you & "be we fortunate or otherwise all these claims will be settled *immediately*." Since then I have had no intimation of any kind from you & there the matter stands. I would have taken the land you offered in the West had it turned out to be "terra firma," but it appears to be *land covered with water*. Have you no offer of the kind to make elsewhere? I do not desire to press you for *money* (badly as I want it) if you can manage it in any other way ...'

There is nothing in Larratt Smith's papers to show whether he received any satisfaction from this particular client. There were, however, plenty of others just like him; most of Smith's evenings at home were spent in writing to them, or going over the ledgers of the ill-fated firm of Crooks & Smith.

But Smith's business worries were more than offset by his happy, tranquil life with Eliza and their little son: '*Tuesday 13th March.* Sonny's Birthday, 1 year old today. Seven of our friends came to dinner including Walter Cassels who gave Sonny a Silver Cup. Sonny walked as far as John Street yesterday, then ran away this morning – brought back by his father – ran away again at night.'

On 23 March 1849 the domestic serenity of the entries is broken.

William Lyon Mackenzie is back in town, the first time he has been seen since the Rebellion 12 years ago. This evening his effigy, with those of Robert Baldwin & William Hume Blake, was burnt by a Tory mob in front of the Inspection building. The howling mob, which included two city aldermen, smashed in the house of Mackenzie's friend Mackintosh & attacked & stoned the residence of George Brown, editor of the *Globe* newspaper; then, worn out by its exertions, the rabble sullenly withdrew.

This incident over, Smith's journals turn to spring.

On Palm Sunday a warm wind sprang up & broke the greater part of the ice then drove it into Privat's corner of Toronto Bay. By Monday the ice had entirely disappeared from the Bay & by Good Friday the *Island Queen* & the Horse boat commenced running to the Island. Very warm weather, 82° in the sun. Having engaged John Daniels to dig the garden for $8, sowed my early peas & finished making asparagus bed before Easter. On the morning of Good Friday, Eliza & I went to St. George's church, then spent the rest of the day with my partner Adam Wilson & his wife. Late on this warm evening a great fire broke out, St. James Cathedral & the old City Hall were both burnt to the ground, also two entire squares on King Street. On Easter Saturday a hurricane blowing from the North West brought cold weather & *several inches of snow fell during the night!*

Smith's entry for 26 April records an even worse conflagration: 'News came by way of the Electric Telegraph of the terrible riots in Montreal yesterday & the burning of Parliament House there.' Smith fails to mention that stones were hurled at Lord Elgin by the same wild Tory mob that set the fire. They stoned him because, in implementing responsible government, he refused to veto the Rebellion Losses Bill. Strange as it may seem, this hated bill (hated because it was drafted as much for the benefit of French Canada as English Canada) was introduced by a responsible ministry and passed by a huge majority, which included a great number of the 'English' members themselves. It is even stranger that Tory defenders of orderly British constitutional government should so readily ignore the constitutional process and rush headlong into lawless violence. On 28 April Smith wrote: 'A noisy Meeting was held in the St. Lawrence Market Place today to Petition Her Majesty, Queen Victoria to recall Lord Elgin. There were, however, plenty of constables & troops on hand & nothing untoward happened.'

Smith turned from political to domestic situations to note that Eliza was expecting another child. In anticipation of the event he made an arrangement with Dr Widmer to enlarge the cottage in return for a raise in rent of £14 a year.

Tuesday 3rd July. Workmen commenced moving the outhouses on Monday 21st May. Result, great disorder. Eliza therefore, took Sonny & his nurse & left for Perth on the *Princess Royal* the following morning, & I came down to Walter Cassels' Chambers at the Bank where I have been sleeping ever since. Thunder, lightning, & rain in torrents, somewhat marred the Excursions on the Queen's Birthday, but the skies cleared for the Illuminations & fireworks in the evening. Capreol's Illumination with Gas, & the fireworks opposite Dr. Widmer's surgery very splendid indeed.

SUMMER 1849

Workmen commenced altering our house on 1st June at 4 P.M., by Tuesday 5th, they had raised the roof by some $8\frac{1}{2}$ feet, & by Thursday 14th, the roof was on, the flag raised & I treated the men. Sent a letter to Eliza today to let her know I will be leaving Toronto on the 9th inst. & that I expect her to come on board the *Lord Elgin* at Brockville on the morning of Tuesday 10th, from whence we will make our holiday excursion to Montreal & Quebec. Enclosed £1 in the letter & gave it to little Macdonald who is going directly to Perth.

Everything turned out according to plan; Eliza duly boarded the *Lord Elgin*, the vessel reached Montreal an hour after sunset, but Lower Canada was in a bad way.

July 20th. We reached Montreal on Wednesday 11th only to find a temperature of 100° in the shade, being the hottest known for 30 years & the Cholera sickness raging. I hastily transacted my business & we left for Quebec in the steamboat *Quebec*. We reached Quebec at 6 A.M. on Friday. Weather intensely hot & many deaths from Cholera. Eliza sick all day.

Myself not well. Saw one or two friends, then left as too much sickness about. We therefore sailed back to Montreal & on to Lachine. Very hot and smoky there. We then set out for Bytown by way of Point Fortune & L'Orignal. Reached Bytown on Tuesday 17th at 10 P.M. & put up at Doran's Hotel in Upper Town which we found very comfortable indeed. After seeing all the sights in Bytown we left at 10 P.M. next day in the *Beaver* for Oliver's Ferry. It was however, too foggy to proceed more than 4 miles so started again at daybreak but ran aground & remained stuck in the mud for 5 hours. We eventually reached the Ferry at 11 P.M. & Perth at 4 o'clock this morning.

During the next ten days at Perth, Larratt Smith took over the management of the Thom estate. Before the untimely death of his brother-in-law, Alexander Thom, Smith had occasionally advised his mother-in-law about her investments and small legal matters, while Alexander had run the farm. But when the latter died he left no will, as Larratt explains in a letter to a lawyer in Bytown written the following year: 'The late Dr. Thom left his real estate to his only son, Alexander who died intestate, leaving two sisters of the whole blood & one of the half. In this case, the whole blood, Mrs. Eliza Smith, and Miss Caroline Thom, take in exclusion of their half-sister Mrs. Vice Chancellor Spragge ... Mrs. Thom, widow of the Doctor, will have to bar her Dower in the 80 acre Lot at Nepean, for which, I understand, you have a purchaser.'

Most of the immediate arrangements for the Thom estate were settled in the summer of 1849. Just before he took his family back to Toronto, Larratt Smith wrote: 'Spent nearly all day Monday seeing parties about running the farm, also supervised the setting up of poor Dr. Thom's gravestone. On our last Sunday, took Eliza to the graveyard in the evening to see the tomb.'

These matters settled, the Smiths left for Toronto. In the interlude at Perth they had almost forgotten about the cholera epidemic, but when the ship docked at Kingston they were horrified to learn that there was cholera in the town, and still more frightened when they arrived at Toronto to find the disease rampant there.

Wednesday 29th August. Cholera very bad. 30 cases in the city & many deaths. Insured my life for £300 sterling in Eagle & Protector office. Stung over the eye by a wasp & feeling most unwell today. I made my Will before my friend Walter Cassels & Helena Potter, our cook, then handed the Will to Cassels for Cameron to keep at the Bank. Tremendous thunderstorm & lightning at night.

Larratt Smith did not catch cholera nor did any members of his household. But domestic life had its distressing moments: '*September 21st.* Turned off Nicholas servant boy for being drunk & swearing at & abusing Helena & destroying trees & knocking down the fruit.'

Nicholas was followed in quick succession by five other boys, none of whom lasted more than a few weeks. Smith appealed to the garrison: 'Wrote Captain Hamilton about a servant & a soldier came at $2 a month.' The nameless soldier left after three weeks when, according to Smith's housekeeping accounts, another soldier, John Hennessy of the Royal Rifle Brigade, took his place and stayed a record five months, after which the procession of servant boys started all over again.

Helena the cook only lasted four months after her tiff with Nicholas: 'Helena received warning yesterday to behave herself or "make tracks," she was, however, very impudent again today, so was paid off & sent away in disgrace for good.'

AUTUMN 1849

The cook and the servant boy may have had their own stories to tell, especially Nicholas, who as hewer of wood and drawer of water was at everyone's beck and call including Helena's. The Smiths' servants never lacked for work. In the autumn of 1849, not only was there fruit to be picked and preserved, winter vegetables to be stowed away, eggs to be packed in salt, and firewood to be sawn before it was stacked in the woodshed (the Smiths burned twenty-five cords of wood a year), but also the cottage was still overrun with workmen: '*Saturday 6th October* – the house has been in the greatest confusion & dirt ever since last Monday when the men commenced putting in coal grates & papering downstairs. Stayed at home all day to see the Drawing-room grate installed & supervise the cleaning. Ordered tin tub to be brought into the kitchen & had a bath there after everyone had gone to bed. Raining in torrents & blowing a gale from the S.E. all night.'

Although Smith's accounts for 1849 continue to record the purchase of immense quantities of wood at eleven shillings a cord, they also show deliveries of coal[2] at five dollars a ton to burn in the new grates and warm the cottage on Front Street.

The Smiths were now ready to receive a visitor: '*Thursday 1st November.* Wrote Mrs. Thom last Thursday & enclosed $10 to enable

Caroline to come up to Toronto. Caro arrived today, she will be good company for Eliza while she awaits her confinement.'

Shortly before the steamboats were laid up for the winter, a distinguished passenger arrived from Montreal to take up residence in Toronto: '*Tuesday 20th November.* Governor General & wife & suite arrived here for good & put up at Ellah's Hotel.'[3] This great statesman was one of Canada's most exemplary governors and helped the country to achieve responsible government.

In view of what Lord Elgin had already done for Canada, his duties in Toronto in 1849 may have seemed trivial: Smith's journals note that not only did the governor of British North America open the St Andrew's Day Ball (tickets £5), he also lent his presence and that of the retinue to other events. Smith noted: 'To a concert on Friday 21st December at Temperance Hall, put on the Choir of St. George's church[4] in aid of the church's organ fund & new heating apparatus (tickets 5 shillings). Altho' the Gov. Genl came with his suite & there were about 175 people in the hall, we only realized £16.14.4½. Eliza there with her sister Caro to hear me sing.'

15: 'Here, there, and everywhere' 1850

WINTER 1850

Despite her advanced pregnancy Eliza also went to the first of the Philharmonic concerts, to a party afterwards at the Camerons, and on New Year's Eve to a reception given by Larratt's partner Adam Wilson. 'Wilson very kindly sent his sleigh, a fine frosty night & a nice party.' The next afternoon Eliza had her own New Year's Day reception. Then, sometime in the evening, 'Eliza taken ill, I went at once for the nurse & Dr. Hodder ...' Very early in the morning of 2 January, Eliza gave birth to another son. The record in the Smith family Bible reads: 'George Cassels Smith, son of Larratt William Violett and Eliza Caroline Smith. Born Wednesday at 20 Minutes to 3 A.M., 2 January 1850. Christened 16 June 1850 at St. George's Church, Toronto, by the Reverend Stephen Lett, L.L.D. (Sponsors Walter Gibson Cassels, Geo. Boyd pro George Smith, England, and Caroline Emily Thom). Died at Barrie at Mr. Chickley's school on Monday 6th June 1859 at 25 minutes past 12 A.M., of intermittent fever terminating with congestion of the brain. Buried in the family burying ground in St. James' Cemetery, Toronto.'

Some nine years and five months before these last lines were written, the child's father had noted: 'Eliza 25 years old today, came downstairs for the first time. Baby doing very well.'

On 13 March the Smiths' eldest son celebrated his birthday – or rather the grownups kept it for him: 'Very wet – raining all day. Larratt 2 years old today. Party in the evening a pleasant affair, 44 present, 36 did not come, weather too bad ... *Saturday 16th.* Walter Cassels took Larratt to the Daguerrean Gallery[1] to have his portrait taken as a birthday treat, but the child would not sit still for even the ten minutes required for a Daguerreotype, so came home again.'

SPRING 1850

Throughout the winter and spring of 1850 the Toronto Amateur Theatrical Company continued to amuse local society with plays from their repertoire. According to Smith, who sang in the burlesque opera *Bombastes Furioso*, and acted in most of the plays, their stock consisted of such productions as *Box and Cox*, *Loan of a Lover*, *Rendezvous*, and a play called *Weathercock*, which served as something of a portent: 'Thursday 4th April. Blowing very hard yesterday from the S.E., raining in torrents. In the evening, I played the lead in 'Weathercock' to a sparse audience. Dreadful night. The storm made great dilapidations in bridges etc. Both the Humber & Don bridges swept away as well as the smaller spans at Thornhill & Hog's Hollow.'

This storm blew itself out. Toronto had a respite until Thursday, 11 April: 'Very stormy & snowing hard all day. Eliza, Caroline & I at Mrs. Nichol's Soiree Musicale last evening. Eliza in great pain today with her left breast bealing. Looking about for a wet nurse for Georgey.' The Smiths soon found a wet nurse, who appears in her employer's journal: 'The wet nurse Catherine had her baby christened on Sunday in St. George's Church by Dr. Lett.'

Very early in the spring of that year, Larratt Smith was elected Pro Vice Chancellor of the University of Toronto. His journal gives only the bare fact, but a letter to his father, written 24 April, is more discursive:

Your humble servant, the Pro Vice Chancellor, is getting well cut up by the Press on the radical side. It is a tolerably uneasy seat after all. I send you the *Globe* now & then, the official organ, that you may see the lies the Editor is capable of writing.

Don't I beg of you hesitate to let Adelaide come out to Canada, if you can possibly manage it – I should like it amazingly & so would Eliza – & of course I would expect her to remain a year. She must come *this* year if she would see the Pro Vice Chancellor, for my tenure of office is but for a year. I am not so terribly reduced but that I can support Adelaide or the whole of you. Don't let that weigh one moment with you – My prospects never were brighter and although I am very hard up at present by force of circumstance due to Crooks' indebtedness to me, I think I may say there's a good time coming. I think it would do *you* good to see me sitting & presiding over the Master & Doctors 'both hearing & asking them questions' – I intend to be Chancellor some of these days. My fees for conferring Degrees already have amounted to some £10 or £12.

Bishop Strachan left New York by the fast Packet of the 17th instant & shocking to imagine must by this time be half seas over. He is gone home with the purpose of proceeding with the King's College Crusade & to advocate its claims. I think it very probable that he will be successful in raising a good deal of money for the Church University – if he should succeed, & the government are mightily afraid he will, away goes the present University at once.

Bishop Strachan's mission to England was successful; he saw all the right people including the Duke of Wellington, obtained a royal charter, raised the money, and founded Trinity College. (Smith's prediction that the University of Toronto would be swept away did not come to pass: on the contrary it grew and flourished and many years later he was again elected Vice Chancellor.) But in 1850 he lost his job: 'Saturday 25th May. Attended Meeting of the Senate of the University – Croft elected Vice Chancellor.'

SUMMER 1850

To his father, on 20 June, Smith wrote:

I have now almost ceased to trouble myself about my Pro Vice Chancellorship. I now leave all these matters to those who have time & are paid for their trouble. My partner Wilson was Queen's counsel for the last assizes, which alone produced during the three weeks of their being held, some £182 odd. Mr. Baldwin evidently throws in our way whatever he can & it is very good of him.

Mr. Baldwin is for a Co-alition with the Conservatives – I see it plain enough when it suits me to come down from my high elevation – I would sooner fraternize with him than with anyone else. I really like Mr. Baldwin & dislike to frustrate his views which I have done to some extent. I am positively certain I should stand a better chance with his party than the Conservatives, but whatever happens I'll hold my independence of both.

The weather in the month of May was most unseasonable; cold & snow on the 20th instant which remained for the Queen's Birthday. The snow went, but the cold staid. Everyone in our house with violent colds till the 1st June. I had not my voice to sing for over six weeks but am now quite recovered.

On Tuesday last, I had the honor of dining with Lord Elgin where I met the Chief Justice Sir John Beverley Robinson & his Lady – Sir Hew Dalrymple & some other officers & members of the House – in all about 15 or 16. Lord Elgin was very attentive to me & most familiarly pressing that I should sing for him. On the whole it has not been a bad move leaving that fellow Crooks, for in every sense I am benefitting by the change and my present position.

I am now at the Head of the Oddfellows Lodge to which I belong, being what is termed Noble Grand of the Lodge. Judge McLean & Jameson, Vice Chancellor of Upper Canada, are among the members.

William Lyon Mackenzie is here in as great a vogue as ever. He is a constant attendant at the Parliament House & even a claimant for losses! Parliament is still sitting & likely to hang together for some time yet.

When you write George, give him our kindest regards & congratulations on the birth of his little one, who we hope, with his mother is doing well. Tell him we have stopped Mr. Munyard from going to Cincinnati & that Mr Boyd has behaved like a trump to him & will finally get him well settled, having already got his sons into employment. He has let him a house, furniture, & fuel free from all rent as long as he likes for himself & family. The Boyds are all well, we see more of them than formerly. We are still on bad terms with the Spragges & likely to be for some time to come, on account of Alex Thom dying intestate, with the result that the money went to Eliza & Caroline & not a penny to Mrs. Spragge. Fanny Kemble is here giving readings in Shakespeare to crowded houses.

The weather has become intensely hot & thunderstorms are the order of the day. Give our fondest love to all ...

The Smiths did not go to Perth in the summer of 1850: Larratt's new partnership with Adam Wilson kept him busy. Eliza was expecting another child, and the renovated cottage on the lakeshore on Front Street was comfortable and cool. As usual there was a good deal of entertainment going on in Toronto.

Monday 15th July. Very fine hot weather, very busy at the office all week. Took time off on Wednesday to go with Eliza & the two sonneys to the Band Concert at Government House. In the evening Cassels took us to the Theatre to 'White's Serenaders,' sat in Boxes. On Friday evening, a Telegraph Company meeting & party at Cameron's. McLean sent his carriage for us. Nice little party. Eliza invited all those who were not going to the Bar dinner on Saturday evening to come to our house. Great Bar Dinner given by Upper Canada to Lower Canada at 8 P.M. at Osgoode Hall. When I got home at midnight, the party at our house had all gone home. Today was very fine & intensely hot. Cassels up at our house as usual.

Although Walter Cassels, as manager of the Bank of British North America, had his own staff of servants in a well-appointed suite of rooms above the bank, he spent most of his time outside banking hours with the Smiths. Larratt's diaries for the summer of 1850 show that Cassels dined at the house on Front Street no less than seventeen times in the month of July alone. In fact he was so often seen in the company of the Smiths that Toronto gossips averred he was in love with Eliza.

Whatever the attraction was, there was also a business connection since

Larratt Smith was the solicitor for the same bank. This association entailed a good many business trips which the manager and the solicitor of the Bank of British North America took together.

5th September, 1850.

Dear Papa:
Since I received your letter on 12th July, I have been here, there, and everywhere. Indeed I have scarcely been home 3 weeks at a time during the summer, much to Eliza's annoyance. Last month I was called away with Cassels to Oswego to look after some failures consequent upon the stoppage of the large New York produce house of Suydam Sage & Co. We improved the opportunity by taking a tour round to Buffalo via Syracuse. There we put up at Rust's Empire Hotel, a most excellent house, the best west of New York. The Theatre there, however, was a horrible affair & we left in disgust. Bugs. The Theatre at Buffalo turned out to be equally bad & we were glad to come home to Toronto.

As soon as I had arrived home & had well nigh found my breath, I was obliged to leave again to examine into the condition of three large Estates in the Niagara District. This occupied me some 10 or 12 days. Whilst there I went to the Whirlpool for the first time. I later fished alongside the American Falls where I caught 2 pickerel, a pike, & a black bass, got drenched through from the spray. On my return to Toronto found all well at our house & 7 Burglars arrested in the town.

AUTUMN 1850

Early in October when Mrs Thom arrived from Perth to spend a month with her daughter Eliza, her son-in-law went off again with Walter Cassels on a very special mission for the Bank of British North America. After it was accomplished, Larratt wrote his father:

8th November, 1850

Your letter of 4th October I received in due course of Mail on my return from Troy, New York, whither I went with Cassels via Quebec, Montreal, Lake Champlain, & Buffalo. We left on our excursion at 1 hour's notice only. Our object being to bring into Canada some £20,000 in gold for the Bank. Since Exchange at New York is 103/4 in London, we easily achieved our purpose.

I spent a delightful week at Quebec. We stayed with Walter Cassels' brother, Dick, who lives in an elegant house on the St. Foy Road, from which the view over the St. Charles River, Beauport, Lorette, Charlevoix, was grand in the extreme. We visited everything worth seeing – the Falls of Montmorenci, the Armoury, which my friend Dobell the ordinance storekeeper enabled us to do to advantage. On Sunday, Dick Cassels took me to the Cathedral where I heard Bishop Geo. Jehoshaphat Mountain preach.

They are splendid fellows the Quebeckers & live like fighting cocks – money no object – with thousands a year when the poor devils in Upper Canada are content with hundreds – I should have been spoilt had I remained there.

On our return to Montreal we spent three days with Mr Paton the inspector of the Bank of British North America, where we received every possible kindness. He lives in great style, as well he might, with an income of between £2000 & £3000 per annum.

From Montreal we went to Troy by way of Lake Champlain on board the *United States* & saw scenery quite equal to views on the continent. After spending the night at the Troy House & making arrangements with Smither's & Virgil's Express we left Troy at 7 A.M. on the cars with 2 boxes of gold & reached Buffalo at 9½ P.M. Imagine 330 miles in one day, in a little over 12 hours with stoppages! We sailed for Toronto on board the *Emerald*. The gold is now safely in the Bank.

Whilst in Montreal, Paton very kindly took us to Dolly's Chop House, the most select public bar in Canada. We then went on to the Industrial Exhibition where we were much pleased with the specimens & productions. The sleighs exhibited were perfect gems & the carriages equally good. A good deal has already been shipped in the *Pearl* to London for the 'Big Show'; the Great Exhibition in the Crystal Palace which Her Majesty Queen Victoria will open on 1st May next year.

How much I should like to come home then & bring Eliza & 'LalLal' with me. The inducements are very great, even in the passage money; the packets have all agreed to carry home & back for $100. exclusive of wines. But the old exclamation 'Je n'ai pas de l'argent' stands in the way and I must wait a few years longer unless Aunt George would open her heart – & though exceedingly kind to me has bestowed what would pay numberless ocean passages upon my brother George. However il n'import, & she has a right to act as she pleases.

Jenny Lind does not intend coming here at all. There have been great facilities offered for parties to go & hear her & many have availed themselves of it – 10$ from Montreal to Boston & back first class seats to the Concert included, was not bad. Another Yankee brought it down to 9$, & besides he offered a Ticket to a Panorama[1] some 3 miles in length; we thought of going, but could not find time.

I am highly pleased with my partner, Adam Wilson, my position & prospects & think I shall yet turn up trumps if I am spared & nothing happens.

Perhaps Aunt George's liberality to his brother was still rankling in Larratt's mind when he answered a letter from George later in the month. In reading it one should remember that Larratt had been offered a place in the family wine business which he had rejected, and this earlier history may account for Aunt George's financial neglect of him.

... I am much obliged to you for asking us to stay with you in the event I should avail myself of the reduced fares to get home to the Exhibition, but I am afraid my circumstances would render it impossible – When I speak of the Exhibition, of course, I only mention it as the means not the object of going home ... First of all, however, to bring Eliza, everything is favorable, for my little one will be weaned & have cut his teeth & what is more she will not be in for it again so as to prevent her travelling. In addition Mrs. Thom has offered to take care of both the children. But the wherewithal to take Eliza 'aye there's the rub.' I should require at least £50 for passage money across the Atlantic, another £15 in reaching Southampton or Greenwich, so that with £200 I should be independent & have funds for every purpose. No dear George I fear that we must not look forward to any reunion for many many years to come. I do not repine at my inability to indulge myself in a trip home, however, for thank God I have enough to eat & drink, very little care, good prospects ahead & I can at all events afford to pay the postage to hear from you all, if I cannot see you when I wish ... From last accounts from Papa I have felt very uneasy about your state of health, why could you not come out after the Exhibition is over – you could manage it if I cannot, & you will be able to avail yourself of the reduction in prices. Why not bring your Mary & Adelaide out with you & spend part of next summer & the whole of the winter with us? Do think about it.

I was pleased to hear that Aunt George with her characteristic liberality had been adding to your comfort, she is truly a kind friend to you, as she undoubtedly is to all belonging to her. I have not time to say more. Think on what I have said about your visit to us next year. Eliza desires her kindest love to your Mary, your little ones & yourself...

Larratt's remark in this letter to George, that Eliza would 'not be in for it,' is unclear, since at the time of writing Eliza was pregnant. On 16 December, Larratt's journal states: 'Eliza ailing for the last six weeks is now rather worse than better. Dr. Hodder has been in daily attendance & sent powders, but to no avail, as her pains came on at 10 this morning & by 11 a miscarriage took place. I went at once to Elmsley Place to fetch Dr. Hodder. Eliza better this evening.'

By Christmas Day Eliza was very much better and on Boxing Day her husband hired a sleigh and took her for an hour's drive. This did her so much good her husband kept the sleigh and the driver until after the New Year: 'Very fine & cold. Eliza took Harriet Boulton sleigh-riding for 2 hours.'

16: 'Sixth Anniversary of our Wedding Day' 1851

WINTER 1851

Soon after the New Year, Larratt Smith's partner, Adam Wilson, suddenly announced his intention to dissolve the firm of Wilson and Smith. This came as a great shock to Smith whose January entries reflect his reaction.

Wednesday 22 January 1851. It is over a fortnight since Wilson first spoke of dissolution. He now proposes continuation till the end of the present year. In the meantime I have declined all invitations, such as Mrs. Nichol's party & the 71st Ball at St. Lawrence Hall, also wrote the secretary of Ontario Lodge that I wished to resign from it. Intensely cold perhaps the coldest day this winter – had my dinner sent to the office at 3 P.M. & remained there till 10 P.M. getting papers etc. ready to go to Niagara to serve ejectments on property at the Falls.

Smith left for Niagara with the thought of the dissolution still in his mind. It was not a good time of year to travel by water.

'Left at 10 A.M. by the steamer *Chief Justice*, reached Niagara a little after 1 after ploughing through fields of ice for miles at the entrance of Niagara River. Obliged to land on the ice because the boat could not get to the wharf.

Tuesday 4th. Drove to Drummondville & Chippewa on Saturday, did my business, then on Sunday drove to Suspension Bridge & to the *Maid of the Mist* in the morning & to church at Drummondville in the afternoon. After transacting my business at Niagara on Monday, I walked about the town, before having wine, tea & oyster supper. Left Moffatt's Neptune Inn at 9 A.M. this morning for a very rough crossing on the *Chief Justice,* reached Toronto soon after 12 o'clock. Found a letter from Papa waiting for me.

He answered his father's letter immediately:

Saturday, 8th February
Your letter of the 6th December has just reached. Before going into your business matters I may as well advise you of the freak Dame Fortune (shall I call her Miss-Fortune) has been playing with me of late. On the 3rd of last month, when I was deeply engaged with our office accounts, Adam Wilson, to my great surprise, stated that he would like a dissolution of the co-partnership to take place on the 1st March next. This announcement, so sudden & unexpected as you may conceive 'knocked me all of a heap' and my first enquiry naturally was to know what could have caused such an alteration in his view. He expressed himself as most friendly toward me, but that a partnership was always furthest from his wishes & that as my business had not proved as lucrative as his own, he would therefore prefer remaining alone as formerly. He assured me that he did not want a single client of mine & would refuse their business, moreover, if I was afraid of losing the bank business, or any good clients, he would continue to assist me with counsel & advice, the first year particularly.

Now, in order to fit myself to conduct my own business, I have commenced going into Court & studying my profession. If I can only continue my business & attend to it myself I think I need not fear but that I can make my own living.

Eliza met with a mishap [a miscarriage] last month much to my surprise. She is now quite well again & I trust there may be no more occasions for anxiety on this head. My little ones are thriving, the second (George) is weaned, being now 13 months old. He walks & talks famously ...

Smith posted this letter in a blinding snowstorm. A few hours later, the snow turned to freezing rain. 'It having rained all night & frozen, I found it very slippery going to church. By evening, the trees were coated with ice & breaking down.'

It was snowing on 13 March 1851: 'Lal Lal 3 years old today. Captain & Mrs. Paterson & Jessie & Cassels dined with us, Susan Boulton & five friends came in the evening for round games & supper.'

Next day, the Smiths most constant visitor repaid their hospitality: 'Cassels not only took the whole of us to the Lyceum to see the Panorama,[1] "Lower Mississipi," but he gave Eliza a Chatelaine,[2] & Lal a handsome toy.'

SPRING 1851

Now that young Larratt had reached the age of three, his parents began to take him about: '*Thursday 17th April.* Up at 6 A.M. & took Lal down to the wharves to see the boats start.' And on a Sunday later in the month: 'Eliza & I took Lal to St. George's Church for the first time ... *Saturday 5th June.* Yesterday Cassels took us all, including little Lal to June & Company's Oriental Circus & Menagerie[3] – camels etc. Today we rowed to the Island, Cassels with Lal in his skiff, and I took Eliza in mine. Splendid picinic despite threatening thunderstorm.'

Early in April, Bishop Strachan came back from England with a royal charter to found Trinity College: '*Wednesday 30th.* Having arranged to change my pew to the Gallery in St. George's Church, I took Eliza, her sister Caroline, & Cassels to the service for the laying the foundation of Trinity College, then to the Lot where Bishop Strachan laid the Corner Stone at 4 P.M. Parson Harris & Cassels dined with us, then all went to Captain Patterson's for an evening of dance & song.'

May 1851 opened with a heavy fall of snow, but Toronto society took little notice of weather: '*Friday 2nd.* Very cold indeed. Office all day. In the evening Eliza & I went to St. Patrick's Ball, a splash affair, we danced till well nigh 4 o'clock in the morning.'

Although the diaries show little of Smith's anxiety about the precariousness of his law practice, he was, in reality, desperately looking about for another means of livelihood. On 8 May he heard of something and immediately wrote to Robert Baldwin who was ill in bed at the time:

Dear Sir –
You were kind enough to say when I spoke to you about the position of my affairs & the precariousness of my connection with Mr. Adam Wilson, that you felt desirous of serving me if it lay in your power.
   I have only this morning received an intimation from Dr. McCaul that the Government will shortly be appointing a Chairman for the Endowment Board of the University, who will be a permanent officer upon a moderate Salary, but whose whole time would be required for the duties of the situation ...
   As regards this appointment, I fully believe, as far as the duties are concerned, that I should be fully equal to them for I am convinced that 14 years drudgery (including the terms of persiflage) must have been beneficial to me in attaining business habits, although it has failed in making me distinguished in Canada ... The president, Dr. McCaul, not only recommended me to apply for the situation, but has kindly offered to support me with what little influence he can command.

As regards any claims I could set up. I could hardly venture to ask for the appointment upon the ground that I was gazetted out of the Clerkship of the Court of Appeals, another is that I have lately been re-elected *unanimously* Pro-Vice Chancellor, a second time, that I am the oldest graduate of the University, & that I hold the highest Law Degree that has been confirmed by the Institution ...

May I then ask you to extend your kindness to me once more to enable me to obtain this appointment, the last favor, if I succeed, that I shall require to ask?

Trusting that you will receive this communication into your kind consideration, and with my best wishes for your speedy convalescence ...

SUMMER 1851

Whether the efforts of Robert Baldwin and Dr McCaul were of no avail, or whether the position never materialized, Smith did not get the appointment. Later, in June, he offered his services as Toronto agent to the Royal Insurance Company of Liverpool. His letter to their actuary, a Mr Percy Dove of New York, has faded into a few faint yellowed lines. Gone too is Mr Dove's answer, which was a refusal.

Still later, in the summer of 1851, Larratt Smith applied for a judgeship in the area surrounding the village of Whitby, once known as the Home District, at this time the newly designated County of Ontario. He had heard of the position through a friend, Judge Joseph Curran Morrison, a 'Baldwin Reformer' and member of the legislature for Niagara, who advised him to write to another influential man, I.S. McDonell of Toronto, which he did on 10 July:

I had intended to have spoken to you personally, but not being fortunate enough to fall in with you, my object is to address you & if possible neutralize any unfavorable opinion you may have of me.

I am not aware that I have ever personally given you offence, if I have it was not intentional on my part, For the truth is I have studiously avoided politics, feeling convinced that a lawyer should abstain from placing himself in a position wherein he might give offence to either party of his clients.

In regard to University matters in which I happened to be mixed up rather more prominently than I desired – as when the efforts to obtain an English Chancellor failed, I named the present one & obtained his return – and to convince you that there was no feeling prejudicial to me – I have been re-elected Pro-Vice Chancellor for the current year, being proposed & seconded by those who formerly opposed me.

I went even further than this, for when the Conservative Party was bent on electing Sir Allan McNab for the sole object of allowing him to decline & animadvert in declining against the Institution & the Government, I called a caucus meeting & opposed it might & main, & the result was that when the Election came on, Sir Allan had but one vote – so much for embarrassing the Government.

Besides my eight years standing in the law, I was Clerk of the Court of Appeals for Upper Canada until the present Chancery Act deprived me of that situation. As regards my present position, I have a very good business and perhaps as respectable clients as any other professional in the country – but I am heartily sick of the practise of my profession and would much prefer 'otium cum dignitate' (Leisure with dignity, Cicero) – and you I believe have it in your power to enable me to occupy a position of honor with a competency for life. I do trust then that you will not allow any slight prejudice to disappoint my expectations ...

Although Smith knew that McDonell disliked him, he was so sure of the judgeship he even mentioned it to his mother-in-law, Mrs Thom:

I am expecting, nay, am almost certain of being appointed Judge of the new County of Ontario, one of the finest counties in Canada, containing the finest Townships in the Province. If I succeed I shall have to remove to Whitby in the course of a year if not sooner. I shall get at once, I suppose, £350 per annum, if not more. The Salary will soon, however, reach to £500, & if I am also made Judge of the Surrogate Court I shall be able to increase it still more. This will suit my complaint well – for I can live there in a beautiful part of the country for $\frac{1}{2}$ it costs me now – keep my carriage in the bargain & be the best man in the County – I'll let you know in due course how the game will end ...

The game ended with someone else getting the appointment. Smith never did go to live in Whitby and he never became a judge.[4] As soon as the judgeship fell through, he settled down to run his own law firm. His diaries for the late summer of 1851 describe the usual journeys over bad roads and voyages over rough Lake Ontario. They tell of sleepless nights in vermin-ridden country hotels, of country clients, city clients, and of long days in Her Majesty's courts of law, not as the timid junior partner – little better than a clerk – but as a barrister conducting his own clients' cases.

He soon acquired a number of articled students, all of whom were made to toe the mark. Those who did not were sent about their business, as this letter of 24 January 1852 shows.

Charles Clark Esq.
My dear Clark:

I have just heard from a second client, that during my absence from indisposition from the office this week, he found the office door locked from the inside at 2 o'clock in the Day, and heard talking going on in the inside.

Now as this is so wholly foreign to the purpose for which I have established myself in business, I prefer that you assign your Articles to some other solicitor. I am forced to this alternative from my sense of the hoplessness of ever being any use to you in your profession, because I well believe that it is useless to expect that you will do anything for yourself.

I regret for many reasons to find you so hopelessly blind to your own interests, but I should be doing a great injustice to the other gentlemen in the office if I allowed you to injure them, by reasons of the bad example you have set to them. The law admits of no trifling.

I shall be prepared to assign your articles whenever you can make an arrangement ...

Six months before he wrote this dismissal, Smith was still in the midst of reorganizing the office and doing the extra work that Adam Wilson's departure entailed. He did not, however, let business intrude on his leisure time with Eliza, or on fishing, picnicking at the island, and going to parties with their friends. He also went to regimental dinners. As a member of the militia he carried out his army duties by importing whisky for the officers' mess at the Toronto garrison through a friend, Robert Eberts, in Detroit. Smith wrote to Eberts on 12 June 1851 to acknowledge the shipment:

Accept my best thanks for your kind attention to my 'whisky interests.' The puncheon has come safely to hand & is now ensconsed within the New Fort under the immediate patronage of Sir Hew Dalrymple, the Commandant, who pronounces it 'prime stuff' ...

These Scottish regiments, you must know, are rather partial to good whisky, which they consider good for finishing off with, after a protracted sitting at mess over Hock, Champagne, Hermitage, Claret, Port, Sherry, Madeira etc., – not to mention Ale in its proper place.

This whisky stands them in between 41 & 42 cents the gallon after duty, freight, & all charges paid. A similar article, not good, is retailed to them here at 2$ a gallon! Therefore I am under many obligations to you ...

Unlike the Duke of Wellington and some of his allies, who had deplored the idea of railways because they might encourage the lower classes to move about, young Smith, from the moment he saw the American locomotives and cars at Lewiston, New York, recognized Canada's need for railroads. One can imagine his delight when Joseph Howe,[5] the provincial secretary of Nova Scotia, who had just made an agreement to build a railway from Halifax to Quebec, came to Toronto: '*Saturday 28th June*. Cassels & I went to the Great Rail Road Dinner given to the Honorable Joseph Howe. Godfrey Spragge very kindly drove us down in his carriage. Fine speeches and a great evening.'

After several months of letter-writing and discussion, Larratt's youngest sister Adelaide came to visit him. They had not seen each other since Mary Violett took her daughters back to England in 1845. In the interim, Adelaide had spent several years at Miss Evill's School for Young Ladies at Bath, later completing her education with her French relatives at Bordeaux in France. She was now twenty-one years old. The first intimation of her coming is in a letter from Larratt to his father written 20 June 1851: 'I am delighted to find that Adelaide is on her way at last. I see the *City of Glasgow* reached home in 21 days, which is stated as being a long passage, so I suppose she will not make the passage quicker than 17, seeing that the Gulf Stream is against them, to which we must add 3 or 4 more days to bring her here from Philadelphia. I shall look for her about the 10th of July ...'

Larratt was not far out in his calculations: '*Wednesday 9th July*. Rained in torrents. Dined with Cassels & sat up till near 2 A.M. then went down to the wharf to see the *Admiral* come in & meet Adelaide who was in the charge of Mr. and Mrs. Gapper of Richmond Hill, all well.'

Although her brother thought Adelaide looked well, their mother, Mary Violett, was not of the same opinion. A few weeks later, in a long confidential letter to Larratt, she remarked:

I cannot tell you how it gladdens my heart to hear you say how much better Adelaide is, how grateful do I feel to the Almighty that He has heard & granted my humble request. I have read her letter to her Cousin, she seems to enjoy herself but I hope she will not visit too much this Winter, late hours and heated rooms never agreed with her and would speedily undo all the change of climate has done for her. My great wish now is to see her return full of health. I shall then be compensated for all I have felt in the parting with her and all the unkind remarks Aunt George has made because I consented to her going.

I am glad dear Adelaide is making herself useful in instructing dear little Lal, your Papa has bought a set of little Books for instructing children and intends sending them by post, which he can do, one at a time, you will therefore receive one by this mail.

I think you had better make up your mind to send Lal back with Adelaide, and let him remain with us at Southampton until he is old enough for College, we will take every care of him, and Adelaide can even complete what she has undertaken ...

Adelaide did not take little Lal back to England as her mother had planned: in fact she did not see her parents again for a very long time, for she fell in love with her brother's best friend, Walter Cassels. They were married at Toronto in 1852, but that is another story. In the summer of 1851 she was doing all the things her mother had told her not to do: '*Wednesday 30th July.* Adelaide spent last Friday evening visiting the Crookshanks, but came back in time for a musical evening at our house. After I finished my work at the office today, Adelaide, Eliza, & I dined with Cassels, then went with him in the evening to the Theatre where we sat in Box seats & saw "All that Glitters is not Gold," & "Laughing Hyena."'

Quite apart from his own legal business in Toronto, Larratt Smith (with some assistance from his mother-in-law in Perth) administered the Thom estate. Although Eliza and her sister Caroline were the chief beneficiaries, Larratt always saw to it that Mrs Thom's dower[6] right was respected and that she had a steady income for life. She, in turn, kept the accounts and advised him of business matters at Perth. Unfortunately all her letters have been lost; one can only guess their contents by Larratt's replies. By the summer of 1851 they were still trying to settle the estate by selling parcels of wild land from a large acreage bought as a speculation by Dr Thom many years before. In a letter to Mrs Thom written 17 June 1851, Larratt wrote: 'I should like you to do something with regard to the Taxes on the land at L'Orignal, for the truth is they are advertised for sale, as I dare say the Nepean lands are by this time, for under the present law the Taxes on wild lands must be paid yearly or they are liable to sale for default for so doing ... when I come, I will visit the Lots for the purpose of sale ... I believe that the Ottawa Lots are worth something ...'

About this time some household effects were divided between Eliza and Caroline. Among the things that came to Eliza was a mangle. This hand-operated machine, with rollers compressed by a large key on top, was used to press newly washed linens, a boon in a household where all the washing was wrung out by hand. After it arrived in Toronto, Larratt wrote to Mrs Thom: 'The things have come from Perth. I have paid Nordheimer for the cartage & taken a receipt, but there is no key for the Mangle – it was lost before they packed it & they cannot supply one here ... By the way, Caroline talks of selling the piano, but would it not be a pity to sacrifice it? Eliza is opposed to the idea.'

At this period Mrs Thom and Caroline were living in the family homestead, while the Thom farm proper was rented to a man named Robert Caldwell, with the stipulation that the rent was to be paid directly to Mrs Thom. There were, however, complications. Larratt wrote to Caldwell: 'Sir, As you seem determined to abandon all the arrangements we agreed upon when we drew up your lease – and continue to annoy Mrs. Thom in the most unmanly way, I have instructed our lawyer, Mr. McMartin, at Perth to hold you strictly to your convenant and, if necessary to protect Mrs. Thom's rights, to take proceedings to eject you, for you will not be allowed to persist in your overbearing conduct towards her with impunity ...' On 31 July Larratt wrote to his mother-in-law: 'If it suits you I could leave for Perth in about a month when I should endeavour to regulate Master Robert Caldwell in some way more satisfactory to you ...'

Owing to Larratt's court cases, the Smiths did not leave for Perth until after the middle of September. Early in the month Toronto was struck by a heat wave.

Sunday 7th September. Very scorching hot with temperature at 88, the hottest day this year. Yesterday we took the children & all went with Cassels to the Island, but returned at 6 in the steamer *Victoria.* Eliza suffering from rheumatism in the head & face. Neither of us went to church today as Eliza in great pain, obliged to send for Dr. Nichol. Adelaide went to St. George's Church morning & evening with Cassels. Eliza better by evening. Still most excruciatingly hot.

AUTUMN 1851

Wednesday 17th. Weather changed on Saturday last with wind blowing a hurricane from the N.E. bringing rain in torrents & cold. Lit a fire in the sitting room the last two nights. Eliza, Lal, & I left for Perth at 1 P.M. today by the steamer *Passport.* Gave Adelaide 50 shillings for housekeeping. She & Cassels came down to the wharf & saw us off. Twohy the Purser gave us the best stateroom in the vessel, Number 1.

Saturday 20th. After stoppages at Oshawa, Darlington, Bond Head, Port Hope, & Cobourg, the ship reached Kingston at 3 A.M. on Thursday, 4 hours late. Left the boat at 7 A.M. for the American Hotel, there to await the

Beaver due at 11 A.M. Did not arrive till 3 A.M. on Friday, we were therefore obliged to sleep at the American Hotel (killed 1 bug in the night). Left Kingston at 8 A.M. in the *Beaver* for Perth. Reached Oliver's Ferry at 8½ P.M. Found Caroline and manservant waiting with buggy & cart since 4 P.M. drove into Perth & reached the farm before midnight. Found all well. Stayed at home all day today reading & sleeping.

The Smiths spent ten days at the Thom farm.

Monday 29th Sept. Gloomy with some rain & blowing hard most of the week. All the womenfolk with colds & swollen faces. I made a little steamboat for Lal, then made a kite & flew it for him. On Friday, Eliza & I called on Parson Harris & found them all flying kites. Mr. McMartin up several evenings to tea & to discuss Estate. I had two confabulations with Robert Caldwell, but failed at the last moment to induce Caroline to come to a new arrangement with him. Eliza, Lal, & I then left for Brockville by the stagecoach at ½ to 2 P.M. A misty rainy drive, but found the road Macadamized nearly all the way from Smith's Falls to Brockville which we reached at 10½ P.M. After supping at Wilson' Hotel, we went to board the American boat, *Northerner*, the fare to Toronto for 2 was 12$. The Band of the 4th United States Regiment on board playing several things. No great shakes. After touching at Kingston at 8 A.M. Friday, we reached Sackett's Harbour about 10 & landed the Band. At Oswego in midafternoon we found a heavy sea running & a strong wind from the N.W., both Lal & Eliza dreadfully seasick. Wind & sea abated before we reached Rochester. Left there at 12, moderate sea & a fine night. The ship reached Niagara & Lewiston on Wednesday 1st October at 7. Breakfasted on board, then took the *City of Toronto* and were home by ½ past 12. Did not go to the office this day.

In the month of October 1851 two historic events took place in Toronto. The Smiths went to them both. The first was the opening ceremony for a railway to link Lake Ontario with Lake Huron (later known as the Northern Railway). The second was the visit of the 'Swedish Nightingale,' the world famous singer, Jenny Lind. Such was Miss Lind's popularity that the promoters of the railroad invited her to turn the first sod. She declined, however, and the spade work fell to Lady Elgin.

Monday 20th. Last Wednesday, Eliza & I went to see Lady Elgin turn the 1st Sod of the Simcoe, Ontario & Huron Railway. A great turnout of everybody & a Grand Parade. Eliza & I, however, were too tired to go to the

Ball, although Rutherford offered us tickets. The Governor General & Lady Elgin & suite left on Saturday for Quebec at 9 A.M. in the steamer *Highlander* to avoid being mobbed, which might have been the case had they taken the *Princess Royal* at 1 P.M.

Jenny Lind arrived today and, to evade the crowds, landed very quietly at the Garrison Wharf where she was met by the city dignatories with carriages & driven straight to Mrs. Ellah's Hotel. Her concert takes place in St. Lawrence Hall. A great rush for tickets – hundreds disappointed.

The Smiths were not disappointed.

Saturday 25th. Jenny Lind gave her second concert on Wednesday night. Macdonald very kindly gave us tickets (at 4$ each!), he & Cassels dined with us, & all including Adelaide, went to the concert. Everyone delighted. Miss Lind gave 3 concerts in all, then left at 7:30 A.M. yesterday morning in the vessel *City of Toronto*, a Band on the Government Wharf playing her off. I saw her off with my Spy Glass. This afternoon a regular fall of *Snow*, the first this season.

Friday 7th November. Snowing & very cold. Meeting of Open Convocation on Wednesday. I could have had my Grace[7] passed for my Degree of Doctor in Common Law, but declined. Eliza & I dined with Cassels & went to the Theatre, 'Serious Family' & 'Rough Diamond.'

NOVEMBER–DECEMBER 1851

Throughout the early autumn of 1851 Eliza appears to have been in good health and to have gone with Larratt everywhere. In his journal for 3 November she has written 'Dick Cassels married' in her round childish hand; no doubt she danced at the wedding. She also went to the market regularly and, according to her husband's accounts, to an auction sale where she bought some preserving pans and a quilting frame. In short, there is no hint of impending doom until Larratt's entry for 22 November: 'Cold with snow. Obliged to call in Dr. Nichol for Eliza who has a dreadful cough & cold which has lasted all this week, day & night.'

Tuesday 3rd December. Eliza's cold still very bad, no sleep at night, no rest by day. At noon on Saturday I commenced giving her Ayre's Cherry Pectoral. She felt better at once, so I took her and the children out for a walk. But on Tuesday, from taking too much Pectoral, Eliza taken very ill. Dr. Nichol in daily attendance. Eliza appeared to be improving until the evening of Saturday the 14th, when she took a bad turn & continued not so well during the night. I read prayers to her & did not go out of the house on Sunday. Dr. Nichol came in the afternoon & pronounced her in extreme danger. Her friend Rose Cameron came & sat up all night with her as I did myself. Blisters etc. applied.

On Tuesday 16th, Eliza appeared better. I telegraphed Mrs. Morris in Kingston to get word to Mrs. Thom. Eliza's sister Catherine Spragge came & brought a nurse, Mrs. Friend, to attend Eliza. Eliza seemed better, fresh blisters applied. But on Thursday about 9 P.M. she took a very bad turn for the worse, and Doctors Hodder & Nichol pronounced her dying. Dr. Stephen Lett, our rector at St. George's Church, came & administered the Sacrament to her & Adelaide & myself. Eliza then distributed all her jewelry among her friends about her & wished all goodbye. By Sunday 21st she appeared to be sinking, rallied, then became worse and died at 5 P.M. without a struggle. My darling was not yet into her 28th year. I went to Spragge's to break the news to the dear children.

Telegraphed poor Mrs. Thom at Brockville, on Monday. Dear Eliza lying in our bed till night when she was placed in her coffin in the dining room. She lay there all day Tuesday, the Sixth Anniversary of our Wedding Day. She was buried at 2 o'clock on Wednesday 24th December. The funeral in St. George's Church was large, for besides our own family, there were many mourners. The Pall Bearers were, Mr. Robert Baldwin, Mr. William Henry Draper & Dr. McCaul, as well as Widder, Vankoughnet & I.H. Cameron. After the service dear Eliza was deposited in Crookshank's vault. Very very wretched indeed.

17: 'Now green in youth, now withering...' 1852

Smith was so wretched and desolate that he immediately gave up the house on Front Street, and, on the invitation of Walter Cassels, he took his little boys, with Flora their nurse, and went to live with Cassels in his suite of rooms above the Bank of British North America. In a letter to Mrs Thom he explained: 'I could not stay in that house & see the many evidences of dear Eliza's presence & feel that she was lost to me . . .'

His journal for 9 January 1852 records:

On the last day of December, I let the house to Bowes. Very busy packing & late to the office. Rose Cameron came up in the evening to help distribute poor Eliza's things. I took the silver & Eliza's drawing-room ornaments & the rest of her clothes with me to Cassels' house. Thunder & lightning very severe, followed by rain & snow. Took my doctorate in Common Law on Wednesday. Auction Sale at my house concluded today, a very miserable state of affairs.

Gave money to Cameron to pay poor Eliza's nurse. Paid off Peter D'Arcy, servant boy, & paid 5 shillings to Davis, a coloured man, to deliver funeral notices. This ends my housekeeping up to 7th February, when Flora came with the children to Cassels' house.

SPRING 1852

Three months later he wrote the following letter to his mother-in-law, Mrs Thom:

The theme you enter upon in the commencement of your letter is indeed painful, heart-rending wherever touched upon, and I really believe that I feel more deeply my dreadful loss as I enter upon each succeeding day.

Whether it is that stupor or excessive excitement, banished at first all outward expressions of grief, I know not, but on each day of rest as it comes round, when I can get time to think of other than business subjects, my extreme wretchedness returns, and do what I will, I cannot contain my feelings. My only consolation is in Him whose thoughts are inscrutable & whose ways past finding out, and most earnestly do I engage in His service, wherein alone is comfort when all other means fail.

But even in church when my thoughts should all be engaged on one subject, I cannot drive from my imagination the spectacle of *our* last sad attendance there, the funeral service. She, the idol of my soul snatched from me in the springtime of life, so gentle, so innocent, so good, lying in the habiliments of the grave. No, I can never enter St. George's Church without thinking of and picturing that sorrowful occasion. There are many many other topics which recall her loved presence to me & bring back all my sorrow afresh.

Still I love to think of her, miserable as it makes me. Would that I could recall the expression of her features, but I cannot. Twice only since her death have I done so, once in my sleep & again, whilst half asleep & awake, it is very very strange. Another thing is equally strange: all my thoughts & recollections of her are of the period before our marriage & they evoke most vividly upon me. Our married life was one unbroken dream of happiness ... all one unruffled calm, without a ripple to disturb the surface. But all is lost for I shall never see her like again.

In the course of a week or two at the furthest, I shall have consigned to their last resting place, her treasured remains. The monument is completed. I enclose you a pen & ink sketch of it. It is cut in Cleveland stone & will stand some 10 feet in height. I shall place it in the centre of my plot which is 30 feet square. The workmanship of the monument is exceedingly beautiful, they are now finishing the inscription. The Latin lines are beautiful to a fault. I took great pains in selecting them & consulted Dr. McCaul. They read in English, 'Go! Too dearly beloved, God calls thee. Go! Best portion of my life. What remains of my existence, in lamenting, will learn to follow.' This, of course, is not literal, but it expresses fully the meaning of the lines.

The last line in Greek is most expressive & contains in one sentence from Homer what Pope so beautifully depicts in his lines commencing,

'Like leaves on trees the race of man is found

Now green in youth, now withering on the ground ...'

The severe frosts we have had here, prevented the man from modelling dear Eliza's bust, he commences tomorrow, but I fear he will make a failure of it, altho' I trust not. My last alternative will then be to have a painting made in England from the Daguerrotype of her dear face which I had taken before our marriage and gave my father. I intend to send him, as I send you, the other Daguerrotype I had taken from Heath's *Book of Beauties*, subject 'Lesbia.' It is most striking. I have had about a dozen taken to distribute among her friends who think the likeness perfect. I should prize one taken from Life even more.

I feel very much disposed to let you have the dear children for a time at all events, as I see no chance of anyone going home to take Lal unless my father came out to Adelaide's wedding which I do not think likely. Moreover in your present desponding state, I think they would be a very great comfort to you. Dear little fellows. I shall miss them terribly, especially dear little Georgey, he is such a sweet little child. Lal, who is nearly 4 years old, is a bully & able to take care of himself & will require a tight rein to preserve the mastery over him – if this is not done, he will be ruined.

Rose Cameron has been ill every since Eliza's death and your stepdaughter Kate Spragge, who as you know is expecting, has hardly been out of her bed all the winter, she is still confined to her room, now better, now worse. I have not seen her for a week, as I positively have not a moment to spare to go to see her. The children spent the day there yesterday. I was mentioning to Mr. Spragge that I had received a letter from you. He hopes that you & Caroline will come up at once & stay with them.

The boats are running regularly now, but as to my coming down, it is absolutely impossible now, besides I feel that it would be a terrible blow for me to go down to Perth alone – so different from my former visits. We are all expecting you up almost immediately. If you want funds, let me know & I will supply them. If you would like to come & stay at the Bank with the children I could give you my room & fit up another bedroom for myself. You had better come up & bring Caroline with you, it will do you the greatest of good, the shock will be great but I hope that time will wear the acuteness off your sorrow. I know moreover that the children will be a comfort to you, their little innocent mirth will amuse you, whilst their presence & society will be a kind of substitute, how poor indeed, for the dear departed one.

When you come, bring a *large* spare trunk with you. I have two if not three of mine now filled with poor dear Eliza's clothes notwithstanding so much was given away, & I should wish you to take them away with you.

The children are in bed hours ago. I think the hooping cough is leaving them after a 3 months visit. They are sadly in want of someone to pay more attention to them than I can. They used to know their hymns & letters but they never say them now ...

Larratt Smith's grief was for a time distracted when he discovered that his sister Adelaide and his friend Walter Cassels had fallen in love and were longing to be married. There were obstacles: although Adelaide had turned twenty-one, she needed her father's consent, not only to the marriage but also as to when and where it would take place. Her mother wanted to have the wedding in England, but the Bank of British North America, being short of trained English staff, had refused Walter Cassels his promised six months' leave of absence. On 26 March 1852 Larratt wrote to his father:

I wrote to you so recently, that but for Cassels' anxiety I should not now be addressing you. He is very unhappy in his present uncertain position & Adelaide is not in a much more felicitous mood. Since it would not be proper for her to stay here with us at the Bank, she is wandering about from house to house – this week at Mrs. Draper's – the next at Mrs. Carthew's, & so on. I feel it would be folly to think of Adelaide going home & leaving Walter uncertain when to follow as the Bank has refused him leave of absence to go to England. I therefore propose that in order to relieve him from this Adelaidemania, you sanction this marriage, to take place, say, in June next, here in Canada. Cassels of course can get a week or ten days for such a purpose ...

Why not come out yourself, the New York Industrial Exhibition is in July & the *Great Britain* will be running fares reduced. Yes, you must come, it will add ten years to your life at least. We can take a long vacation in July & I'll introduce you to a small pond with every luxury, Scugog Lake ...

Captain Smith, who by this time was seventy years of age, did not come to Canada for his daughter's wedding. There was, however, a good deal of correspondence about the marriage. Later in the spring young Larratt Smith warned his father: 'You have mortally offended Mrs. Boyd in your last note to her by saying Adelaide can be married "in Toronto." Of course I see your delicacy in the matter about *wishing it*. But she flared up & said, "Do they think us nobody in this matter? Are we not to be consulted? I love my niece as much as my own children & am I to hear that she is to be married at a stranger's," and so forth ...'

SUMMER 1852

Just a week before the wedding, on 10 June, Larratt wrote again:

We have had a world of difficulty & annoyance with the Boyds regarding Adelaide's wedding. As the last boat leaves Toronto at 1 P.M. it would have been impossible for the *bridesmaids & lady guests* to be getting up at daylight at the Boyds' farm at Richmond Hill & scampering some 18 or 20 miles in the dash to the ship so as to enable Cassels & wife to leave Toronto the same day. I therefore proposed that the wedding should take place in town. The Boyds offered their town house, with a room not big enough for a man to swing his leg round in without hitting the wall, & containing no table big enough, cracked cups & saucers, no plate, no dishes glasses or anything else, so that in fact I should have gutted the Bank suite to supply the necessaries for the wedding breakfast...

I wrote to Mrs. Boyd that the *wedding in the country* would not answer as to time. That the wedding in *town* would not answer for *want of conveniences*. I thanked her for their willingness & kind intentions & said that it must take place at the Bank, *my own* residence – where I had at command perhaps the most elegant suite of rooms in Toronto & the largest, & where I commanded glass, plate etc. & the best attendance. The truth is that you & I are to be at the expense of the affair & the Boyds want the credit.

The Boyds, Mr. & Mrs., acquiesced, but the girls (cross-grained, perverse Eleanor & Mary) said that it was 'highly improper' & 'illicit,' & that they would not go to the wedding, *even if their Papa ordered them to do so*. John Boyd & the other brilliant youths followed suit & there was a hubbub. I had to give in or mortally offend the Boyds. And so I have had to send everything to their 'town mansion,' where the wedding breakfast is to take place after all.

To add to the annoyance from these young cubs, they worried Adelaide to death by talking of me to her & saying what stories were in circulation about me, but refusing to give their authors. These stories (I really believe invented by themselves) were to the effect that 'I was on the Cricket Ground on the Queen's Birthday'!! What a crime! That 'Cassels was the mourner & I was looking out for a wife' – I who have not spoken to a girl except Miss Draper since dear Eliza's death – & then it was of a Sunday at dinner there, having declined three times previously I, who have refused everybody's pressing invitations, who could have gone to the theatre every night this season & not been seen, the stage box being placed at my refusal, & declined, who was offered by the Mayor the exclusive use of a private room off the Court Room, where I could have heard Catherine Hayes[1] & seen her without being seen, & without paying a farthing, I who have never missed my church morning or night, or turned my back on the Sacrament table since poor Eliza's death. Every friend I have denounce so wicked a report. I believe the Boyds are jealous of Adelaide & myself & therefore take a delight in annoying us. Well, well, let it pass...

The wedding will come off on Thursday next at half past 10 A.M. at St. George's Church where my dearest Eliza lay for the last sad rites – a comparison of serious & melancholy consideration. I shall give Adelaide away. Her bridesmaids are Kate Crookshank, Eleanor & Mary Boyd, & Fanny Parsons. The groomsmen, John Boyd, Geo. Crookshank, & young Parsons. The bridesmaids will go to the church in Crookshank's carriage, Adelaide & I will go together, whilst Cassels & his party can go as they please. The party will afterwards adjourn to the Boyd's town house where breakfast will be held for about 20 at the very outside – I wish it to be quiet, most quiet.

Cassels & Adelaide will leave Toronto by the afternoon boat for Buffalo – thence,

I know not. I cannot help but agree with you that it will be a most fortunate & happy union. They have most elegant quarters in the Bank of British North America with every possible comfort about them; very handsome furniture, splendid crystal chandeliers for gas – in fact, gas in every room in the house, bedrooms, kitchen, pantry. Cassels has a large elegant gilded mirror in the drawing room. I have purchased a piano for you to give Adelaide, a Chickering with rounded corners, & although not the most expensive, it was the finest toned instrument in Nordheimer's Establishment. The price, including a music stool of rosewood covered with hair cloth, came to £105. In short, everything in the Cassels' house is as handsome as it can be & the Boyds are furiously jealous as usual. Mrs. Geo. Boyd particularly so, is disgusted with her own establishment, which is very handsome notwithstanding ...

Smith went on living with Adelaide and Walter Cassels at the Bank of British North America for the next two years. His little boys remained with their grandmother, Mrs Thom, on the farm at Perth. On 10 August 1852 Smith wrote to his old schoolmaster John Kent in England:

I think you would be pleased with the appearance of things in Toronto – this town is improving so fast. There are 2 Railroads running into it, one from Lake Huron, the other in process of construction from Guelph. Next year there will be an esplanade along the whole front of the city from the Garrison Wharf to the Windmill at a cost of £100,000, which will give the city a uniform frontage & all the annoyance of stagnant water will be obviated as the esplanade will be carried out to 8 or 10 feet of water.

You will also be gratified in the appearance of the public & private buildings put up in the last few years. I'll venture to say there is not a town in England of the same size to compare with it. The population has been ascertained at 35,000, a trifling difference since you & I remembered it as 'dirty little York' with a population of but 7,000. A late Boston newspaper has just admitted that there is a greater amount of tonnage in steamers entering the Port of Toronto daily than there is in Boston.

Since I last wrote you I have been most deeply afflicted. I have lost what I valued most on earth my dear departed wife, & from having a happy cheerful home am now bereft, my household broken up & scattered – my children some hundreds of miles away from me with their mother's family. I am now living with my favourite sister Adelaide since her recent marriage to one of the most esteemed friends I possess in the world, Walter Cassels, the manager of the Bank of British North America of which Bank I am the Solicitor. The profession of the Law is not as lucrative as it used to be, still I can make a competency ...

18: 'Leave everything to circumstance & opportunity' 1853

Early in February 1853 Smith sent his mother-in-law, Mrs Thom, a statement of her affairs:

I received your long letter several days since. When did you last pay anything on your wild lands on the Ottawa River? I wish you would let me know as I fear they may have been sold for Taxes. I would rather pay the Taxes myself than that the land should be lost ...

I cannot imagine how it is that you are all so susceptible to colds. Can it be that you keep the house too warm? My first idea was to suggest removal, but where I could not say. Here in Toronto it is perfect ruination. All meat is 10 pence a pound, flour 8$ a barrel, & house rent perfect ruination. Houses in Bay Street similar to the Boyd's which could have been got for £35 & £40 cannot be got for £75 a year!

In addition to all this Toronto is not healthier than Perth. My sister Adelaide is very ill from influenza & confined to her bed. Dr. Nichol is attending her daily. We have had a very mild open sickly winter & influenza has gone through every family here. Miss Agnes Munroe, 15 years of age, had died after a 48 hour illness from cold caught from going on the ice. She died after intense suffering from suffocation, quinsy, having set in.

The season is very fatal to old people as well as to children. Dr. Lett announced in his sermon at St. George's last Sunday that no less than three members of the congregation who had been alive & well on the Sunday previous, were dead & buried.

I trust the dear boys are now safely over their colds. I intend going to Quebec early in the summer & shall take the opportunity of seeing them on my way. I should very much like for you & Caroline to come up to Toronto & stay with us for a month or so in the summer & bring the boys with you. Kiss them for me. How are they off for toys?

Both of these visits evidently took place, as, after the summer, Larratt sent a note to his sister-in-law, Caroline Thom, at Perth: '... Ask your Mamma if she recollects seeing a large handsomely bound copy of Spencer's *Faerie Queen* in my room at the farm. I borrowed it from Adelaide who prizes it. I fancy I may have left it with some other books on the table in my bedroom ... I have just discovered a nightcap of your Mamma's which she left behind while staying with us at the Bank ...'

About this time, Larratt replied to a letter from his father:

Thank you and Mamma for all your kind enquiries. Both my boys are well, although Mrs. Thom was obliged to birch them one day.

I have every reason to be thankful for my success in money matters. Ever since dear Eliza's death, besides paying off several hundred pounds of debt, spending about £200 on her monument in St. James' Cemetery, purchasing my own Law library, & paying my own & my children's board, finding them & myself in clothes, also purchasing a piano, I have over £1000 invested besides some £400 of debts to collect.

I mean to get out of Cassels' house as soon as I can & this is the chief inducement to work. I hate the law & have always disliked it. It is not fit for a gentleman, but it is a glorious field for scoundrels & swindlers. If I can only feel my way into £500 per annum without it, I would not be long in it.

Mamma mentioned in a note to me that I had cheered her by not using black-edged paper & a black seal in writing to her about Adelaide. I have never used anything else since Eliza's death ... Tell Mamma I am very pleased with the slippers & waistcoat. The slippers are particularly handsome, the waistcoat I should have preferred had it been black, as I have made no alteration in my mourning since dear Eliza's funeral, & do not intend to until I am engaged again. When that will be, I cannot give you the remotest idea.

I like a hint Mamma gave me in her note & I think if all goes well & I do not get into difficulty on this side of the water, I will take a run home next year & see what is to be done in England. I must have a house of my own before long. I miss my boys dreadfully. At the same time I have made up my mind (unless a pretty face makes a fool of me) that my better half that is to be, 'must bring some grist to the Mill.' Now don't imagine that I crave Fortune's arrivistes, for I detest the species, & I could not marry the richest woman in the world if I could not win her affection, but I feel that the chain once broken is not the same, & that, bringing as much love as one can, there may be other qualifications not wholly to be disregarded. Now, unless Mamma pitches into me, I shall leave everything to circumstance & opportunity.

19: 'She certainly strikes my fancy' 1854

Circumstances and opportunity did not present themselves until late in the winter of 1854, when Smith dropped in one evening to see his sister-in-law, Kate Spragge, and found Mr and Mrs Murney of Belleville with their daughters, Bessie and Isobel, staying with the Spragges. Larratt Smith had known the Murneys for some time. They were considered prosperous, a condition that was likely the result of the efforts of a forbear, Captain Henry Murney, who had been brought from England in the 1790s to command the schooner *Governor Simcoe* on Lake Ontario. Captain Murney later served in the War of 1812 as master of the *Prince Edward*, a schooner he had built himself. This shipbuilding expertise, combined with other interests, had brought financial success to his family.

When Smith met the Murneys in March 1854, they were known to have a sizeable bank account. They also had a houseful of daughters, nine in all. Isobel, the second of these girls, was said to have been very pretty and extremely vivacious. Smith's journal for that date makes no remark about Isobel Murney except that he spent a pleasant evening singing with her.

On 27 August 1954 he wrote: 'Last Monday I was most unexpectedly ordered off to Belleville on a Court case. Upon reaching Belleville, I put up at the Dafoe House, did my business, then called on the Murneys who insisted on my staying with them. Spent the rest of the week boating, singing, & dancing in the evenings. Saturday being rainy, I spent all the morning in the Arbour with Isobel, & the afternoon reading *The Adventures of Mr. Verdant Green*[1] to the ladies in the house. Sang in the evening & played Lanterloo.'

Shortly after this, Smith wrote to his friend John Kent in England: 'In the early part of this month, I spent a week very pleasantly at Murney's in Belleville. I have rather taken a fancy to his second daughter, Isobel.

Isobel will make a fine woman, but is very young, not yet 16, whilst this department is 33. There is nothing in it though she certainly strikes my fancy ...'

Smith did not see the Murneys again until early in November: 'Whilst crossing from Prescott on the Mail steamer, found Mr. Murney on board. Made me promise to visit them at Belleville on my way back to Toronto.'

The visit was not a success. 'The ship docked at Belleville before the Murneys were out of bed. Very cold & blowing hard – trifled away the day shopping with Isobel. Dull evening, making words from cards, no music. Left on Monday, reached Cobourg only to find the sea running too high for any boat to come in. Took passage in stage for Toronto, 2 horses, 2 seats & 11 passengers. Never suffered so much in all my life. Arrived at Toronto dirty, wretched & fatigued.'

20: Always carefully chaperoned 1855

On 4 January 1855, Isobel Murney's father brought her to Toronto to enrol her in Mrs McNally's school. Smith notes meeting her at the Spragges' house. He also met another of Mrs McNally's pupils, a young girl from Montreal named Mary Elizabeth Smith: 'Spragge drove us all in the big sleigh to a merry party at Barrie's – had a lot of fun there with little Minny Smith.'

By midwinter, however, Larratt Smith had forgotten Minnie Smith as his entire attention became absorbed by Isobel Murney, a concentration helped by the skilful manœuvring of her mother. Mrs Murney, like most Victorian women of her class, knew that the only future for her numerous daughters was marriage, and, despite Isobel's youth, she was looking for a husband for her. Mrs Murney had decided that Larratt Smith was a good catch. Her first tactic was to write a letter asking him about a minor legal matter. On 23 February 1855 he answered:

I have been happy to have performed this trifling service ... I have not seen or spoken to Isobel since the day before she went to Mrs. McNally's. I make frequent enquiries of Paige, the singing teacher as to her progress. He says that she has decided talent & is most anxious to improve herself, that he can make a singer out of her. He complains of the want of facilities afforded him by the McNallys which prevents Isobel from practising with ease & freedom, that 'old McNally' won't sit in the room when she is getting her lesson, but leaves the door half open so that any number of impertinent listeners are about & in the next room, which distracts Isobel's attention & makes her nervous. If Paige shuts the door they open it again ... I am going to sing for the Patriotic Fund Concert on Tuesday next with Mrs. John Beverley Robinson. I have selected a song by Balfe from the opera '*Jeanne D'Arc*,' 'I would be a soldier still.' The concert promises to be a most spirited affair.

In a second note, Smith wrote to Mrs Murney:

On Saturday, thinking that Isobel would like to go to the Concert, I dropped her a note at Mrs. Sullivan's where she was spending the day, & asked her if she could get leave from Mrs. McNally, & having obtained it, Cassels & I took her – or rather I took them both, Cassels to do 'Papa' & I think she was highly gratified, for in truth it was one of the most successful affairs we have ever had in Toronto. There were 60 or 70 performers (including choral & instrumental performers), besides the Stars & Satellites. The room was most elegantly decorated with flags, Muskets, bayonets, swords & shields, besides a splendid illumination over the orchestra displaying in 'red' lights the word 'Alma' and other devices. Mrs. Beverley Robinson never sang better, & all passed off with great éclat. Mrs. Robinson & myself were honoured with an encore, but for particulars I must refer you to the papers I send by the Mail which includes the Programme. I suppose we shall clear for the Fund at least £150.

Poor Isobel was told by Mrs. McNally to be home by 10½ P.M. or be locked out. It was about 11 before the Concert was over, & 12 before we arrived at McNally's, & so she actually *was* locked out, & had to return to my brother-in-law Cassels' quarters at the Bank. My sister Adelaide, who is recovering from her last confinement was fast asleep, servants ditto, spare room bed not made up. So Cassels had to set to work & really all things considered he did very well, for in the morning it was discovered that Isobel had been sleeping between two tablecloths! Isobel was off by daybreak, long before any of us were out of bed. Whether Mrs. McNally gave her a dressing down this Department cannot say ...

Why don't you give me the full benefit of that euphonious cognomen which my Godfathers & Godmother gave me, you spell Larratt thus, not Laratt.

I am about fast asleep, fagged, tired, & stupid. Good night, God bless you all. Love to Yorkshire & the babes in the wood.

                                                Larratt
                                                with two r's

Mrs McNally's school closed for the summer. Isobel Murney stayed on in Toronto until the middle of July. In that time she saw a good deal of Larratt Smith (always carefully chaperoned), and even stayed with his sister Adelaide Cassels at the bank. Towards the end of August, after taking his sons on an excursion to Quebec, Smith went to Belleville: 'Arrived at midnight & to my surprise, found the Murneys sitting up waiting for me. Stayed there 4 days partying & boating with Isobel, but just as I was packing up to go with them to New York, I received a telegraph to go to Cobourg on urgent business.' Smith was back in Belleville in October at the wedding of Isobel's older sister. A few weeks later he wrote to Mrs. Thom: 'I have been to Belleville since I last wrote you, to Minny Murney's wedding. It was a gay affair & I enjoyed myself as I always do, amazingly. I notice what Caroline says with regard to Isobel & the gossip she heard. The woman is wrong, there is no engagement whatsoever between us ... Isobel is a fine girl, a remarkably fine girl with excellent qualities, but she is a perfect child ...'

Smith says nothing more about Isobel Murney until after the New Year. His diaries for the last of 1855 are preoccupied with business, and Canada's new form of transportation: '*Toronto & Hamilton Railroad opened for traffic on 3rd December*. On the 7th, I went by train to Hamilton in *1 hour & 35 minutes*. Thousands are arriving from every part of Canada & the States for the Dejeuner & Ball to be held in the Northern Railroad Works. Walked up with Cassels to see the preparations for the grandest affair ever seen on this continent.'

21: 'Behaving as strangely as usual' 1856

By 1856, Larratt Smith had been a widower for more than six years. He was still wearing a black waistcoat. His journal for 16 January reads: 'Poor Eliza would have been 31 years of age today had she lived.' In this sombre mood he wrote to his sister-in-law, Caroline Thom: '... there is nothing new here. A good many parties, but I prefer declining them as the "hugger muggering" system finds no favor in my eyes, not, at all events, in the ballroom. I agree with Dr. Lett, who when he stopped the Polka at the Charity Ball for the Orphans Home [in Toronto], & a married lady insisted that she would dance in spite of him, said, "Madam if you must dance this disgusting dance, I recommend you to go home & dance with your husband in your bedroom."'

To his journal, however, he confided: 'Yesterday I sat to Augustus Sullivan for my photographic likeness to be sent to Belleville. Wrote Isobel a note & enclosed it in a letter to her mother. I had barely done this when Mrs. Murney telegraphed me to meet the Stage-coach, went down there but she did not come. So spent the evening at the theatre & saw "Still Waters run Deep."'

Mrs Murney arrived in Toronto in April. She brought three of her younger daughters (but not Isobel) for a stay of six weeks. When the time came to leave for Belleville, she coaxed Larratt Smith to come with them. In doing this she was enticing him still further into the strange courtship of her daughter Isobel. '*Tuesday 28th May.* Am now writing up my journal after spending 6 delightful days with the Murneys. Walked every day with Isobel, boated when Lake Ontario was not too rough, & sang in the evenings. Intended to have left on Sunday but was persuaded to remain till Tuesday. Took Isobel out in the boat on our last afternoon together. Great romping in the evening.'

From then on a steady stream of letters passed between Mrs Murney in Belleville and Larratt Smith in Toronto. On 30 June he wrote to his father:

... I have actually made since poor Eliza's death, over £6000 ... but I have worked hard for it night & day, including Sundays. No wonder then that I have bethought me of matrimony once more, for what is the good of riches if my life is to be spent like a horse in a mill & deny myself the enjoyment of humanity. My boys 200 miles away, seen for but once a year & without a place I can call home.

The only sunny spot that I have had to turn to has been Belleville, where I have always been received with the greatest kindness & hospitality, & there, what of any affection I have left is centered. I am engaged to Murney's eldest unmarried daughter.

I am only just engaged & scarcely that, for the young lady is still in the hands of her governesses – & like most damsels of her age is shy & coy. She will only be 18 years of age tomorrow, so that I suppose I shall not be married for another year at least, which gives me plenty of time to get my affairs arranged.

I actually engaged myself by letter to Isobel's mother with whom I have corresponded for many years & whom I knew as a girl when I was a boy at Upper Canada College. I have not seen Isobel Murney since I was accepted. If I could get away I should not lose a moment in going to Belleville to give her assurance which I cannot do in correspondence. She will make a splendid woman, indeed she might easily pass now for 20. It is my misfortune that I am twice her age, but I shall have the satisfaction of moulding her views to my wish, which I could hardly do with some antiquated 'tabby' of a spinster.

Isobel's father Mr. Murney is connected with all the best families in the country & his influence is very great. He has been Member of Parliament for the County of Hastings for the last 20 years, & is a man of means, with, I dare say, £50,000, although there is a large family, some 9 or 10, of whom but one is a boy.

The Murney family is a most affectionate set, & as Isobel has sisters – several younger than Lal & Georgey, & one an infant, I have every reason to believe that she will be all that a parent could be to my boys. I expect to get away to Belleville in about 10 days. I shall go to Perth, & perhaps bring the boys with me to Belleville, as Mrs. Murney wishes me to bring them ...

By this time, Larratt was writing to Isobel every day. She did not, however, always answer his letters.

16th July. Letters from Mrs. Murney but no letter from Isobel till yesterday when one came. Telegraphed her & left for Belleville at once. Reached there, but received a cool reception from Isobel whom I found out driving with Hutton. Had a talk with her & gave her a brooch & a bracelet. Isobel then insisted on going to a party at Ponton's – she is as usual dancing mad! Next day Mrs. Murney returned me all the presents I gave Isobel. Had another talk with the latter, in which she requested 6 months delay on our engagement, starting from the 1st of August. I agreed & left for Toronto.

Unlike the Murneys, for whom Larratt Smith was all they could wish for in a son-in-law, the Smiths in England (who must have had wind of the affair long before Larratt told them) thoroughly disapproved of Isobel Murney as a daughter-in-law. Captain Smith's letter on the subject has been lost, but his son's reaction was immediate:

I received your somewhat severe note of 4th July whilst at Perth on a visit to the boys. You do me injustice by supposing that I had not reflected! My choice of Isobel Murney was the result of the nicest reflection. The disparity in years I accounted as nothing. In this country, where women are prematurely old, haggard, wrinkled and toothless at 30, a man of 40 will always outlast a woman of 20. I selected Isobel from the position her father holds in the country. I considered also that being brought up in the country with homely habits & ideas, without notions of the extravagances of city life, and as yet uncontaminated by the world, my prospects of happiness would be secured.

As regards solid accomplishments, you are well aware that few if any girls in this country possess them in any degree. Isobel, however, has had a fair education & possesses great musical taste & talent. I do not therefore think that I have made the worthless selection you seem to consider it, or that the lady is as 'contemptible' ...

Perhaps you will be glad to learn that 'as the course of true love never did run smooth,' Isobel Murney has of her own free will, required our engagement to be suspended for six months, for the reason, that being young & inexperienced she needs time to reflect if she likes me sufficiently to be united to me.

I am therefore under an engagement neither to see nor correspond with her in any way until after the 1st of February next. This is all her own doing & contrary to the tears, wishes & protestations of her mother & every member of her family. I have great misgivings that this affair will come to nothing. I regret this more on Mrs. Murney's account than on any other. She is a most fascinating & accomplished woman – no woman in Canada can write such a letter. I correspond with her as usual & shall probably join her at the seaside at Portland, Maine before my vacation is over.

Smith spent ten days in August with the Murneys at Old Orchard Beach, a fashionable resort in Maine, where they were holidaying with some wealthy friends, the Gildersleeves of Kingston, Upper Canada. He later wrote to his mother-in-law, Mrs Thom: 'How the boys would have enjoyed the bathing at Old Orchard Beach with the surf rolling in from the boundless Atlantic! & who knows you might have liked it also. I never enjoyed myself more. Boating, fishing, shooting, & picnicking every day. We used to drive a coach & four with 20 in it for 15 miles over the finest sand as hard as iron without leaving an impression. At night, private theatricals, charades, & songs – telling my thoughts of it unsettles me ...'

During this period there is no mention of Isobel Murney either in Smith's letters or his diaries. But in October 1856, after attending the Kingston assizes, he broke the pact: 'Arrived at the Murneys' on Friday. Isobel behaving as strangely as usual. Gave me her Ultimatum. I kept to my room most of that day & went to bed early. Left for Toronto this morning on the *first trip of the Grand Trunk Railroad.* Isobel relented & saw me off.'

Isobel Murney continued to blow hot and cold with Larratt Smith. By December of that year the courtship had grown cold: 'After receiving letters from Mrs. Murney, Bessie, & Annie, yesterday, I dined with Mrs. Beverley Robinson & took advice. After the office today, I wrote Mrs. Murney & returned all Isobel's letters, mementos etc. & sent Mrs. Murney some Hyacinth bulbs & glasses, Annie, a gold pencil case, & Nina, a silver bouquet holder, & gave the parcel to Miss Watson to take to Belleville. Gave Mrs. Beverley Robinson my goldfish & globe.'

22: One passage to Southampton 1857

One would have expected the affair to end then and there. But in the spring of 1857 the Murneys turned up in Toronto with Isobel in tow. Smith met them coming out of church and once more fell under the spell of Isobel Murney. Isobel, however, was under no spell.

10 April 1857 Yesterday as we walked home from St. George's Church, Isobel deliberately told me that she never thought of me until I returned! & that she hates all Englishmen whom she stigmatizes as being 'cold & mean.' She then became upset & said she did not mean it. After we got back to the Spragges I gave her a Bouquet, bracelets, a brooch, & a fan. I spent the following evening with Isobel & gave her a parasol, but after a most unsatisfactory talk & a sleepless night, I wrote her that our engagement must be broken off & wrote Mrs. Murney what I had done. Isobel sent for me at once & professed herself sorry at having annoyed me. Her father then called to see me & said that the matter must be determined one way or the other. He proposes to give Isobel & me a trip to England after being married in New York. Murney then drove me to Spragge's house *& Isobel consented in the presence of both of us*. Thereupon I left off my mourning & took a walk to see the centre piece of my new house in St. George's Square which is now finished.'

In the time when he and Eliza were living in the rented cottage on Front Street, Smith made regular contributions to a building society. Now, after more than six years, he was building a house of his own. Had he finally determined (no matter what happened) to make a home for his sons, or was the house an inducement to Isobel Murney to marry him? The house, it appears, meant nothing to Isobel: 'When I went to see Isobel today, she told me that she had changed her mind & wished matters postponed for a year or two. I declined & took leave of her with the full understanding that everything was broken off between us *for ever*. She then wished me to take back my presents myself. I declined – told her she might *send* them back ...'

Mr Murney's offer of a trip to England suggested to Larratt Smith that he buy himself a passage to Southampton. He left New York in the packet *Indiana* on 10 June 1857. Except for his brief unhappy visit in 1838, Larratt had not seen the country of his birth since as a boy of eleven he had embarked with his family in a sailing ship for a six weeks' voyage to Canada. Now, many years later, the *Indiana* under steam and sail reached Southampton in sixteen days: '*Wednesday 24th June.* When the ship weighed anchor in Southampton water I went ashore in the steam tender & found Papa whom I had not seen for ten years, on the wharf in the Docks waiting for me.'

Young Smith spent three months with his family both in and out of Southampton. He went to Greenwich where he visited his brother George, and lost no time in calling on Aunt George with whom he later dined. George drove Larratt in his carriage to the great exhibition at the Crystal Palace in London. Later in London Larratt dined with his uncle William Violett with whom he went to the theatre: 'Left Drury Lane Theatre in disgust for the Haymarket where we saw, "Fiddle-dee-dee, leave her to me."'

By the end of July Larratt had been to Plymouth, seen his birthplace at Stonehouse, and met countless relatives and friends. On 10 August Captain Smith and Larratt went to France to see the great fête in honour of Napoleon III.

Papa & I left Southampton in the steamer *Albania* for Le Havre. Beautiful night, comfortable berths & a clean ship. Detained at Havre & missed two trains by French customs searching baggage & viséing passports. Reached Paris & put up at Grand Hotel de Louvre, 4th flat, 2 bedrooms, 8 francs. Very good & handsome. Dined & went to the Theatre du Palais Royale, poor affair.

On Friday we went to the Place Carousel & witnessed the opening of the Louvre by the Emperor Napoleon in great state, attended by 30,000 troops under arms. Saw the Emperor & the Empress Eugenie & all the French court very distinctly.

On Saturday, the great day of the Fête Napoléon, we strolled about all day; through the Louvre, the Tuileries gardens & the Champ-de-Mars. Saw Balloon ascent & heard the military bands play in the gardens. In the evening we went to L'Opera Comique to see 'l'Etoile du Nord,' a very splendid theatre & performance, 100 in the orchestra. Whilst in Paris, besides churches, galleries & gardens in the day, Papa & I went to the theatre every night, the Gaieté & the Vanité Theatres, & to the opera 'Guillaume Tell' & the new opera 'Le Prophète.'

On our last day, we went to the Church of St. Sulpice, finished the Louvre, dined at the Palais Royale, then left for Boulogne. Embarked in the *Triton* for London via the Thames. Very rough passage, no beds or anywhere to sleep below – forced to sleep on the deck in the rain.

By the end of July, Larratt had been up to London several times with his father; they called at the head offices of the Canada Company[1] and the Bank of British North America, saw all the sights of London, and dined with relatives. Larratt went once by himself for a rendezvous and an evening of theatre with his army friend, Lieutenant Woods. On one of these trips he bought a quantity of china, glass, and other furnishings for his new house in Toronto, the residence Isobel Murney had disdained.

After arranging to ship his purchases by the *City of Hamilton* lying in the Thames estuary, Smith went back to Southampton where he spent three more weeks with his family. Then, after what he described as 'A terrible leavetaking,' he left for London on the first lap of his journey to Liverpool.

Thursday 24th September. Embarked yesterday from St. George's Pier Liverpool, in the tender, *Sailor King*, for the ocean vessel *Anglo Saxon*, 126 passengers & 148 steerage on board.

The pilot left at 2 P.M. Sailors dipped the colors, fired 2 guns & made all snug. Saw my last glimpse of England. Porpoises playing about the ship.

After a stormy crossing, in which everyone on board the *Anglo Saxon* was seasick, including the diarist, he wrote: '*Friday 2nd October*. We reached the Straits of Belle Isle at 5 P.M. The ship fired a gun which was answered from the lighthouse. Passed through the Straits, a brilliant Aurora in the sky.'

Perhaps the Aurora Borealis was a good omen, for the rest of the journey was smooth and pleasant. Larratt Smith arrived home in time for the Toronto assizes where he took two cases. He also lost no time in arranging the finishing touches to the house in St George's Square: 'Walked with Cassels to see my new house. Ordered cross-bars to the windows & gave carpenters orders to fit up shutters.' He then engaged a housekeeper and moved in promptly.

On the first of December, Larratt's mother-in-law, Mrs Thom, and his young sons Larratt and George came to live with him. There was a joyful reunion. Larratt took the little boys to the pantomime, showed them off to his friends, and enrolled them in the preparatory school at Upper Canada College.

In the meantime another match-making mother had noticed Larratt Smith. This was none other than the wife of the commissioner of the Canada Company, the most famous hostess in Toronto, Mrs Frederick Widder. Smith wrote the day after he returned from England: 'Somewhat to my surprise, on coming out of St. George's Church, after singing in the choir there, I met Mrs. Widder & her daughter. They insisted on my lunching with them, then took me to the afternoon service at St. James Cathedral. Dined with the Widders, who later very kindly sent me home in their carriage.' On Sunday, 8 November, he wrote again: 'Walked home from church with Miss Widder & dined with her parents for the second time.' These overtures became the prelude to a shower of invitations to dinners, musical evenings, and parties at the Widders' elegant house, Lyndhurst.

But Smith's attentions to the Widder girl (we are not told her name) were desultory. He gave her some pieces of music and a copy of *The Merchant of Venice*; he took her to the theatre, and on one occasion gave her a bouquet. By the following spring he stopped going to Lyndhurst. The courtship – if it could be called one – had come to nothing.

23: Meanwhile Mrs Thom is packing 1858

Eventually there was another courtship that did succeed and led to a marriage, as the Smith family Bible states: 'Larratt William Violett Smith married secondly, Mary Elizabeth Smith, eldest daughter of James Frederick Smith and Mary (nee Sanford), *by the name of Minnie*. The wedding taking place at the residence of her father in Bay Street, Toronto, on Thursday 19th August, 1858, the Reverend Henry Grasett officiating.'

Larratt had come to know Mary Elizabeth, or Minnie as she preferred to be called, when he was courting Isobel Murney and Minnie was a pupil at Mrs McNally's school. She was, in fact, about the same age as Isobel Murney.

Minnie was born in Montreal in 1838. Her father, James Frederick Smith, who claimed descent from Rob Roy Macgregor, the famous Scottish freebooter and outlaw, was a well-to-do merchant and one-time president of the Bank of Montreal. According to his descendants, this Mr Smith was a dour man and a stern father. Minnie's mother, Mary Sanford, came of a New England pioneer family who, when the American Revolutionary War broke out, remained loyal to the Crown. In 1776, Mary's grandfather, Ephriam Sanford, abandoned his estates in Salem, Massachusetts, to raise a company of soldiers in the service of the King. He and his son were later awarded a land grant in Lower Canada, where Mary was born. Mary Sanford Smith was later to die in childbirth when her daughter Minnie was eight years old.

Apparently Larratt Smith did not begin to court Minnie until the summer of 1858. The journal entries for the spring of that year are terse and dull. He records office work, court sessions, levees, theatre, and parties in monotonous order. He notes minor household repairs and the settings of hens on clutches of eggs. He complains of his sons' lack of progress at Upper Canada College preparatory school, of the difficulty of keeping them at their lessons, and of their misbehaviour: 'Obliged to send Lal to bed for bad conduct at the dinner table. Georgey also behaved very badly. Resolved to enroll both boys in Mr. Chickley's Grammar school at Barrie, where it is to be hoped they will learn some manners.' Shortly after this entry, he and Mrs Thom went up to Barrie, inspected Mr Chickley's premises, and arranged for the boys to enter the school on 13 July.

Late in June, Smith gave his first party at the new house in St George's Square. His journal records his notice of Minnie: 'Party at my house a great success – 60 out of 80 came – the Spragges brought Minnie Smith & we had great fun together. On the way to my boat this afternoon, I met Miss Smith, forgot about the boat & walked home with her. Resolved not to go to England this year.'

From that day forward Larratt Smith's journals mention calling on his future bride at her father's house on Bay Street every evening. Nothing in his short, taciturn entries strikes a note of urgency; judging by them one might assume these visits were but a prelude to a lengthy, punctilious courtship. I was told by several relations that, in pressing his suit, Larratt was aided and abetted by Minnie's father who had made up his mind that it was time his daughter of almost twenty was married. James Frederick Smith had decided that Larratt Smith, although eighteen years older than Minnie, was the right man for her. What Minnie thought of this choice of bridegroom will never be known. How one wishes that she had kept a diary.

James Smith's determination was crowned with successs. Larratt's laconic journal for the end of July begins to hint of marriage: his entry for the 24th of the month is written in Greek, and translates into giving Minnie a fan, some ornaments, and a bracelet, and taking her to the opera. Meanwhile, at the house in St George's Square, Mrs Thom is packing her trunks to go home to Perth.

On Thursday, 19 August 1858, Larratt and Minnie were married in the drawing room of her father's house on Bay Street, and left for New York immediately after the ceremony. This wedding journey was made, not by stage-coach, but in a railway car in style.

Another family tradition has it that when Minnie signed the marriage register, Larratt teased her by saying: 'Because you have written Minnie instead of Mary, you are not properly married.' Whereupon the young bride burst into tears.

After this tearful beginning, Minnie Smith turned out to be more than a match for her husband. Not only could she speak French as fluently as he, she was also very musical and consequently moved with ease among his circle of friends. Only ten years older than her eldest stepson, Lal, Minnie showed him and his little brother George great kindness and sympathy throughout their short lives, and her own children adored her.

The house in St George's Square sheltered five of the eleven children born to Minnie and Larratt Smith. In 1867, the year of Confederation when Upper and Lower Canada embraced the reluctant Maritimes, the Smith family moved to their new residence, Summer Hill. Later still Canada was to take on five more provinces, and the Smiths to produce six more children – one of them, my father, was born in 1872. By that time Larratt Smith, like his country, was no longer quite so young.

The Accession of Queen Victoria

The Upper Canada College
Prize Poem for 1837

BY LARRATT SMITH

And has another kingly spirit fled
To swell the mansions of the silent dead?
Yes; to that bourne whence no return is known,
Suppliant to stand before a mightier throne,
Earth's mightiest monarch wings his upward flight,
And leaves a nation plunged in sorrow's night.
Blest with a kindly heart, a gen'rous soul,
How mild his sway; how gentle his control;
E'en while the tide of life was ebbing fast,
The call of mercy moved him to the last,
E'en at that solemn hour, his falt'ring voice
Bade the doom'd felon's downcast heart rejoice;
His latest accents breathed a patriot's prayer;
'God shield my people with thy heavenly care';
And oh; while throbs with grief a nation's heart –
While death delays, yet shakes his threat'ning dart,
Thy presence Adelaide, thy tearful smile,

Thy voice, with Christian solace fraught, beguile
The soul's departing anguish of its sting,
Till faith, victorious, lends his angel wing.
With many a pearl, with many a costly gem,
resplendent gleams thy queenly diadem,
But brighter far thy virtue's lustre cheers,
A monarch's exit from this vale of tears;
For in that hour when flattery's homage palls,
And on the ear of Death unheeded falls,
Did England's Church forsake her father king,
Or fail religion's soothing rights to bring?
See the meek Prelate points to realms above,
And speaks of mercy through a Saviour's love;
The peace divine his voice had often shed
With healing balm round many a lowlier bed;
The prayers, that oft had fervent utterance sought
For dying peasant of the straw-built cot,
Now float in tones seraphic, and prepare
A monarch's soul in endless bliss to share –
Church of the king and peasant – Church of God,
O lightly on thee fall affliction's rod –
Still teach the king and peasant how to live,
How win a crown that world's can never give.

    But as we wistful gaze, admiring yet
The mellow glories of the sun that's set,
Hail to the rising star that cheers the scene,
Shedding around new light and joy – Our Queen;
Our virgin Queen; the herald loud proclaims,
Hark to the burst of feeling, when he names
Britannia's mistress; How the countless throng,
lusting with loyalty, the shout prolong;
Auspicious day; while gladness lights each face,
The Rose of England droops with modest grace;
No vain exultant pride of new born power
Awakes bold thoughts, that like the eagle tower;
No rising lust of empire fill'd the breast,
By change so awful and so vast, oppress'd;
But tears roll'd down, with humbler feeling fraught,
And wrapt she stood in sad and silent thought.

The Accession of Queen Victoria / 181

Say, pensive, then, did not her prayers ascend
To God, the monarch's and the peasant's friend, –
A prayer for heavenly dews to bless the land,
Whose sceptre trembled in her youthful hand?
And did not one, 'neath whose maternal care
The Royal Oak had gain'd a growth so fair? –
Did not she, too, in supplication's tone,
Approach the footstool of the Eternal Throne,
And fervently implore the King of Kings
To shield her child beneath his fostering wings.

   Reflections, sad, may curb a nation's pride,
But chast'nings do not check the loyal tide;
For, swifter yet, as now, it onward flows,
A nobler front our Constitution shows,
When rising proudly from its recent shock,
It rides the crested wave, or shuns the threat'ning rock;
Grim death may drive the pilot from the helm,
Another quick succeeds to guide our realm;
And onward still the gallant vessel steers
Her course undevious, mid the wreck of years.
Not so in countries less with Freedom bless'd,
Beneath Democracy's stern yoke oppress'd:
When one short rule has spun its weary round,
Does noisy Faction raise her barren sound;
'Neath rival names, whole hosts, array'd in strife,
Distract the land, with wrath and hatred rife.
But Albion, when thy monarch sinks to rest
With peace and social order still thou'rt bless'd;
When fades one star of Brunswick from the skies,
The undying flame another quick supplies;
As son to sire, as day succeeds to night,
Unbroken flows the stream of Royal right;
George sinks to rest, William the good succeeds,
He wins a heavenly crown for earthly deeds;
Victoria 'plucks allegiance from men's hearts,'
And treason vainly barbs his venom'd darts.
While others boast the Sovereign people's sway,
Mine be the pride a Monarch to obey;
Mine be the chivalry, that Sidney fired,

That Raleigh spurr'd, and Shakespear's muse inspired; –
Mine be the banner, from whose folds unfurl'd,
Fair freedom wafts her blessings o'er the world:
Let that bright ensign o'er me living wave,
And when I die, float peaceful o'er my grave.

   Victoria reigns:– the voice of discord's fled;
Britannia lifts her sad and drooping head.
They err who say that chivalry's no more,
Save in the page of legendary lore;
It dwells on castled Ainwick's lofty steep;
From Edgcumbe's groves it sweeps across the deep;
It looks from Belvoir on the vale below;
It lives and breathes on Cheviot, capp'd with snow;
From hill to dale it spreads, – from Liffey's waves
To where old ocean moans in Thule's caves;
It floats from spire, it peals from Turret gray –
It swims o'er distant seas, far, far away,
To where Canadian woods exclude the day.

   Deem not the sterner sex alone can guide
A nation's weal, or curb a nation's pride:
A woman's softness and a woman's might
Have soothed in peace; – have baffled in the fight;
When Deb'rah rose 'a mother in the land,'
Proud Sis'ra 'bow'd and fell' 'neath Jael's hand:
A prophet Queen, the tribes in peace she sway'd,
And justice dwelt beneath her 'palm-tree' shade.
Zenebia scorn'd thy yoke, imperial Rome;
And fought though vainly, for her marble home;
And still Arabia's sandy deserts trace
Gigantic piles upon her swarthy face –
A woman's boast – Which time can ne'er efface.
Had not a woman's mind, to kindred height,
Soar'd with Columbus in his lofty flight,
The world's cold sneer, mistrust, and doubts that freeze,
Had quench'd the sprit of the Genoese;
He told his tale – fair Isabella smiled,
Columbus track'd the ocean's pathless wild,
And Earth, rejoicing, hail'd her new born child.

The Accession of Queen Victoria / 183

Mid realms laid waste, mid battle's disarray,
When ruin yawn'd to clasp her destined prey,
Fair Austria's daughter, smiling through her tears,
Undaunted stood before the Hungarian peers;
Woman; 'twas thine to rouse the sleeping fire
Of knightly courage, and a nation's ire.
Hark; how the bold Hungarian chieftains fling
Defiance fierce to proud Bavaria's king:
Pro Rege nostro; shakes the startled walls,
Rings through each baron's old ancestral halls;
Then darts, like fiery cross from fell to fell,
From shelter'd cot to bristling citadel:
A woman leads embattled hosts to war,
Resistless, on she speeds, while triumph guides her ear.
But why repair to foreign clime to show
That manly vigour may with softness grow?
Britannia, great Elizabeth was thine;
(No nobler name have hymn'd the immortal Nine)
She awed proud Callia's hosts and humbled Spain,
Bade British commerce tempt the daring main.
Turn we to Anna's reign – on Churchill's brow
Bright shines the laurel worn by Wellesley now.
With heavenward spire, full many a rising fane
Sheds Christian lustre o'er a woman's reign:
While Steele and Addison, those twins of fame,
The Augustan age on earth revived, proclaim.

   Queen of the Isles: anointed from on high,
Vice-Sovereign of a King beyond the sky,
All hail to thee; nursed by thy tender youth
With holy heavenly thoughts and princely truth.
May great Elizabeth's capacious mind,
With Anna's zeal and Charlotte's worth combined,
And every royal virtue of thy race,
Victoria's name with fadeless lustre grace;
Methinks, as down the vale of length'ning years
I gaze, suspended 'twixt my hopes and fears,
I trace the historic page, with trophies bright
Of nations snatch'd from Superstition's night,
And basking in the noon of Gospel light,

Hush'd is the voice of war – the Church upheld –
Law sacred – Merit crown'd – Sedition quell'd: –
These by thy glories – thus the holy fire
Of loyalty and truth shall ne'er expire.
Thus while thy presence gilds this earthly scene,
Each Briton loud will shout, GOD SAVE THE QUEEN.

Toronto, 1 December 1837

From the Montreal *Gazette*, 10 February 1838

INTRODUCTION

1 Scadding, *Toronto of Old*, 424–5

CHAPTER 1

1 Bernard Smith to Violett Georgina Smith, 18 Aug. 1941. All the quotations in this chapter are from the same source.
2 Sir John Colborne, lieutenant-governor of Upper Canada, 1829–39, was made governor-in-chief of British North America in 1839, but was succeeded by Poulett Thompson in the same year.

CHAPTER 2

1 A French trading post, Fort Rouillé, commonly known as Fort Toronto, was built on the north shore of Lake Ontario about the middle of the eighteenth century and was maintained for several years. After the fall of New France, the British under Col. John Graves Simcoe established a townsite in the area in 1793 and named it York in honour of a military victory in Holland by the Duke of York. In 1834, when the place was incorporated as a city, it was renamed Toronto, a name that originated in an Indian language.
2 Bernard Smith to Violett Georgina Smith, 18 Aug. 1941
3 The area known as the Home District was settled about 1796. It was bounded on the north by lakes Simcoe and Couchiching (spelled Goughchin in the *Gazetteer*), on the east by the Newcastle and Colborne districts, on the west by the Simcoe, Wellington, and Gore districts, and on the south by Lake Ontario. Toronto was

the principal town in the district. Wm. H. Smith, *Smith's Canadian Gazetteer* (Toronto: H.W. Rowsell 1846)
4 Kent to Larratt Smith, 23 Aug. 1897
5 Scadding, *Toronto of Old*, 461

CHAPTER 3

1 Dickson and Adam, eds., *A History of Upper Canada College*
2 Bernard Smith to Violett Georgina Smith, 18 Aug. 1941

CHAPTER 4

1 Rose's *Cyclopedia* provides a useful summary of Smith's law career: 'When Larratt William Smith arrived in Toronto in 1833 he entered Upper Canada College, and here remained for a period of five years ... In Michaelmas term, 1838, he entered the Law Society as a student of the senior class, and was articled for five years to the late Chief Justice Draper. In Michaelmas term, 1843, he was admitted an attorney; and in the following term was called to the bar. In 1843, at the opening of King's College, he matriculated in arts, and, passing on to law, took his degrees of B.C.L. and D.C.L., the latter in 1852. Shortly after being called to the bar he purchased a junior partnership in the legal firm of Smith, Crooks & Smith, of Toronto. Since that period he has practised his profession in partnership at different times with the Honourable Chief Justice Wilson, James H. Morris, Q.C., and Samuel George Wood, LL.B. At the present time [1886] he is senior partner in the firm of Smith, Smith & Rae. Dr. Smith has not allowed the practice of his profession to absorb the whole of his attention, but in several important enterprises of a public as well as a private nature, has taken a prominent part.' Rose, ed., *A Cyclopedia of Canadian Biography*, 426–7
2 The murderer, James McDermott, was publicly hanged in Toronto on 21 November 1843. Smith wrote: 'I went down at 7 A.M. to the Gaol to see McDermott hanged, but it was postponed till 12 & as I was obliged to be in Mr. Draper's office, did not see it. Saw the body at the University later.'
3 Larratt Smith to Thomas Coltrin Keefer, 20 Jan. 1840
4 Col. Fitzgibbon gave full credit for the defeat of the Americans at Beaver Dam to Mrs Laura Secord, the intrepid Queenston housewife who walked eighteen miles through the Black Swamp to warn him of the impending attack.
5 Finch's Tavern stood on Yonge Street where Finch Avenue is now. It was a useful stopover where farmers and travellers could get accommodation for themselves and their horses overnight as well as food and grog at the bar. This inn was very popular with the half pay officers and their families from the farms in the Yonge Street area.

6 The wife, daughter, and son of Francis Boyd whose farm adjoined the Smiths' farm on Yonge Street near Richmond Hill. Boyds and Smiths may have been kin, but in spite of the reference to 'Aunt' Mary, and a later one by Mrs Boyd claiming Larratt's sister Adelaide as her 'niece,' the family connection was not that close.

7 The *Gore* and another regular passenger ship, the *Transit*, were built in the Niagara shipyards. These schooner-rigged, wood-burning steamboats were part of a fleet of lake vessels that criss-crossed Lake Ontario linking Toronto with the small towns around the lake from Niagara to Kingston and beyond to Montreal.

8 John George Lambton, first Earl of Durham (1792–1840), was governor-in-chief of British North America and lord high commissioner from 8 May to 1 November 1838. His research into Canadian affairs in those few months resulted in his famous report which led to the union of Upper and Lower Canada and the achievement of responsible government in the colonies whereby executive power was entrusted to a ministry responsible to Parliament, and the electorate, as in the British system.

9 The lake vessel *St George* was advertised as 'a beautiful ship, propelled by a low-pressure engine of Ninety Horse-power, is schooner-rigged & has accommodation for 60 passengers.'

10 Charles Poulett Thomson (1799–1841), first Baron Sydenham, was the son of an English merchant who had a business in St Petersburg. Young Thomson spent some years in Russia working for his father. (Larratt Smith later refers to a droshky which Thomson had specially built in Canada.) Poulett Thomson was appointed governor of British North America in 1839, and died at Kingston on 19 September 1841 as the result of a fall from his horse. Larratt Smith often follows the contemporary custom of calling the governor, the 'governor-general'; this latter title for the chief officer of the crown in Canada became official at Confederation in 1867.

11 The Parsons family emigrated from the County of Dorset, England, with the Thornes to whom they were related, settling at Thornhill in 1820. Thornhill is named after the Thorne family.

12 The Rev. John McCaul (1807–87). A renowned scholar, McCaul was born in Ireland and educated at Trinity College, Dublin. He was principal of Upper Canada College in 1839. In 1843 he was appointed professor of classics and belles-lettres at King's College. From 1853 to 1880 he became president of the newly organized University College. Dr McCaul was said to have come of royal lineage, but this rumour has never been verified.

13 The Ridout Brothers, hardware merchants, were members of the same family as surveyor-general Thomas Ridout and John Ridout, the ill-fated duellist.

14 A stick provided with a guard or basket, used for fighting, fencing, or exercise. *Shorter Oxford Dictionary*
15 Molasses pull toffee
16 A small sleigh or sledge
17 The widow of Col. Heath of the Honourable East India Company Service, owner of the estate, Deer Park.

CHAPTER 5

1 The Sandwich Lands mentioned here were in King Township and should not be confused with the settlement near the Detroit River and Lake St Clair.
2 There was no Canadian silver currency at this time: specie was made up of English (sometimes European) and American coins. New York shillings, worth about twenty-five cents, or ten cents if defaced, were in common use in Canada and often known as 'yorkers.'
3 On Keefer's later career, see *Philosophy of Railroads and Other Essays, by T.C. Keefer*, ed. H.V. Nelles (Toronto: University of Toronto Press 1972).
4 The Rev. Charles Stephen Matthews (1800–77), MA, Cambridge, 1828, was an original member of the teaching staff of Upper Canada College.
5 The original Constitutional Act of 1791 had decreed that an area one-seventh of all lands granted to settlers in Upper and Lower Canada was to be kept for the support of a Protestant clergy. This touched off a series of social and economic grievances that went on until 1840 when the act Smith writes of came before the House. It was, however, disallowed. The Clergy Reserve question was finally resolved in 1854 by secularizing the lands and dividing the profits among the municipalities. A certain amount of these profits was set aside for clerical pensions.
6 A lively dance in $\frac{3}{4}$ time
7 Sir Roger de Coverly, named after the squire in Joseph Addison and Richard Steele's *Spectator*, was a kind of quadrille usually danced by four couples. Sir Roger was danced in Toronto until the 1920s when it went out of fashion.
8 Another observer who had been on the voyage to Queenston averred that he saw six steamboats abreast on the Niagara River. Perhaps young Smith, carried away by the excitement of the spectacle, was counting rowboats and canoes.
9 Sir Richard Downes Jackson (1777–1845), administrator of the government of Lower Canada, was a veteran of the Peninsular War where he attained the rank of lieutenant-general. In 1839 he commanded the British forces in North America. He would have been sixty-three years old when he came in from Niagara on that hot summer day in 1840.
10 Scadding, *Toronto of Old*

Notes / 189

11 A vehicle which in England was called a 'break'; a kind of private stage-coach with seats inside and on top
12 A brown, globular, hard candy usually flavoured with peppermint; for 'yorker', see note 2 above
13 The Hon. John Hamilton (1802–82), senator and shipowner, was a prominent figure in shipping circles; he owned steamboats on Lake Ontario as well as the Upper St Lawrence River.
14 Scadding, *Toronto of Old*
15 This was in lieu of a written examination, there being no law school at this time: King's College did not open until 1843. William Draper later gave Larratt Smith written examinations, a process which sometimes took several hours.
16 William Hume Blake (1809–72) was born in County Wicklow, Ireland, educated at Trinity College, Dublin, and came to Canada in 1832. After being called to the Bar in 1838, he became known as the foremost counsel in Upper Canada.
17 Henry Rowsell's Book and Stationery Shop, 222 King Street West, Toronto, ran a circulating library, importing the latest books from England. *Nicholas Nickleby* by Charles Dickens, published in 1838, had probably just become available in Canada when Smith got it at Rowsell's. Smith kept the book for six days, which cost him sevenpence halfpenny.
18 One of the sessions of the High Court of Justice which were observed in Canada just as in England. The others were Easter, Trinity, and Michaelmas.
19 Sir Allan Napier MacNab, Baronet (1798–1862), was born at Newark (now Niagara-on-the-Lake), educated at the Home District Grammar School, bore arms as a teenager in the War of 1812, and during the Rebellion of 1837 commanded the 'Men of Gore.' Knighted for services in suppression of the rebellion, in 1858 he was created a baronet. Called to Bar of Upper Canada 1826, elected for Wentworth County to Assembly of Upper Canada 1829. Speaker 1837–41. After the union of Upper and Lower Canada as the Province of Canada in 1841, MacNab became the Conservative leader. Elected Speaker of the House 1844–8 and again in 1862; premier of Province of Canada 1854; resigned 1862.
20 Arthur Acland was a young Englishman who began his law career in the office of William Henry Draper where he and young Larratt Smith became friends. Acland was later awarded a judgeship at Goderich, Upper Canada. It was said to have been Acland who dubbed Draper 'Sweet William.'
21 The wife of Sir John Beverley Robinson (1791–1863), Chief Justice of Upper Canada. The Robinsons were originally United Empire Loyalists who forfeited their estates in New York and Virginia and came to Canada after the Revolutionary War. For his services to his country, Robinson was created a baronet in 1854.

CHAPTER 6

1 Champagne made for home consumption. *Shorter Oxford Dictionary*
2 Sir George Arthur (1784–1854), the last lieutenant-governor of Upper Canada, left for England 18 March 1841, never to return.
3 The North American Hotel, which stood on Front Street near Scott Street, was a four-storey building with a flat roof from which the opposite shore of Lake Ontario could be seen on clear days. This hostelry, while of moderate price, was said to be both elegant and convenient. Connected with it was a large one-storey addition which served for assemblies and balls and, for a time, as a theatre.
4 So called because the creek which ran through the village was forty miles from the Niagara River. After the War of 1812 the Forty was renamed Grimsby by Col. John Graves Simcoe, lieutenant-governor of Upper Canada.
5 A military corps of coloured men embodied in 1840, and engaged to hack a passable road through the forest between Canboro and Cayuga. These men were the descendants of former slaves, brought to Canada by the Loyalists, who had fought side by side with their former masters in the wars against the Americans. These black men had no particular regiment of their own, but were members of the various Loyalist regiments such as Butler's Rangers and were called, with pride, the Black Defenders. When young Larratt Smith drove over the Cayuga road in 1841, the Black Defenders were still there, living in huts they had built themselves. The subaltern whom Smith met at De Coo's Tavern was Henry George Augustus Powell, a white man who had served some six years with the regular army.
6 This tavern belonged to a descendant of a Loyalist family, which sometimes spelled its name De Cou or De Cew.
7 Sir Francis Hincks (1807–85), statesman and reformer. Despite young Smith's antics in pulling down his placards, Hincks was elected to the first Legislative Assembly of United Canada in 1841. He was receiver-general in the first Baldwin-Lafontaine government.
8 The *British Colonist*, a Toronto newspaper, was founded by Hugh Scobie in 1838.
9 The seat of the capital reverted to Toronto in 1844.
10 Later known as the Palmer House, this hotel stood at the corner of King and York streets.
11 A solution of soap in alcohol with camphor, oils of origanum, and rosemary. The name Opodeldoc was beliefed to have been used by Paracelsus (1493–1541), the celebrated Swiss physician and alchemist.
12 Lieutenant-general John Clitheroe (1782–1852) was a veteran of the Peninsular War. After the sudden death of Lord Sydenham, Clitheroe administered the government of Canada until the appointment of Sir R.D. Jackson.

13 'Vingt un' or 'vingt et un,' called 'Twenty-one' today and still played; 'Lanterloo,' a round card game, now called 'Loo'.
14 A folio consisted of seventy-two to ninety words taken as a unit in reckoning. *Oxford Shorter Dictionary*. In 1841, Larratt Smith was writing with a quill pen.
15 The gardens belonged in part to the descendants of Daniel Claus (1727–87), a Loyalist who married Nancy, daughter of Sir William Johnson, Bart. (1715–74), superintendent of Indian affairs in New York State before the American revolution. His son, Sir John Johnson, was a prominent Loyalist.

CHAPTER 7

1 This must be the Temple of Sharon, a large wooden structure erected by David Willson in 1835 for the Children of Peace, an offshoot of the Society of Friends. See Scadding, *Toronto of Old*, 486.
2 Sir Charles Bagot, Baronet (1781–1843), was appointed governor of British North America on the death of Lord Sydenham. During his short term and despite ill health, Bagot made important constitutional changes leading to responsible government, carried out by his successor, Sir Charles Metcalfe.
3 A special kind of straw hat imported from Leghorn in Italy.
4 This house, called Caer Howell after the Powell family estate in Wales, had double-decker verandahs surrounded by extensive gardens. The Royal York Hotel was built on the same site.
5 Dr James Sewell was a son of the Hon. Jonathan Sewell (1766–1839), a Loyalist from Cambridge, Massachusetts.
6 Jacob Maler Hirschfelder (1819–1902) was born at Baden-Baden, Germany, and came to Canada in 1837. He became tutor in Hebrew when King's College opened in Toronto.
7 Dr Norman Bethune, father of the Rev. Malcolm Bethune, and grandfather of the famous Dr Norman Bethune, the hero of revolutionary China.
8 The wife of Frederick Widder of the Canada Company. The Widders owned a stately mansion called Lyndhurst and were renowned for their lavish entertainment.
9 Cylindrical heat chamber into which ran a pipe from a stove on a lower floor; above the dumb stove was another pipe running from it into the chimney.
10 One of the Smiths' servants.

CHAPTER 8

1 The Rev. Adam Townley (1808–82), a former Methodist minister who was ordained to the ministry of the Church of England by Bishop Strachan.

2 Christopher Alexander Hagerman (1792–1847), attorney-general of Upper Canada, appointed puisne judge of the Court of the Queen's Bench in 1840.
3 A theology based on human reasoning rather than revelation
4 List of cases in court for trial, and/or names of parties with cases pending
5 A roll of parchment containing entries of the proceedings in an action-at-law up to the entry of the judgement

CHAPTER 9

1 Canniff, *History of the Province of Ontario*, 633
2 Founded about 1826, named after Colonel John By of the Royal Engineers who designed and built the Rideau Canal; name changed to Ottawa 1855; selected as seat of government by Queen Victoria, 1858; became capital of new Dominion of Canada in 1867.
3 A polite way of saying goodbye, the letters standing for 'Pour prendre congé' were written at the bottom of a calling card or note. This custom continued until sometime into the twentieth century.

CHAPTER 10

1 The senior partners in the firm of Crooks & Smith were Robert Crooks, son of James Crooks, merchant of West Flamboro, and John Shuter Smith, whose father lived at Port Hope.

CHAPTER 12

1 Judge Christopher Alexander Hagerman died on 14 May 1847, and William Henry Draper did indeed succeed him as puisne judge of the Court of the Queen's Bench.
2 James Bruce, eighth Earl of Elgin (1811–63), governor-general of British North America, 1847–54. Lord Elgin worked in harmony with four different ministries to achieve responsible government in Canada.
3 John Beverley Robinson (1821–96), second son of Chief Justice Sir John Beverley Robinson, became lieutenant-governor of Ontario after Confederation. His wife, Mary Jane Hagerman, was said to have a very beautiful voice. When Larratt Smith wrote this, he little knew that he would soon be singing duets and organizing concerts with her and that she would become one of his greatest friends. The codicil to his will mentions 'My long gold seal given to me by Mrs. Beverley Robinson.'
4 The fashionable resort in the United States.

Notes / 193

CHAPTER 13

1 A feminine high collar often made of fine material or lace and finished with a small ruffle
2 The Yonge Street tollgate was first set up about 1820 on the northeast corner of Bloor and Yonge streets; it remained there until 1850 when it was moved to the northwest corner of Davenport and Yonge streets.
3 The steamboat *Brothers* (owned in Chatham) left Amherstburg every Tuesday, Thursday, and Saturday at half past seven in the morning for Detroit and Chatham; the fare to Detroit was 50 cents, to Chatham $2.50.
4 Many hotels in the country were named after Albert, the Prince Consort.

CHAPTER 14

1 Adam Wilson (1814–91), jurist, was a partner of Robert Baldwin from 1840 to 1849; mayor of Toronto, 1859; solicitor-general in the Macdonald-Sicotte administration, 1862–3; judge of the Court of the Queen's Bench, 1863; in 1878 chief justice of the Court of Common Pleas; and in 1884 Court of Queen's Bench in Ontario. He was created a knight bachelor in 1887.
2 Coal also had its disadvantages: '*Thursday 7th February.* Chimneys so dirty I was obliged to clean them by firing my pistol into each flue.'
3 A comfortable hotel kept by Mrs John Ellah who came to Canada from Plymouth, England, where she had been housekeeper to Lord Seaton. Ellah's Hotel, known earlier as the New British Coffee House, was located in the Chewett Buildings at the corner of King and York streets.
4 The Church of St George-the-Martyr was designed by the architect Henry Bower Lane and built in 1844; Smith later subscribed ten shillings towards the cost of the bell. St George's was destroyed by fire in 1955.

CHAPTER 15

1 This was probably Eli J. Palmer's Dome Light Premium Daguerrean Gallery situated on the corner of King and Church streets.

CHAPTER 16

1 A picture of a landscape, etc., either arranged on the inside of a cylindrical surface round the spectator, or unrolled so as to pass before him in successive portions. *Shorter Oxford Dictionary*
2 An ornamental appendage worn by ladies at their waists; attached to it were short chains of keys, scissors, penknife, thimble case, etc.

3 June, a New Englander, was one of a group of circus owners to originate the full tent circus, and the first to import wild animals for his own use; it was not until 1851 that a circus and a menagerie were exhibited at one price of admission. The menagerie was added to overcome the prejudice and puritanical hostility evoked by circuses.

4 Larratt Smith did go on to have a long and distinguished professional life. According to Rose's *Cyclopedia*, he '... acquired an enviable reputation as a good financier, an able manager, an excellent office lawyer, and a shrewd, straightforward business man; and his various positions in the management of different financial institutions indicate that these qualities are appreciated. He has been clerk of the Court of Appeals for Upper Canada; pro-vice and, subsequently, vice-chancellor of the University of Toronto; has been president of the Building & Loan Association since its incorporation in 1870; is vice-president of the Toronto Consumers' Gas Company; was vice-president of the Canada Bolt Company; a director of the Bank of Upper Canada; and a director of the Canada Landed Credit Company; is a director of the London & Canadian Loan & Agency Company; of the Hand-in-Hand; and of the Anchor Marine Insurance Company; was a director of the Merchants Building Society; of the Grand Trunk Telegraph Company; of the Ontario Peat Company; has been a local director of the Life Association of Scotland; is a life senator of the University of Toronto; a bencher of the Upper Canada Law Society; is president of the Lake Superior Silver Mining & Land Company; vice-president of the Sovereign Fire Insurance Company; director of the Glasgow & London Fire Insurance Company; director of the North American Life Insurance Company; and has been solicitor of the Bank of British North America since 1845 ... He is a member of the Church of England, and a churchwarden of Christ Church, Yonge Street.' Rose, ed., *A Cyclopedia of Canadian Biography*, 427.

One of Larratt Smith's funeral notices, in the *Globe*, 20 September 1905, mentions his membership in even more companies, including his favourite utility the Consumers' Gas Company, of which he became president before his death. Gas, to Smith, was an even more remarkable invention than the 'Electric Telegraph'; when he bought Summer Hill he made sure that the entire house was piped with gas (I well remember offering to blow out the gas jet in the night nursery, and my mother's shriek of consternation).

Smith was also a shareholder in the gas company. When news of Thomas Edison's invention of the incandescent lightbulb reached Toronto in 1879, I was told, Smith flew into a great rage and rushed home to Summer Hill crying 'Minnie, I am ruined.' Needless to say, he was no more ruined by the invention of the electric lightbulb than he was by losing the Whitby judgeship in 1851.

5 Joseph Howe (1804–73), a statesman of Loyalist ancestry, was the son of a

Halifax printer, worked in his father's printing shop, and was almost entirely self-educated. In 1836 he was elected to the Legislative Assembly of Nova Scotia and was the foremost advocate of responsible government. In 1848–54, under the Uniacke government, he became provincial secretary of Nova Scotia. Although the scheme that Smith mentions in 1851 fell through, it gave impetus to railway building and Joseph Howe became chief commissioner of the railway board in 1854.

6 In 1833, an act known as the Dower Act was passed to afford greater facility in forcing a married woman to bar her right of dower to participate in one-third of her husband's estate. But Larratt Smith was careful to protect the interests of his mother-in-law. This is made clear in a letter to Mrs Thom written 17 June 1851: 'You will have to bar your Dower to the Lot in Nepean sold to Hallahan. I have written in pencil where you sign to execute the Deed. In these sales of wild land I propose to invest $\frac{1}{3}$ of the whole price for your benefit during your lifetime.'

7 The permission which a candidate for a degree was required to obtain from his College or Hall.

CHAPTER 17

1 A world-renowned Irish singer

CHAPTER 19

1 A novel by Edward Bradley, published 1853

CHAPTER 22

1 A land and colonization company instigated by John Galt in 1824

Bibliography

UNPUBLISHED MATERIAL

Larratt William Violett Smith, Diaries, 1839–58, Toronto, Upper Canada; in the possession of the Canadian History Department, Metropolitan Toronto Library, Toronto

Miscellaneous letters saved by chance (in the possession of the author):

Bernard Smith, Bournemouth, England, letters to his cousin Violett Georgina Larratt Smith, Toronto, Canada, 21 August 1938 and 28 August 1941 (originals non-existent, copies in my possession)

John Kent, Funchal, Madeira, letter to his friend Larratt William Violett Smith, 23 August 1897

Larratt William Violett Smith, letter to Thomas Coltrin Keefer, Thorold, Upper Canada, 20 January 1840 (my copy may be a xerox)

George Smith, Greenwich, England, letter to his father (Captain) Larratt Smith, Esq., Richmond Hill, Home District, Canada, via Halifax Mail, 18 July 1841

Captain Larratt Hillary Smith, Twickenham Farm, Home District, Upper Canada, letter to his son Larratt William Violett Smith, Mrs Howe's Boarding House, George Street, Toronto, 25 November 1842

Captain Larratt Hillary Smith, Southampton, England, letter to his son Larratt William Violett Smith, Front Street, Toronto, 10 November 1847

Larratt William Violett Smith, Toronto, letter to Colonel Homer Young, adjutant-general, Montreal, 8 September 1846

Letterbook (in the possession of the author):

Larratt William Violett Smith, letters taken from his letterbook, beginning 19 February 1847 and ending 8 September 1856

SOME SECONDARY SOURCES

Arthur, Eric. *Toronto: No Mean City.* Toronto: University of Toronto Press 1964
Canniff, W.M., MD. *History of the Province of Ontario (Upper Canada).* Toronto: A.H.Hovey 1872
Dickson, George, and G. Mercer Adam, eds. *A History of Upper Canada College, 1829–1892.* Toronto: Rowsell & Hutchinson 1893
Edgar, Matilda. *Ten Years of Upper Canada in Peace and War.* Toronto: William Briggs 1890
Firth, Edith, ed. *The Town of York, 1793–1815, 1815–1834,* 2 vols. Toronto: The Champlain Society for the Government of Ontario, University of Toronto Press 1962, 1966
Fitzgibbon, Mary Agnes. *A Veteran of 1812: The Life of James Fitzgibbon.* Toronto: William Briggs 1898
Guillet, Edwin C. *Pioneer Days*, 1933; *Pioneer Inns and Taverns*, 1954, 4 vols.; *Pioneer Settlements*, 1933
Kirby, William. *Annals of Niagara.* Toronto: Macmillan of Canada 1927
Lizars, Robina, and Kathleen Macfarlane. *In the Days of the Canada Company.* Toronto: William Briggs 1896
Mackenzie, Ruth. *Laura Secord; The Legend and the Lady.* Toronto: McClelland and Stewart 1971
Minhinnick, Jeanne. *At Home in Upper Canada.* Toronto: Clarke, Irwin & Company 1970
Morgan, Henry J. *Sketches of Celebrated Canadians and persons connected with Canada.* Quebec: Hunter Rose & Company 1862
Robinson, C. Blackett. *History of Toronto and County of York.* Toronto 1885
Rose, Geo. Maclean. *A Cyclopedia of Canadian Biography,* 2 vols. Toronto: Rose Publishing Company 1886, 1888
Scadding, Henry, DD. *Toronto of Old.* Toronto: Adam Stevenson & Company 1873
Story, Norah. *The Oxford Companion to Canadian History and Literature.* Toronto: Oxford University Press 1967
Taylor, Conyngham Crawford. *Toronto Called Back from 1886 to 1850.* Toronto: William Briggs 1886

Index

Acland, Arthur (in William Henry Draper's office) 47, 65, 70, 71, 189n
Alma, Esq. (election officer for Niagara) 54
Americans: some antagonism to 19, *see also* Yankees; business relations with 122; soldiers 67; war with Mexico 120
Amherstburg 127
Animal magnetism 84
Arthur, Sir George 24, 37, 39, 40, 53, 190n
Assemblies 84
Ayre's Cherry Pectoral (cough medicine) 153

Baby, Charles (clerk of the peace at Sandwich) 127
Bagot, Sir Charles 76, 191n
Baker (friend) 79, 80, 81
Baldwin, Robert 56, 57, 61, 123, 138; as attorney-general assigns Crown Docket to Smith 86; burnt in effigy 131; and firm of Wilson & Smith 130, 138; letter to, from Smith, on job hunting 145; pallbearer for Eliza Smith 154

Baldwin, Dr William Warren 56–7
Banks: *Bank of British North America*: elegant apartment for manager 139, 155, 159, 160; managed by Walter Cassels 122; pays excellent salaries 141; Smith solicitor for 108, 129; transfers gold from New York to Toronto 141; headquarters visited in London, England 174; *Commercial Bank* 128; *Bank of Upper Canada* 42, 60, 61, 69, 90
Barber (friend) 18
Barrie, Mrs (entertains Eliza Thom) 93
Barwicks (friends in Thornhill) 18, 30, 35, 40, 44
Beckett's (drugstore, wine merchant) 48, 110; employer of George Boyd 110
Bedbugs 18, 41, 63, 64, 65, 67, 79, 124, 152
Bell, John (a poor shot) 39
Belleville, *see* Murney, Edmund
Benson, Amy, *see* Violett, Amy Benson
Berthon, Theodore (portrait painter) 10
Bethune, Norman 79, 104, 191n
Beverley 97

Bible, Smith family records in 96, 120, 136, 176
Billings (friend) 25, 27, 34
Billings, Miss (girl left behind) 62
Black, Miss (at Mrs Robinson's party) 49
Black Regiment 55, 190n
Blake, William Hume 45, 94, 120, 131, 189n
Blitz, Signor Lyman (conjurer) 56
Bond Lake 30
Bonshaw, *see* Irving, Captain Jacob Aemilius
Book of Beauties 156–7
Books, *see* Reading
Borthwick (friend) 80
Boulton, Charles 77
Boulton, Mr and Mrs D'Arcy 51
Boulton, Harriet (friend of Eliza Smith) 142
Boulton, Henry 74, 92
Boulton, Mr H.J. (head of Niagara Commission) 67, 68
Boulton, William 45
Boulton's Racecourse 77, 78
Bowmanville 98
Boyd, Francis (closest neighbour at Richmond Hill): attractive home of 9, 10; degree of kinship with Smiths uncertain 187n; cattle imported by 10; chairs Richmond Hill meeting on Durham Report 21; owns a Holbein 10; host to militia officers 78; attends public dinner 53; on Queenston excursion 37; serves on Grand Jury 77; as justice of the peace 59; a founder of Toronto Club 22
Boyd family (Mrs Francis 'Aunt Mary,' Eleanor, Elizabeth, Mary, Frank, George, John, Walter): as neighbours 18, 30, 34, 40, 48, 52, 59, 70, 73, 78, 94, 100, 139, 187n; criticism of Smith by 159; gossip about Eliza Smith repeated by 159; Adelaide Smith's wedding arrangements 158–9
Boyd, George (partner in Beckett's, drugs, wines) 110, 136
Braham (English tenor) 69–70
Breakenridge (friend) 42
Bridgeford (friend) 40, 67
British Empire, and protection 122
Brock (friend in Niagara) 54
Brock's Monument 36, 37, 38
Brockville 124, 132, 152
Brough (in Draper's office) 42, 45, 47, 84
Brown, George (editor of the *Globe*) 131
Bucknell, Mary Charlotte Pingo, *see* Smith, Mary Charlotte
Buffalo 125, 140, 159
Bytown 93, 133, 192n

Caer Howell gardens 79, 191n
Cameron, Colin (friend of Captain and Mrs Larratt Hillary Smith) 92
Cameron, John H.: manager of Commercial Bank 130; pallbearer for Eliza Smith 154; takes charge of Smith's will 133; useful in Crooks affair 130
Cameron, Rose (Mrs John Cameron): best friend of Eliza Smith 100; New Year's Eve party 128; present at birth of Larratt Alexander 121; and Eliza's death 154, 155, 157
Canada Company 174, 194n
Canadian Rifles 116
Capreol (fined for assault) 104
Carthew, Edmund (neighbour at Richmond Hill) 21, 37, 41, 50, 51; bedbugs in home of 41; inherits fortune

107; measles in home of 57; son's death from measles 59
Carthew, Mrs Edmund 41, 107
Cassels, Richard 'Dick' (brother of Walter) 140, 153
Cassels, Walter (manager of the Bank of British North America): 'a very warm friend' 122; accompanies Smith on business and holiday trip 140–1; godfather to George Cassels Smith 136; gossip about, and Eliza Smith 139, 159; inspects Smith's new home 174; marries Adelaide Smith 157, 158, 159; shares bank apartment with Smith 132, 155, 160; shares family and social life of Smiths 131, 136, 139, 144, 145, 150, 153; usefulness as chaperone 166
Cavendish, Mr (first Toronto practitioner of mesmerism) 84
Cayuga 55
Champlain, Lake 140
Chatham 127–8
Chicago 115, 116
Cholera, see Diseases
Christie (maid at Twickenham Farm) 83–4
Church of England: Lenten customs of 101; pew renting 20; pew sharing 18, 20, 45, 48; Sunday gloom of 20
City Hall, old 100, 131
Clark, Charles (dismissed student) 148
Claus and Lyon's gardens 67, 191n
Clergy Reserves 32, 188n
Clitheroe, General 66, 190n
Clothes: fashions in wardrobes 27, 34, 48, 84, 92, 119, 193n; Smith barters clothes with Irving 43, 73; borrows from father 26; buys 26, 28, 42
Cobourg 60, 64, 151, 164, 166

Cockburn, James 51
Cockburn girls (friends at Richmond Hill) 49, 51, 73, 80
Colborne, Sir John 6, 7, 8, 9, 185n
Collins, Mrs 49
Collyers, Mrs 48
Colonial Life Assurance 113
Cotter, Colonel and Mrs (friends near Bonshaw) 43, 44
Couchiching, Lake 8
Cox, Miss (at Thornhill party) 30
Cozens, Mrs (godmother to Mrs Draper's fourth daughter) 22, 92
Creighton's, Captain, counter irritant (ointment) 62
Crest, Smith family 3, 77, 109, 185n
Cronyn, Rev. Benjamin (St Paul's Church, London) 128
Crooks, Robert: law partner in Smith, Crooks & Smith 95; partner in Crooks & Smith 104, 129, 130; 'that fellow Crooks' 138
Crooks & Smith (second law partnership) 104, 129–30
Crookshank, George, and sister: entertained by Smiths 105; members of Adelaide's wedding party 159; family vault, temporary resting place for coffin of Eliza 154
Crozier (bandmaster of 81st Regiment) 113
Cull (friend) 80
Currie, Mrs (housekeeper) 96, 99

Daguerrean Gallery 136, 193n
D'Alton, Captain (and amateur theatricals) 86
Dalrymple, Sir Hew (commandant, New Fort) 138, 148
Dancing 26, 35, 119, 168, 188n; Smith

as bachelor 35, 41, 59, 64, 70, 73, 80, hornpipe 41; balls and dances 47, 74, 92
Davenport, Miss (actress) 19
David's Temple 75, 191n
Davis, Edward 26
Davis, Mrs (housekeeper) 23–4, 33
Dean and Forests' Theatrical Company 81
De Coo's Tavern 55, 190n
Deer Park, home of Colonel and Mrs Heath 27, 188n
Deering's Theatre 86
Dickens, Charles 58, 77, 78
Diseases: cholera 132, 133; 'hooping' cough 157; influenza 161; measles 57–9; scarlet fever 49; typhus fever 114, 117
Dixon's (post office) 27
Dodsworth (landlord, shoemaker) 26, 27, 41, 48, 49
Dolly's Chop House (Montreal) 141
Downs, Captain and Mrs (hosts at Niagara) 67, 68, 69
Draper, Augusta (Mrs William Henry Draper): background of 20; birth of seventh child 77; encourages Smith's singing talent 20; lends unhelpful pony 81; music copied for 71, 81; sharp note written to Smith by 82; party-going by 30; parties given by 47, 70, 71; piano moved for, by army fatigue party 82; social advice to Smith given by 26; visits Mr Draper in Kingston 72
Draper, Caroline Matilda 77
Draper, William Henry: accepts Smith as articled student 14, 20; appointed attorney-general 34; on Eastern Circuit 42; entertains Sir Charles Bagot 76; inherits large sum 108; gazetted judge, Court of the Queen's Bench 113; gives sons Shetland pony 69; improves office heating system 82; moves to Kingston with government 60; pallbearer for Eliza Smith 154; persuasive speaker ('Sweet William') 14; returns from Kingston 82; shares church pew 20, 45, 48; speaks in debate on Union of Canadas 27
Drummondville 54, 55, 56, 143
Duelling 17, 65, 93
Dunlop's restaurant 48, 49
Durham Report 21, 187n
Dyett (friend) 52, 58, 62

Eagle and Protector (insurance) 133
Eighty-First Regiment, 'the red coats' 112, 113
Elgin, Lord 109, 113, 116, 131, 132, 135, 192n; dinner given by 138; and Lady Elgin 152–3
Ellen (maid at Benje's) 65
Erie, Lake 55, 114–15
Exhibition at Crystal Palace, London 173

Family Compact 57
Fashions, *see* Clothes
Financial affairs (Smith's): as bachelor 16, 24, 25, 26, 32, 33, 40, 41, 47, 69; as married man 101, 102, 103, 107, 112, 129; financial security established 162, 169
Financial transactions in Upper Canada: coins used 30, 188n; exchange rates 119–20; funds, transfer of 122–3; gold and silver, bank use of 123; land deals, by exchange 120, by

lottery 108; specie, transfer of 140–1; taxes on wild lands 113, 150
Finch's Tavern (on Yonge Street) 19, 26, 46–78 *passim*, 186n
Fitzgibbon, Colonel James: attractive Toronto house of 17; military record of 16, 186n; moves to Kingston with government officers 63; returns to England 16
Fitzgibbons (three brothers, friends): attended Upper Canada College 17; companions in Happy Go Lucky Club 16, 17, 18, 19, 27, 35, 49; special dinner for James 36; sister 17
Fletcher, Mr (on phrenology) 78–9
Forty Mile Creek 54, 56, 190n
Fortye, Anna 99; and husband 100
Foster, Miss (at Robinsons' dance) 47
Front Street, cottage on (home of Larratt and Eliza Smith): description of 95; enlargement of 132, 134, 139; domestic arrangements of 102; domestic chores at 100, 103; furniture bought for 96; gardening at 102, 131; laundering at 150; livestock at 95, 103; owner of 95; rent of 95; rent raised 132; servants in 96, 99, 102, 121–2, 134; supplies bought for 95–6, 103

Galt, Thomas 62
Gamble, Clarke 74, 84
Gapper, Mr and Mrs (friends in Richmond Hill) 26, 29, 35, 73; bring Adelaide back from England 149
Garrison Common 15, 25; cottage on (bachelor home of Smith): discomforts of 19, 24, 34; entertaining in 40; furnishings of 15, 25; known as Happy Go Lucky Club 17, 23, 29, 40;

housekeeping in 16, 22, 23, 25, 28; owner of 14; rent of 16; servants in 23, 24, 28, 33; rows in 27; shared with Hind brothers 15, 16; vacating of 40, 41; *see also* under Fitzgibbons, Hind, Jarvis
Garrison Players 86
Garrison Wharf 27, 48, 153, 160
Gas: introduced 73, 194n; great gas illumination 74, 132; luxury in Cassels' apartment 160
Gildersleeves (friends of Murneys in Kingston) 171
Gilkison, Mrs David (landlady, singing teacher) 70, 86, 88; and mesmerism 84; misfortunes of, 'per usual' 71, 77, 86, 87; husband 87
Gillespie (chancery clerk, Smith, Crooks & Smith) 101, 107
Grand River 55
Grasett, Bayley 58
Grasett, Rev. Henry 58; marries Larratt and Minnie Smith 176
Greenland Fishery (tavern) 14
Greenwich, England (home of Smith wine merchants) 13, 173
Green Room (at Summer Hill) 101

Hagerman, Christopher Alexander 17, 23, 31–32, 35, 88, 107, 109, 192n; last illness 109; son's shocking behaviour 109
Hagerman, Mary Jane (Mrs John Beverley Robinson) 22, 192n
Hale (in Hamilton) 31
Hamilton 54, 128
Hamilton Amateurs 101
Hamilton, Dr 117
Hamilton, Hon. John 187n
Happy Go Lucky Club 17, 23, 29, 40

Harrington (in Draper's office) 54
Harris, Rev. Joseph (principal of Upper Canada College) 9
Harris, Parson Michael (Perth): marries Eliza Thom and Larratt Smith 97–8; kites flown by 152; Larratt Alexander christened by 120
Harris, Susan (Eliza's bridesmaid) 93
Harvey, Jane (friend of newly-wed Smiths) 100
Head, Sir Francis Bond 12, 25
Heath, Miss (at Robinsons' party) 47
Heath, Mrs (owner of Deer Park) 57
Henderson, 'old' (at Davidtown) 51
Henderson, Sarah (Davidtown) 32, 51
Hennessy, John (soldier servant) 134
Hepburn, Mr and Mrs (friends) 25, 34
Heward, Augustus (friend at Regatta) 80
Heward, Mr and Mrs (friends of Captain and Mrs Smith) 43, 79
Hill, George (farm near Bonshaw) 43, 44
Hincks, Sir Francis 55, 190n
Hind, Edward and Thomas: co-founders, Happy Go Lucky Club 17; cottage-mates on Garrison Common 14, 16, 19, 27, 30, 40, 58; friendship with Smith 42, 43, 48, 53; visits to Hinds' farm 36, and Twickenham Farm 30, 34, 40; work in government offices 16, 33, 57, 58, 62, 75; sister 25
Hirschfelder, Jacob (musical friend) 79, 191n
Hocken, Miss (amateur singer) 87
Hodder, Dr Edward Mulberry (family physician) 105, 106, 136, 142, 154
Holland Landing 8, 43, 44
Home District 9, 185n
Hotels, inns, taverns of Upper Canada, visited by Smith: American Hotel, Kingston 151; Barrington's Hotel, Niagara 54; Benley's Hotel, Hamilton 54; Dafoe House, Belleville 163; Dayfoot's Tavern, Forty Mile Creek 56; De Coo's Tavern, Cayuga 55; Doran's Hotel, Bytown 133; Dulmage's Hotel, Kingston 97; Fralick's Inn, Drummondville 55; Hastwell's Hotel, Beverley 97; Neptune Inn, Niagara 67; Newmarket Inn, Newmarket 51; Prince Albert Hotel, Windsor 127; Royal Exchange Hotel, Chatham 128; Western Hotel, London 128; *see also* Toronto, hotels
Howe, Joseph 149, 194n
Hunter's Lodges 32, 37
Huron, Lake 114–15
Hyde (music teacher) 38

Immigrants 111–12
Irving, Aemilius 'Hickory' (friend with variations): arrival in Canada with family 22; betting of 47, 48; birthday dinner of 58; boards with Smith at Upper Canada College 22; at Dodsworth's 45; at Duffill's 52; almost fights duel with Smith 65; financial transactions of 43, 48, 53; frequent companion of Smith 43, 52, 60, 64, 65, 70, 75; hasty temper of 44, 48–9; insolence of 65; and Smith's infatuation with sister, *see* Irving, Miss D.; reckless driving and riding of 75; visits England and West Indies 32, 122
Irving, Miss D. 43, 51–4, 57, 59, 61, 64, 72–82 *passim*
Irving, Captain Jacob Aemilius: background and characteristics 22, 43;

Bonshaw, home near Newmarket 22, 43, 44, 51, 61, 73, 75; at cattle show, Toronto 44; expert with horses 43, 44; gracious host 44, 72; justice of the peace 59; a founder of Toronto Club 22

Irving, Mrs Jacob Aemilius 43, 53, 70, 72

Island, Toronto 38, 49, 80, 145

Jacques and Hay (furniture) 96

Jameson (vice-chancellor of Upper Canada) 138

Jarvis, Augusta 60

Jarvis brothers: companions at Happy Go Lucky Club and at home 18, 25, 35, 36, 43, 53, 58, 59, 64; *George*: forgets invitation 45, 48; raffles pony on steps of Ontario House 49; plays violin 51; *William* 85–6; boat owner 42, 43, 59; at birthday party at Twickenham Farm 30; junior to Smith in Draper's law office 31; marries D. Irving 76; *Samuel*: in law office of Christopher Hagerman 31; tries making latire 27, 188n; at party at Twickenham Farm 52

Jarvis, Samuel Peters 17

Jarvis, Sheriff (father of George, William, and Samuel) 18, 94

Jones, Jonas (judge) 23, 84

June & Company's Oriental Circus & Menagerie 145

Keefer, Thomas Coltrin (schoolmate at Upper Canada College) 16, 31–2, 188n

Kelly, Frederick 48

Kemble, Fanny 139

Kent, John (friend, journalist, schoolteacher) 186n; family friendship with 9, 18, 71, 78, 88; helped in duelling incident 65; letters to, from Smith 160, 163; headmaster, Upper Canada College preparatory school 9

King's College 87–8, 116, 137; chapel 120

Kingsmill, Charles 'Charlie' (schoolmate) 31

Kingston 60, 62–3, 96, 125, 190n; cholera in 133

Kingston Mills 97

Kinnear, Thomas (landlord on Garrison Common) 14, 15, 186n

Lake steamers, *see* Shipping

Larratt, Mary, *see* Smith, Mary Larratt

Latire 27, 120, 188n

Lees, two Miss 30

Legal activities (Smith's) *as articled student*: articled to Draper 14; education 14, 21, 42, 44; attending court 22, 23, 45, 46, 77; carrying Writ of Election 54; in charge of Crown Docket 25, 34, 82, 86, 88, 192n; clerk to Draper 34, 42; out-of-town trips 29, 54–6; clerk of Niagara Commission 66, 67, 68, 191n; office jobs 17, 18, 25, 30, 42, 45, 61, 63, 86, 88, 192n; *as practising lawyer*: appointed Notary Public 108; out-of-town business trips 127–8, 147; special business plus holiday trip with Walter Cassels 140–1; moves to new offices 101, 107; setting up individual practice 144, 147; appointed solicitor to Bank of British North America 108, to Colonial Assurance Company 113; taking on articled students 147; working long hours in office 129, 130; *see also* Smith, Crooks & Smith; Crooks & Smith; Wilson & Smith; *law career* 186n, later years 194n; Smith on law and lawyers 147, 162

Lett, Rev. Stephen: christens George Cassels Smith 136; and wet nurse's child 137; at deathbed of Eliza 154; objects furiously to the polka 168

Lewis (pianos) 112

Lewiston, New York 67, 68

Lind, Jenny 141, 152, 153

Lodgings (Smith's): Bell's 89; Benje's 63, 65, 66, 79; Dodsworth's 41, 46, 49, 52; Mrs Duffill's 52, 60; Mrs Gilkison's 86, 88; Mrs Howe's 79; King's 88, 89; Wallis's 95

London (Canada) 128

London (England) 173, 174

Loring (friend) 17, 19

Lower Canada, possible uprising in 123; Smith on 123

Lyndhurst, home of Mr and Mrs Frederick Widder 80, 175

Lyon's Cottage 89, 90, 92

Macara (unsatisfactory client) 104, 109

McCaul, Rev. John (scholar and administrator) 187n; examines Smith for admission to King's College 87, 89; tries to assist Smith in job hunting 145; consulted about Latin lines on Eliza Smith's tombstone 156; involved in university politics 120; pallbearer for Eliza 154

McCormack (friend) 68

Macdonald, Sir John A., *see* Ridgeway affair

McDonald's Wharf 59

McDonnell, Alexander (schoolmaster at Upper Canada College) 17, 19, 42, 95

McDonnell, I.S. 146

MacKenzie (friend) 61, 65, 66, 74

Mackenzie, William Lyon 12, 32, 131, 139

McKyrs, B. (at St Catherines) 54

McLean, Judge (friend) 138, 139

McLeod's Tavern (Yonge Street) 29

McMicken (returning officer at Queenston) 54

MacNab, Sir Allan Napier 46, 63, 189n

Mail: arrangements for sending 45, 47, 109, 113, 126, 132; cost of 18; damage to 24, 122; problems of 96, 116, 119, 126

Malden 127

Markham 21, 32

Matthews, Rev. Charles Stephen (teacher at Upper Canada College) 31, 188n

Mesmerism 84

Metcalfe, Sir Charles 91

Michigan, Lake 114–15

Michillimackinac, Fort 115

Mill of Ogle (Scottish home of greatgrandfather) 4

Mills Livery Stable 77

Mob action, *see* Violence

Moffat, Mary Jane (daughter of owner of Neptune Inn, Niagara) 67

Moffat, Mrs (godmother, Mrs Draper's child) 77

Montreal 131, 132, 140, 141

Moodie, Georgina ('pretty friendly') 41

Morris, Hon. James 124

Morrison, Judge Joseph Curran 146

Mountain, Bishop George Jehoshaphat (in Quebec) 140

Muirhead, Deborah (in Niagara) 67, 68, 69
Murchison's (tailor) 26, 42
Murney, Edmund (father of Isobel): affluence of 163; Belleville home of, visited by Smith 163, 166, 169; influence and importance of 169; large family of 163; inducements to persuade Isobel to marry Smith 172
Murney, Mrs Edmund: boyhood acquaintance of Smith 169; corresponds regularly 169; described enthusiastically by Smith 170; entertains Smith at Old Orchard Beach 170; guest at Spragge home in Toronto 163, 172; letter to, from Smith 165; matchmaking of 165, 168, 170, 172; receives gifts from Smith 171
Murney, Isobel: age of 164; attractions of 163, 169; choice of as second wife defended by Smith 169, 170; first meeting with Smith 163; immaturity of 167, 169, 170; at Mrs McNally's School 165, 166; pursued by Smith 169–72; singing lessons of 165, 166
Murney, Mrs (friend of Mrs Thom) 96, 98
Murray (friend) 51
Music: popular 53, 61, 64, 81, 113; Smith plays violin 34, 41, 42; *singing* (Smith, counter tenor): in amateur theatricals 86, 137; at amateur and charity concerts 87, 135, 165; in choral groups 20, 22; in church as choir member and soloist 20, 35, 175; concerts 100, 153; with friends 44, 51, 56, 58, 59, 64, 68; singing and piano lessons 38

Nelles, Warner 55
New York 7, 90, 123
Newmarket 41, 51
Niagara 25, 54, 127; falls 112, 114, 143; river 37, 188n
Nichol (friend in Niagara) 54
Nichol, Dr 151, 153, 154
Nichol, Mrs 137
Nordheimer's (pianos) 160

Ocean steamers, *see* Shipping
Oddfellow's Lodge 138
Old Orchard Beach, Maine 170
Oliver's Ferry 124
Ontario, Lake 7, 15, 55, 95, 147; *see also* Shipping
Opodeldoc (patent liniment) 62, 190n
Orangemen 21, 69, 79
Orillia, *see* Oro
Oro, Township of (first Canadian home of Captain and Mrs Smith) 7, 8, 9
Osgoode Hall 58–9, 139; barracks 79
Oshawa 151
Oswego 7, 125

Paget, Mrs (friend of Mary Violett Smith) 26
Papineau, Louis-Joseph 32, 120, 123
Paris, France 173–4
Parsons, Harriet, John, Mr and Mrs 24, 28, 30, 59, 64, 73, 187n
Paton, Mr (inspector, Bank of British North America) 141
Patrick ('our man') 41, 49
Perth (home of Dr and Mrs Alexander Thom): difficult to get to 96–7, 151–2; and to leave 104, 124–5, 152; holiday visits to, by the Smiths 103, 124,

132, 151; home for Smith's sons after mother's death 160; location of 93; Smith's marriage to Eliza Thom 97–8
Philadelphia 149
Port Hope 151
Potter, Helena (cook) 133, 134
Powell, Harry (subaltern in Black Regiment) 55
Powell, John (mayor) 32
Powell, William 25
Price, 'the Reformer' 57
Prices, sampling of: coal 134, 193n; concert ticket (Jenny Lind) 153; brandy 42; dress coat 42; drinking warer delivered 103; excursion to Niagara 114; fares, ocean crossings 141, 142; fee for wet nurse 121; fishing rod 66; flour 161; gardener 102, 131; head reading (phrenology) 79; hotel rooms in Paris 173; man's hat 78; lodgings 41, 63; meat 161; notices delivered by hand 155; oats (horses) 92; piano 112, 160; potatoes 107; red stockings 27; rent for cottage 16, 95, 132, for house 161, for office 113; servicing cow 103; sheet music 53; whisky 148; wood 134; wages of servants 96, 102, 121, 134; spy glass 68; teapot mended 102
Primrose family (friends) 41, 43–4, 49, 78, 79

Quebec 7, 132, 140; cholera in 133
Quebec Industrial Exhibition (in Montreal) 141
Quebeckers 141
Queen Victoria 11–12, 35–6
Queen's Own Regiment 120
Queen's Wharf 15
Queenston 37, 54, 55; Heights 32, 36, 37

Racquets Club, burlesque sport at 45
Radenhursts (friends) 56, 59, 76, 79, 81, 93
Railroads: Grand Trunk, first trip of 171; Smith's interest in 149, 167; 'two railroads running into Toronto' 160; Simcoe, Ontario and Huron (later Northern) 152; sod turning by Lady Elgin 152; Toronto and Hamilton, opening of 167
Reading (Smith, non-legal texts) 48, 49, 71, 74, 77, 78, 163; buys books 45, 70–1; books as presents 71; mislays *Faerie Queen* 162
Rebellion in the Canadas 11
Rebellion Losses Bill 131
Religious observances (Smith): churchgoing 27, 28, 34, 35, 42, 44, 48, 59, 71, 83, 96, 128, 140, 159, *see also* St George's, St James', Church of England; prayers at home 24, 46, 59, 70, 78, 99, 154
Richey's Methodist Chapel (visited with Rattan, a friend) 48
Richmond Hill 8, 15, 17, 18, 21, 29, 30, *passim*
Rideau: canal 93; lake 97; river 112
Ridgeway affair 120–1
Ridout, Georgina (friend) 79, 80
Ridout, John 17
Ridout's (hardware) 25, 187n
Rifle Brigade 116, 118, 125–6
Riots, *see* Violence
Robinson, Christopher 36
Robinson, John Beverley (second son of chief justice) 47, 192n; marries Mary Jane Hagerman 113–14

Robinson, Sir John Beverley (chief justic) 77, 88, 109
Robinson Mrs, later Lady (wife of chief justice) 47
Rogers, Miss (girl left behind) 62
Rooster, Tom (servant boy) 102
Rowsell's Library 45, 189n
Russell (tailor) 84

St Catherines 54, 56
St George's Church 131, 145, 151, 154, 156, 159, 175, 193n
St George's Society 76
St George's Square, house on (first home of Larratt and Minnie Smith): building of 172, 174; dull existence for widower in 176–7; first party in 177; shopping in England for 174
St James' Cemetery 105, 120; Eliza's monument 156, 162
St James' Church (later Cathedral) 20, 35, 39, 44, 71, 77, 131
Sampson (friend) 42
Sandwich 127
Sandwich Lands 19, 188n
Sanford, Ephraim (great-grandfather of Minnie Smith) 176
Savigny (treasurer of St George's Society) 76
Saxon (friend, likes theatre) 79, 81
Scadding 66
Schioghoff (juggler) 36
Schools for girls in Toronto: Mrs Blake's 26, 27, 29, 59; Mrs McNally's 165–6; Mrs Rankin's 87, 90; education of Canadian girls 170
Scott's (grocers) 30
Servants: availability of 10; duties of 10, 134; 'frolicking' with 65; problems with 33, 60; frequent changing of 102, 134; see also under Front Street and Garrison Common cottages
Sewell, Dr James 79, 85, 191n
Sharpe, Mrs and Miss (friends) 30, 73
Shaw, George and William 22
Shaw, Miss 81
Sherwood, Judge Henry 66
Shipping: *lake*: extensive use of 21, 24, 25, 37, 39, 42, 47, 59, 60, 62, 63, 67, 107n; first sight of propellor boat 79; Island run 131, 151; party ship for regatta 80–1, 83, 90, 94, 109, 112, 153; bad weather for 25, 39, 42, 83, 100, 109, 113, 124–5, 127–8; *ocean* 18, 149, 173, 174; crossing times of 111, 126, 149, 173; fares of 141, 142
Simcoe, Lake 8, 9, 38
Skerrett's Company (of actors) 112
Smith, Adelaide (sister, later Mrs Walter Cassels): arrives in Canada 7, 8; at Mrs Rankin's school 87, 90; concert treat arranged by Smith 87; departs for England 93, 94; European education 94, 149; returns to Canada to visit Smiths 149; teaches Larratt Alexander 149–50; wedding 157–60, 166
Smith, Bernard (nephew in England) 3, 4, 8, 12, 13, 185n
Smith, Eliza Caroline (née Thom), (first wife): background 92, 93; courtships 93–4; marriage 97–8; active as young matron 100, 101, 112, 153; attends husband's amateur performances 100, 135; avoids letter writing 121; bandmaster's tribute to 113; bears three sons 105, 120, 136; church-going of 100, 128, 131; death of baby son 105; described by husband 121, 156–7; fond of father-in-

law 121; entertains friends 100, 105, 124, 129, 131, 144, 148, 150; gossip busy with 139; helps soldier's wife 126; inherits from brother 139, from father 102; miscarriage 142, 144; stays with Rose Cameron 128; suffers from colds 106, 138, 153, from mastitis 106, 137, from facial rheumatism 151, from sickness in pregnancy 114, 120; travels with husband 112, 115, 132; undaunted by pregnancy 105, 136; visited by mother 140, by sister 117; visits to Perth, see Perth; death 154; monument 156, 162

Smith, George (Scottish great-grandfather) 4

Smith, Goerge (Scottish grandfather) 4

Smith, George (uncle in England) 4; business (wine merchant) and home in Greenwich 12, 13; offers place in firm to Smith brothers 12; suicide of 13, 88

Smith, Aunt George (in England): on generosity of 110, with reservations 141; debt owed to 95, 110; Indian gifts sent to 117; letter to 107–8; unkind remarks made by 149; visited in England 173

Smith, George (brother): arrives in Canada 7; attends Upper Canada College 7; future decided by father and uncle 12, 18; leaves for England 21; letter from 13; letters to 109–10, 115, 116–17; marriage of 13; succeeds as wine merchant 13; takes Smith to exhibition at Crystal Palace 173

Smith, George Cassels 'Georgey' (third son): birth and christening 136; death 136; disposition at two 157;

'hooping' cough 157; with grandmother in Perth 160; with father and grandmother in Toronto 174–5; school 136, 177

Smith, Isobel Wilson (great-grandmother) 4

Smith, James Frederick (father-in-law) 176, 177

Smith, John Shuter (senior partner in Smith, Crooks & Smith) 95, 99, 104, 107

Smith, Captain Larratt Hillary (father) 3, 4; army background 4; and battle of Queenston Heights 5; bride found in Bordeaux, France 6; characteristics of 5, 10, 20; first choice of land not a good one 7; buys Twickenham Farm at Richmond Hill 9, 10; visits Toronto from farm 26, 27, 29, 40–1, 70, 78, 80, 81, 86; director, Bank of Upper Canada 61; a founder of Toronto Club 22; godfather to grandson Larratt Alexander 120; letter from 126–7; letters to 106, 108, 113, 119, 121, 124, 144, 158, 169, 170; objects to Isobel Murney as daughter-in-law 170; organizes future of son George 12, 18; present at Richmond Hill meeting on Durham Report 21; serves in militia 12; on Grand Jury 9, 77; shares interests with son: circuses 40, concert-going 69, phrenology 78–9, regattas 80, theatre 86, 89; sightseeing in Buffalo 125, in Paris 173–4; sudden return to England 89; trusts son's judgment in business matters 30, 77, 89–90; unannounced visit from England 125; visited by Smith in England 173–4; see also Twickenham Farm

Smith, Larratt William Violett ('young Mr Smith'): arrives in Canada 7; composes prize-winning poem 11, 179–84; education (general), Upper Canada College 7, 11–12, King's College 87, 88, 95, 189n; youthful visit to England 12; enlists in militia 12, 37, 38, 78; family rows about future 12, 13, 141; firefighting (volunteer) 48, 61, 66, 70; fond of cats 16, 18, 22, 68; visits to Twickenham Farm 24, 29, 34, 46, 64–86 *passim*; chores at farm 21, 40, 63, 64; and personal hygiene 27, 33, 34, 49, 60, 71, 76, 102; and infatuation with Miss Irving, *see* Irving, Miss D.

Life as bachelor: boating 42, 43, 59, 64, 79, regatta 80–1; cricket 18, 103; circuses 40, 79; drinking 33, 35, 58, 78, 79; duelling 17, 65; 'frolicking' 65; Olympic Games 15; picnics 68; playing cards 18, 22, 24, 33, 44, 48; 'playing the fool' 20, 48, 62, with doorknockers 63, 64; sailing 42, 49; shooting 19, 26, 38, 42, 44, at unexpected targets 29, 35, 75; skating 49, 73; sleighriding 27, 33, 34, 73; swinging the ladies 59; entertaining at cottage, expenses of 40; special dinner 36; being entertained in homes of friends 17, 25, 35, 41, 48–79 *passim*; paying calls 21, 26, 47, 60, 92; record number of calls 92; 'quite tired of parties' 32; home as bachelor, *see* Garrison Common

Married life with Eliza Thom: ceremony in Perth 97, 98; difficult arrival and departure 96, 98; three children born 105–6, 120, 136; home, *see* Front Street cottage; death of first son 105; elections as pro vice chancellor 137, 138, 146; family outings 139, 145, 151, 153; fire in offices 101, 107; dinners 138, 139, 149; fishing 103, 140; party-going 112, 117, 118–19, 128, 136, 137, 145; picnics 145; sight-seeing with father 125, with Walter Cassels 140; holiday trips to Bytown 133, Montreal 132, Niagara Falls 114, Port Credit 112, Quebec 132, tour of Great Lakes 114–15, *see also* Perth; job hunting 145–6; life insured and will made 133; management of father's Canadian affairs 89–91, 108, 113, 119–20, 122; management of Mrs Thom's affairs, *see* Thom, Mrs; militia activities 148; unannounced visit from Captain Smith 125; visit from Adelaide Smith 149; wife's last illness and death 153–4, 155–6

Life as widower: shares Bank apartment with Cassels 155; with Adelaide and Walter Cassels 160; children live with Mrs Thom in Perth 157, 160, 162, 169; designs monument for Eliza 156; follows mourning customs 159, 162; leaves off mourning 172; pursues Isobel Murney 169–72; quarrels with Boyd family 158–9; resents gossip 159; new house, *see* St George's Square; sons and Mrs Thom brought to Toronto 174–5; Mrs Widder and matchmaking 175; visits England and France 173–4

Marriage to Minnie Smith: wedding 176; eleven children born 178; St George's Square first home 178; Summer Hill second home 178; wedding journey, uses railroad 177;

Smith on second marriages 162, 169
  See also Clothes, Dancing, Financial affairs, Legal activities, Lodgings, Music, Reading, Religious observances, Theatre
Smith, Larratt (first-born son) 105, 106
Smith, Larratt Alexander 'Lal' (second son): birth, christening, and confirmation 120; death 120; disposition at four 157; health and energy of 136; 'hooping' cough 157; with grandmother in Perth 160; with grandmother and father in Toronto 174–5; school 177; serves (later) in militia, Queen's Own Regiment 120
Smith, Mary (sister): at Mrs Blake's school 26; called on at school by Smith 31, 41, 42, 44, 57; celebrating marriage of queen 36; go-between with Miss Irving 53, 59; to dentist 41; guest at Bonshaw 72; hostess to Miss Irving at Twickenham Farm 64; returns to England 93–4; sleigh rides with Eliza and Larratt 93
Smith, Mary Charlotte (sister-in-law in London): cork fortune of 13; 'expansive' letters of 121; Indian gifts for 117; large family of 13
Smith, Mary Elizabeth 'Minnie' (second wife) 165, 176–8
Smith, Mary Larratt (Irish grandmother) 4
Smith, Mary Sandford (mother of Minnie Smith) 176
Smith, Mary Violett (mother): background and Bordeaux girlhood 5, 6; arrives in Upper Canada 7; as pioneer 8, 9, 10; second home at Twickenham Farm 9; illness of 18; letter from 149–50; social etiquette of 94; portrait of 10; may be reason behind duelling incident 65; rejoins husband in England 93, 95; sends supplies to family members in Toronto 19, 21, 26, 29, 42; Sunday School classes of 8, 46; visits Toronto occasionally from Twickenham Farm 26, 29, 41; stays briefly in Toronto 93; wants Adelaide to marry in England 157; wants to bring up grandson in England 150; wants Larratt to remarry 162
Smith, Violett Georgina (daughter) 3, 8
Smith, William (uncle) 4
Smith, Crooks & Smith (first law partnership): arrangements for partnership 95; busy days for junior partner 99; fire in offices 100–1; funds borrowed from Aunt George Smith 95; partnership dissolving 101, 104
Smith's (grocers) 27, 42
Smythe, Patrick (Eliza Smith's grandfather) 93
Smythe, Thomas (possible ancestor) 3
Snook (farmer) 29
Southampton (English home of Captain and Mrs Smith) 90, 93, 94
Spragge, Catherine Thom 'Kate' (Eliza Smith's half-sister) 93; bears twins, boy dies 102; estrangement from Smiths 139; friendship with Smiths 100, 104, 105; large party 119; and Eliza's last illness 154; hostess to newly-wed Smiths 98, 99; pregnant and ill 157; takes Minnie Smith to housewarming in St George's Square 177
Spragge, Godfrey John (married to Catherine Thom): estranged from Smiths 139; gardening of 102; home damaged by fire 104; home near cot-

Index / 213

tage on Front Street 99; host to mother-in-law, Mrs Thom 96, to Murneys 163, 172, to newly-wed Smiths 98, 99; on Queenston excursion 37; takes Walter Cassels and Smith to Great Railroad Dinner 149; vice chancellor of Upper Canada 99
Stanton, Caroline 116, 119
Stanton, James 77
Steamers, see Shipping
Steer, Miss (at Jarvis's party) 35
Stevenson (friend in Niagara) 54
Stewart, 'Pollywog' and wife (friends) 73
Stowe, Montague 48, 58
Stowe family 57, 59, 60, 80
Strachan, John 46, 70, 76, 87, 88, 117, 137, 138
Stratton, Charles Sherwood, see Tom Thumb
Street, Thomas 55, 56, 58, 61, 62, 65
Street family (Drummondville) 55, 56
Stuart, George Okill (archdeacon of Kingston) 39
Sullivan, Augustus (photographer) 168
Summer Hill (second home of Larratt and Minnie Smith) 5, 17, 101, 120

Tarbutt (friend) 52, 58, 62
Taverns, see Hotels
Tay River 93
Taylor, Zachary 127
Telfer, Dr 79
Telegraph, electric 111, 114, 131, 139, 154, 169
Theatre (Smith): joins Toronto Amateurs (Civilians) Company 20; amateur acting 86, 87, 100, 101, 109, 137; guest actor with Garrison Players 86; theatre-going 20, in Buffalo 125, in Detroit 127, in London, England 173–4, in Paris 174, in Syracuse 140, in Toronto 19, 40, 79, 81, 86, 100, 112, 150, 153, 168
Thom, Alexander (brother-in-law) 93; companion on fishing trips 103; death 128; godfather to Larratt Alexander 120; leaves no will 133, 139
Thom, Dr Alexander (father of Eliza Smith) 92, 93, 96
Thom, Mrs Betsy Smythe (second wife of Dr Alexander Thom, Smith's mother-in-law) 93; accident of 112; business affairs managed by Smith 96, 133, 150–2, 161; cares for grandsons at Perth 160–2; godmother to Larratt Alexander 120; guest of stepdaughter in Toronto 96, and of daughter 140; inspects Mr Chickley's Grammar School at Barrie 177; letters to 147, 150–1, 161; makes home in Toronto with Smith and grandsons 174–5; packs for return to Perth 177
Thom, Caroline (sister-in-law) 93; characteristics of 117; godmother to George Cassels Smith 136; inherits with Eliza 150–1; letters to 162, 168; lives with mother in Perth 151, 152; visits Smiths in Toronto 117, 135, 137, 145
Thom, Catherine, see Spragge
Thom, Eliza, see Smith, Eliza Caroline
Thom, Harriet Smythe (first wife of Dr Alexander Thom) 93
Thomson, Charles Poulett (Baron Sydenham) 22, 24, 25, 34, 69, 187n
Thomson, Miss (friend of Mary Violett Smith) 86

Thomson, Mr (of Indiana) 55
Thorne, Mr (of Thornhill, friend of Captain and Mrs Smith) 24, 29, 30, 67, 68, 73
Thorne and Barwick 108
Thornhill 18, 24, 28, 30; violence feared 57
Tinnings Wharf 59
Toilet facilities: at cottage on Front Street 103; at Rifle Brigade Ball 118
Tom Thumb, General 123
Toothbrushes, use of 102
Toronto 111, 160; cattle show in 43; fire hazard in 100; flooded bridges in 137; spectator sports in 53, 54, 77; *fires*: old City Hall 131; two squares of Yonge Street 131; St James' Church 131; Shelden and Deutcher's foundry 61; Sheriff's Distillery 66; Smith, Crooks & Smith (offices) 102, 107; Godfrey Spragge's house 104; Webb and Barwick 101; section of Yonge and Newgate streets 61; *garrisons*: amateur acting of officers 86; bands play in churches 20, 39, 48, in public places 39, at private parties 30, 47, 60; important effect on Toronto 32, 89; matrimonial rules for 62; results of rules 62; provide fatigue parties and servants for private citizens 82, 134; serenading officers of 86; *hotels and taverns*: Black Swan Inn 44–5, 53; City Hotel 40; Ellah's Hotel 135, 153, 193n; Mansion Hotel 61, 190n; North American Hotel 53, 81, 86, 190n; Ontario House (later Wellington Hotel) 21, 26, 49, 53; Paterson's 56; Stowe's Hotel 91; Finch's Tavern 19, 26, 46–78 *passim*, 186n; Greenland Fishery 14; McLeod's Tavern 29; Stewart's Tavern 60; *newspapers*: *British Colonist* 59, 108, 113, 190n; *Globe* 119, 137; *Toronto Herald* 58, 116; *tollgates*: Cook's 53; Lot Street 42; Thorn Hill 81; Yonge Street 62; Yorkville 26
Toronto Bay, rescue from 80
Toronto Civilians Theatrical Company (amateur) 87, 137
Toronto Club 22
Toronto Debating Club 86
Townley, Parson (at Thornhill) 70, 86, 191n
Trinity College 138
Turquand, Miss (at Robinsons' dance) 47
Twickenham Farm (second Canadian home of Captain and Mrs Smith) 9; annual parties at 50, 52, 73, 85; attractive appearance of 9, 10; birthday party for Captain Smith at 30, for Larratt Smith 71; Christmas Day at 49, 50; haying at 40; hospitality of 58; move from 90; passenger pigeons at 38; pig-killing at 29; sale of 89, 90,
Typhus fever, *see* Diseases

Union, Upper and Lower Canada 27, 53
University of King's College 87, 88
University of Toronto 138
Upper Canada College 17, 22, 27, 31, 34, 75, 76; fees of 9; founding of 7; subjects taught at 9, 11

Vankoughnet, Philip 154
Vaughan: Hunter's Lodge held at 32; meeting on Durham Report 21, 71

Violence: after Durham Report meeting 21; in Montreal 131; at Thornhill 57; in Toronto 58
Violett, Amy Benson (maternal grandmother) 5
Violett, Mary, *see* Smith, Mary Violett
Violett, Robert (maternal uncle in France) 5, 6
Violett, Sr, Robert (maternal grandfather) 5
Violett, William (cousin in England) 110
Violett, Sr, William (maternal uncle in England) 66, 110; letter to 110–11; visited by Smith 173

Wacousta (novel) 115
Wakefield's Book Auction 70–1
Wallach, James William (actor) 112
Webb and Barwick (fire) 101
Westmacott ('shabby' host) 18
Wet-nurses 121–2, 124, 137
Widder, Frederick (commissioner of Canada Company) 175
Widder, Mrs Frederick: daughter's death 130; entertaining by 80, 191n; home of 80, 175; matchmaking of 175
Widder, Miss 175
Widmer, Dr Christopher (landlord, Front Street) 69, 95, 132
Wilkinson, Dr 33–4

Whitby 146, 147
White, Miss (at Thornhill party) 30
Wilgress (friend) 71, 79, 80
Wilson, Adam, later Sir Adam (former law partner of Robert Baldwin): accepts Smith as partner 130; friendly relations with 130, 144; requests dissolution of partnership 143; *see also* Wilson & Smith
Wilson, Isobel, *see* Smith, Isobel Wilson
Wilson & Smith (third law partnership): encouraged by Robert Baldwin 130, 138; partnership dissolved 143; reactions of Smith 143, 144
Windsor 127
Women, aging of 170
Woods, Lieutenant (friend) 112–13; letters to 118–19, 125; visited in London, England, by Smith 174
Wright (friend) 25

Yankees: ironic attitude towards 54; moderate approval of 126; war rumour about 72
Yonge Street 8, 9, 15, 21, 29, 34, 37; 'all the Yonge Street people' 43; accidents on 69, 72–3
Yonge Street Wharf 80
York (later Toronto) 7, 185n; 'dirty little York' 160
York, village 55

PICTURE CREDITS

Toronto harbour 1835: Metropolitan Toronto Library (MTL) B 3-20a

King Street 1835: MTL JRR 262

Captain Smith: MTL 971-26-11

Mary Violett Smith: MTL 971-26-10

Parliament Buildings: MTL B 1-17b

Upper Canada College 1842: MTL JRR 848

Robert Baldwin: MTL E 1-45h

William Henry Draper: The Law Society of Upper Canada

Princess Royal: MTL X 25-6

Toronto harbour 1849: MTL B 9-10b

Ontario House: MTL JRR 692

Yonge Street 1840s: MTL JRR 679

Bank of British North America: MTL Z 2-8

John Street 1851: MTL JRR 793

King's College: MTL JRR 2815

Deering's Theatre: MTL JRR 854

Toronto Bay 1852: MTL JRR 517

Toronto 1854: MTL JRR 338

Williams Omnibus: MTL JRR 3510

Dundas Street tollgate: MTL JRR 932

St Patrick's Market: MTL JRR 514

Government House: MTL JRR 296

Provincial Exhibition: MTL JRR 3519B

Queen's Own Rifles: MTL X 22-4

Family photographs not listed here are in the possession of the author.

www.ingramcontent.com/pod-product-compliance
Lightning Source LLC
Chambersburg PA
CBHW020404080526
44584CB00014B/1169